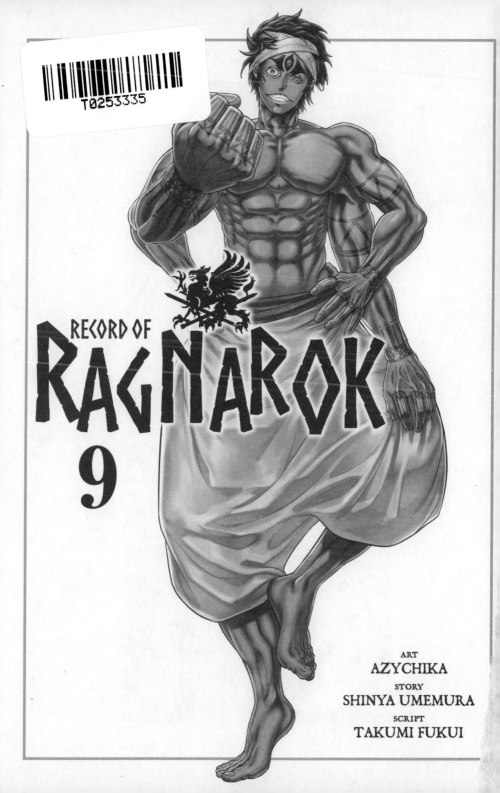

RECORD OF RAGNAROK

9

ART
AZYCHIKA

STORY
SHINYA UMEMURA

SCRIPT
TAKUMI FUKUI

9

RECORD OF RAGNAROK

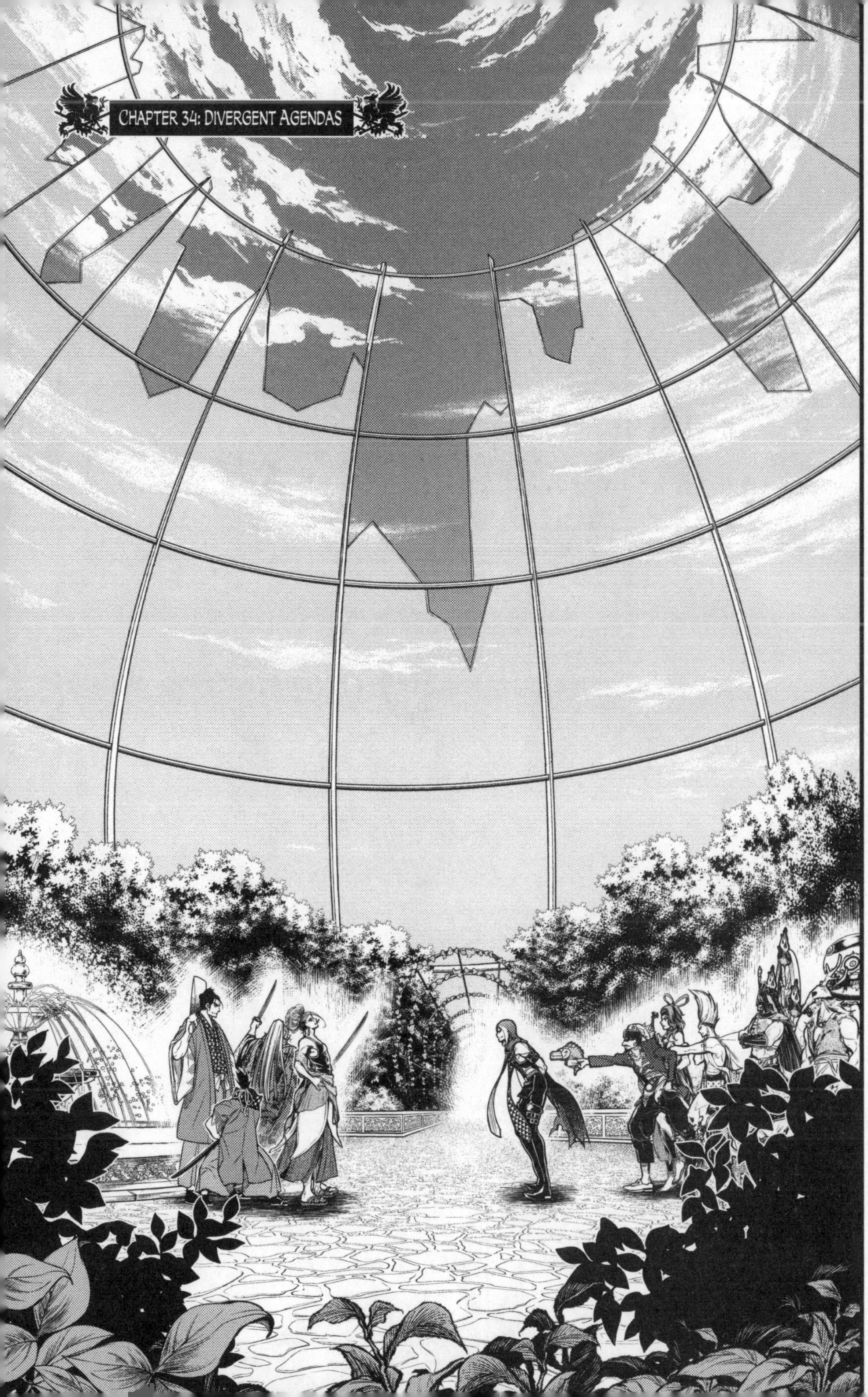
CHAPTER 34: DIVERGENT AGENDAS

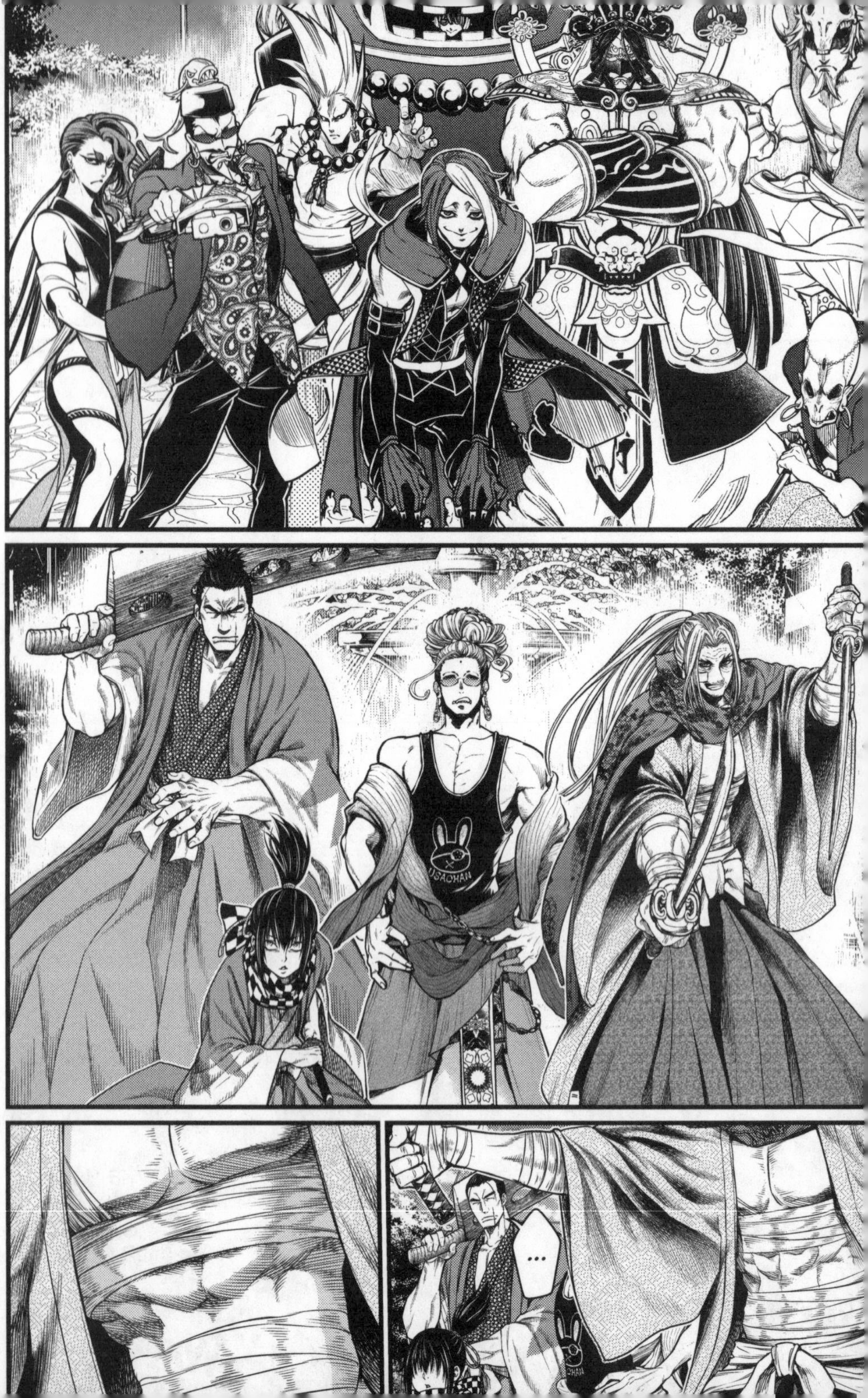
USAOHAN
...

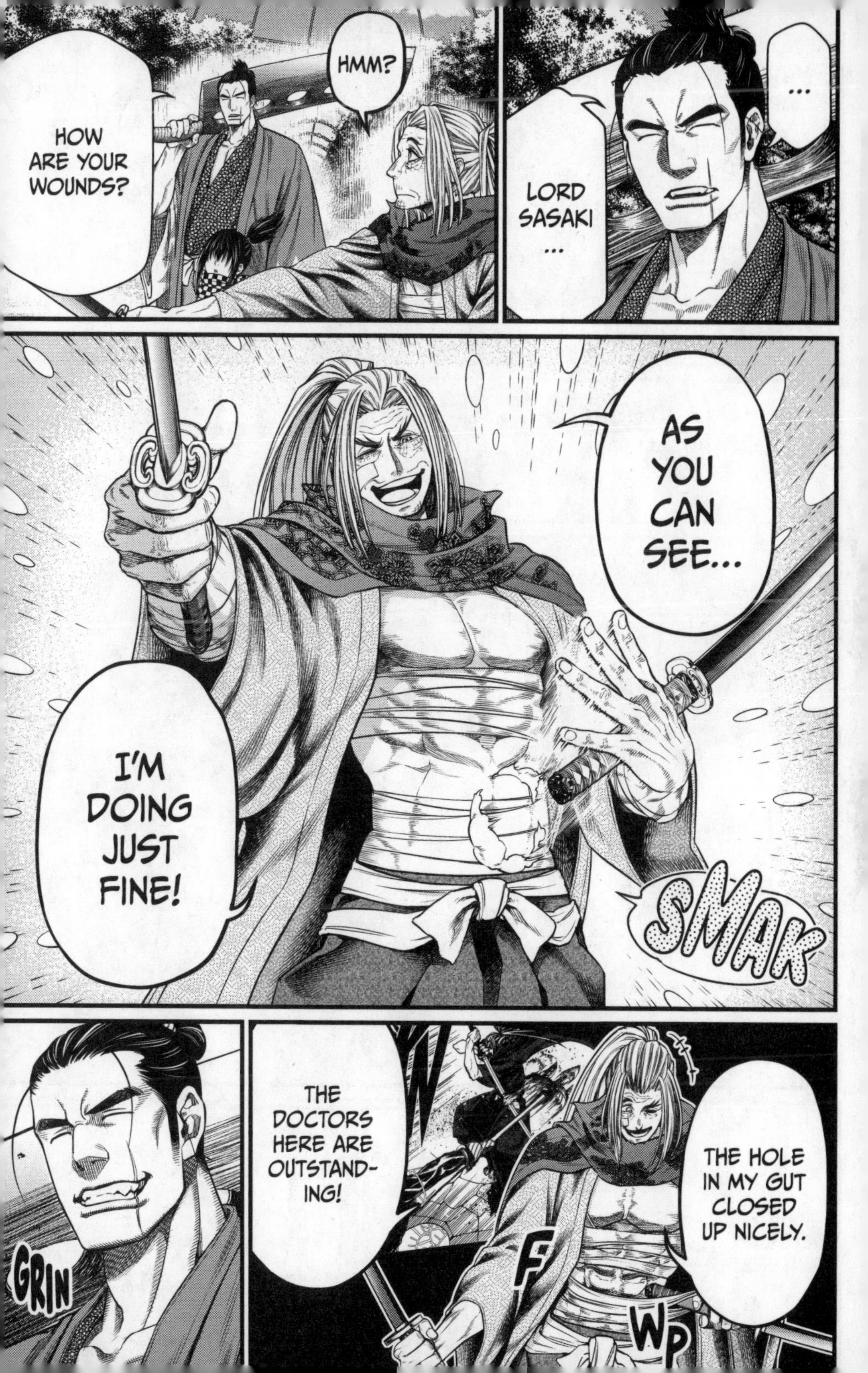
...
LORD SASAKI ...
HMM?
HOW ARE YOUR WOUNDS?
AS YOU CAN SEE...
I'M DOING JUST FINE!
SMAK
THE HOLE IN MY GUT CLOSED UP NICELY.
THE DOCTORS HERE ARE OUTSTANDING!
F
WP
GRIN

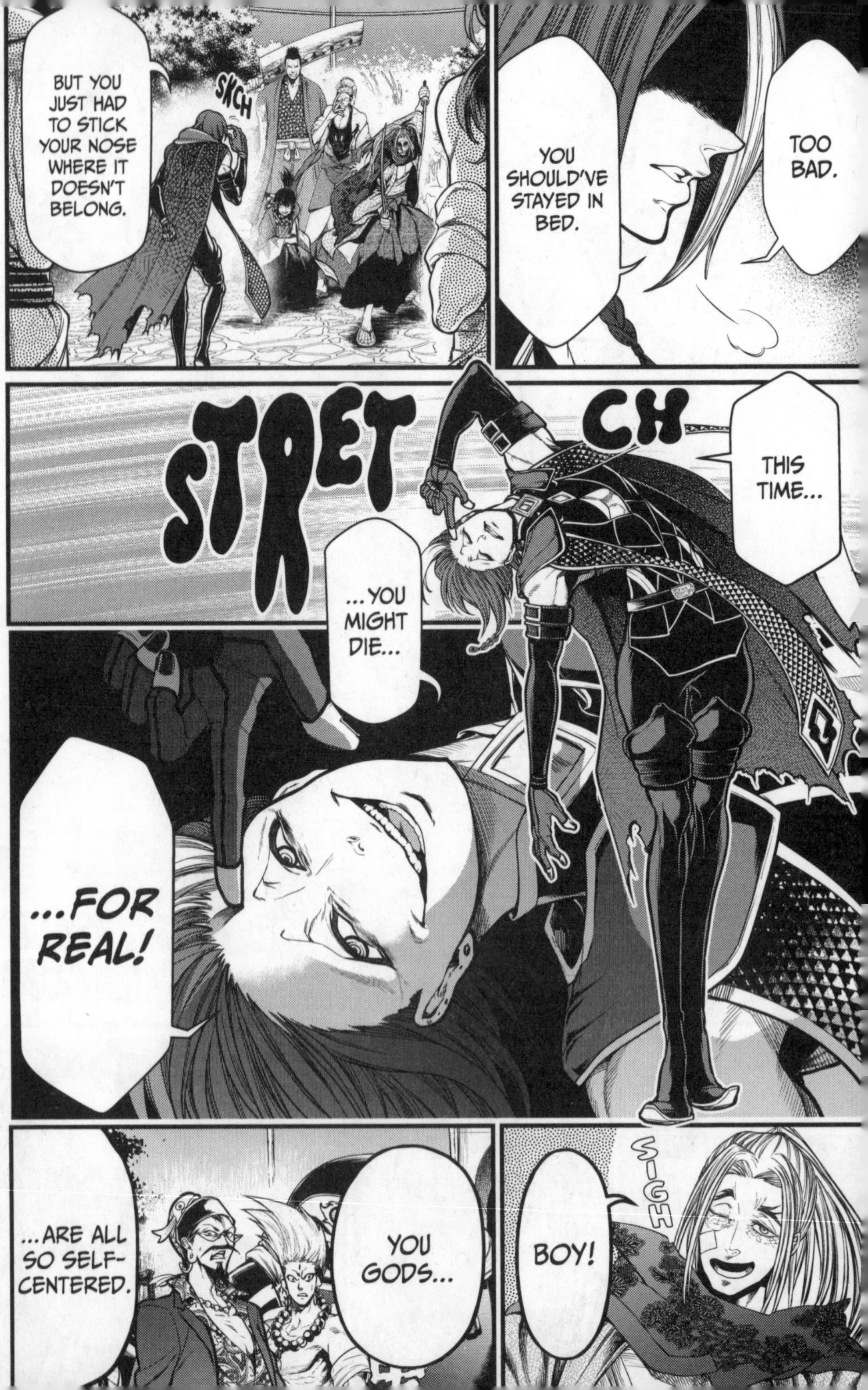
TOO BAD.
YOU SHOULD'VE STAYED IN BED.
BUT YOU JUST HAD TO STICK YOUR NOSE WHERE IT DOESN'T BELONG.
SKCH
THIS TIME...
STRETCH
...YOU MIGHT DIE...
...FOR REAL!
SIGH
BOY!
YOU GODS...
...ARE ALL SO SELF-CENTERED.

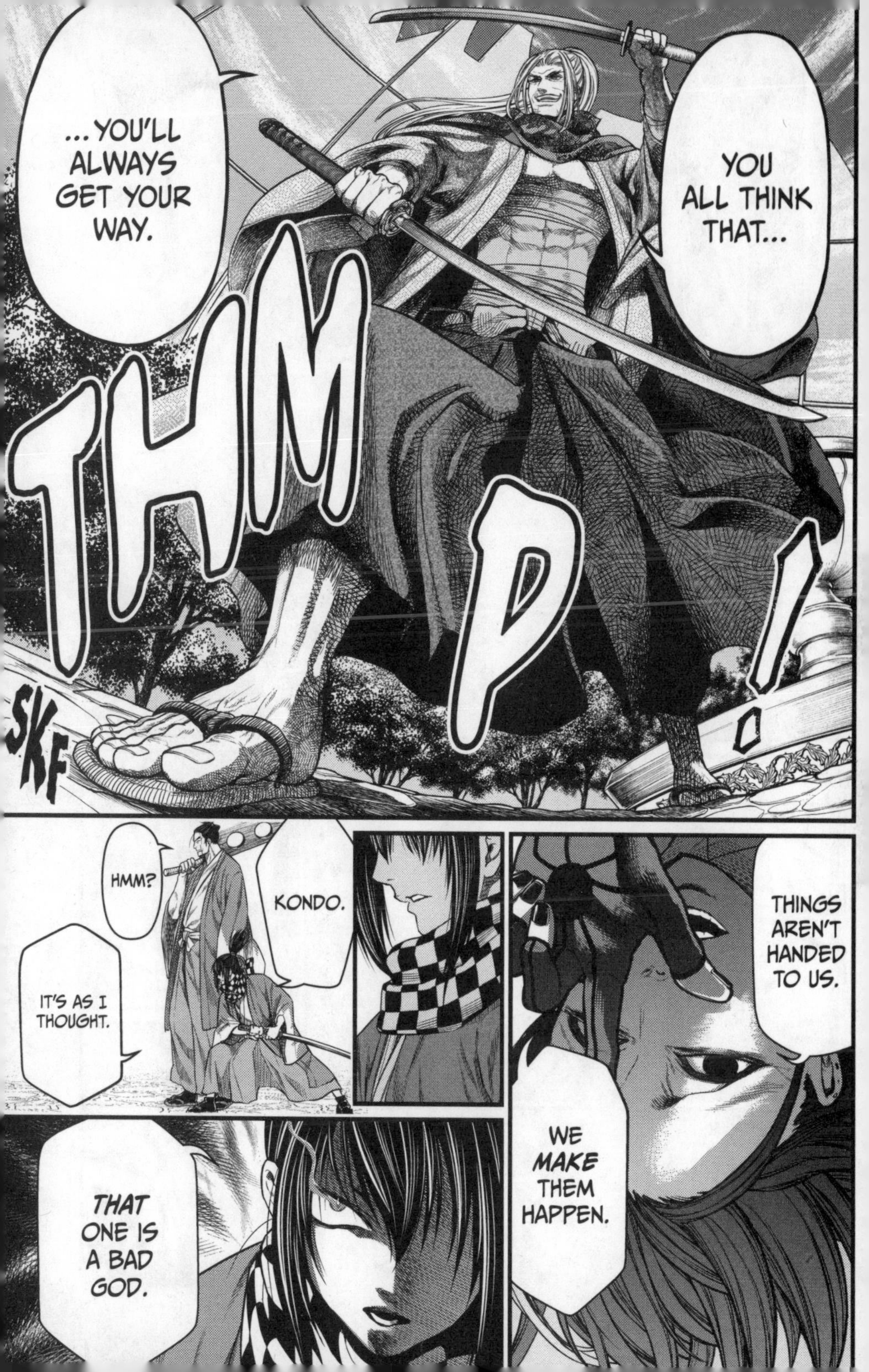
YOU ALL THINK THAT...
...YOU'LL ALWAYS GET YOUR WAY.
THMP!
SKF
THINGS AREN'T HANDED TO US.
WE *MAKE* THEM HAPPEN.
KONDO.
HMM?
IT'S AS I THOUGHT.
THAT ONE IS A BAD GOD.

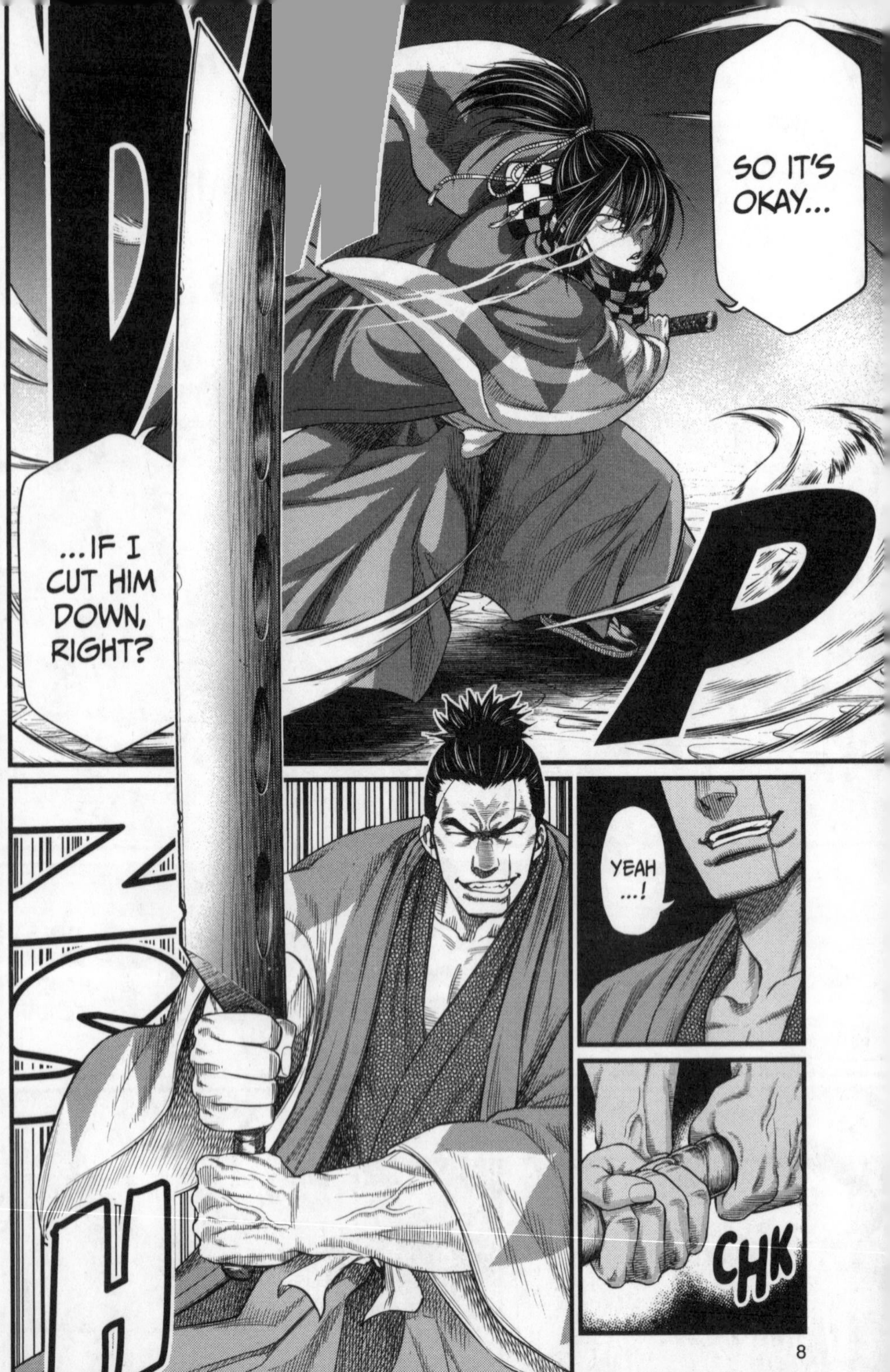
SO IT'S OKAY...
...IF I CUT HIM DOWN, RIGHT?
YEAH ...!
CHK

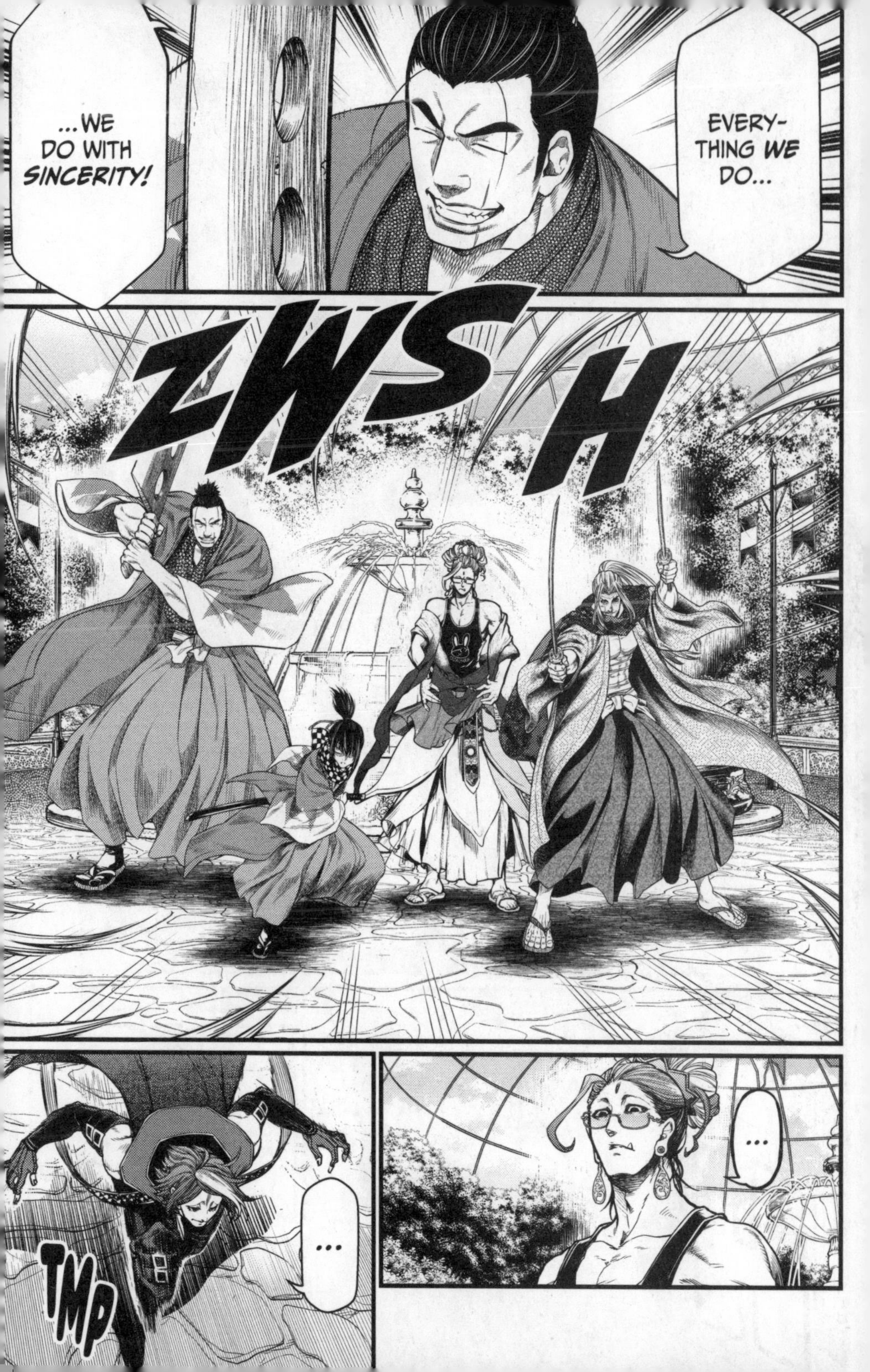
EVERY-THING WE DO...
...WE DO WITH SINCERITY!
ZWSH
...
...
TMP

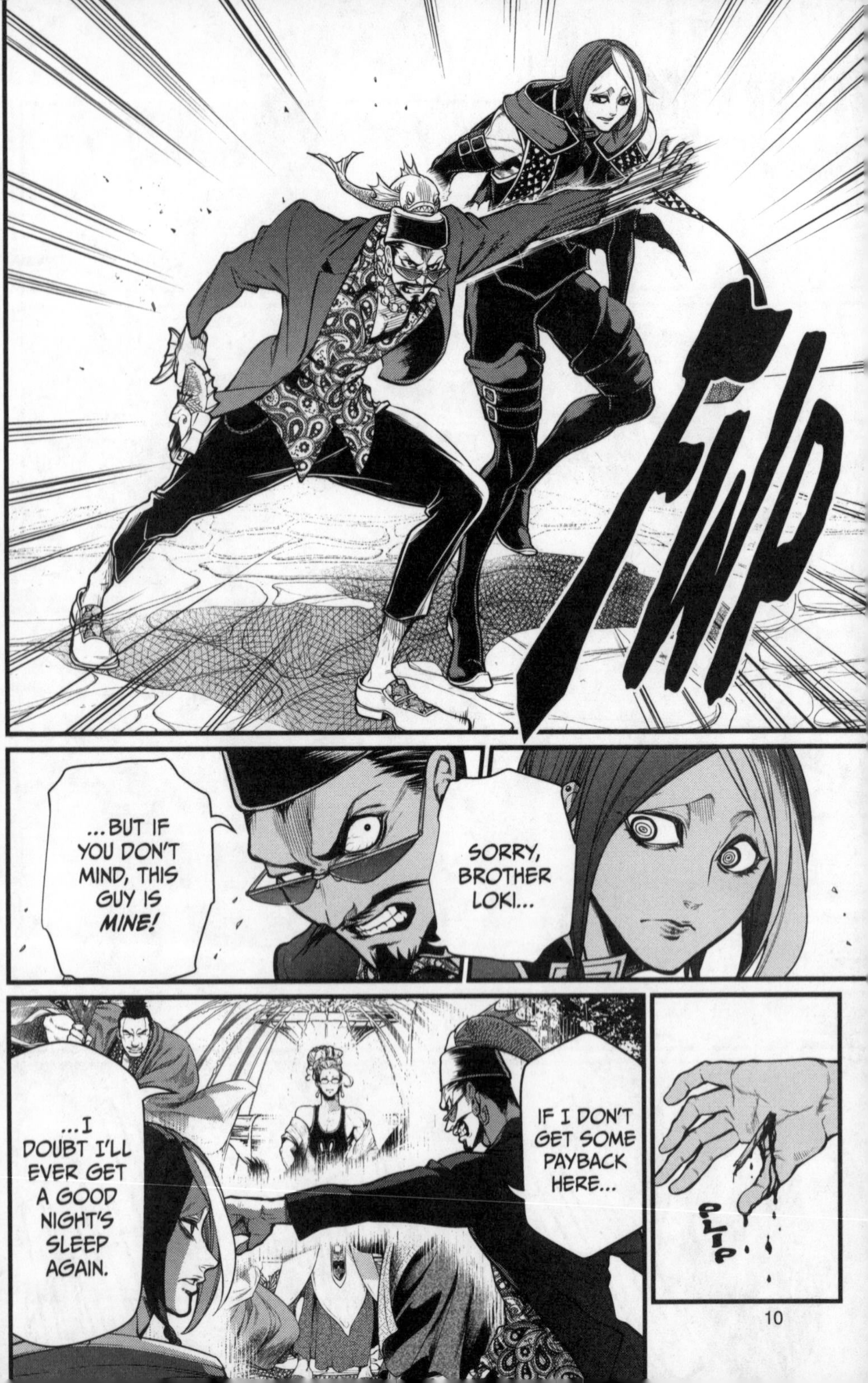
FWIP
SORRY, BROTHER LOKI...
...BUT IF YOU DON'T MIND, THIS GUY IS *MINE!*
DRIP
IF I DON'T GET SOME PAYBACK HERE...
...I DOUBT I'LL EVER GET A GOOD NIGHT'S SLEEP AGAIN.

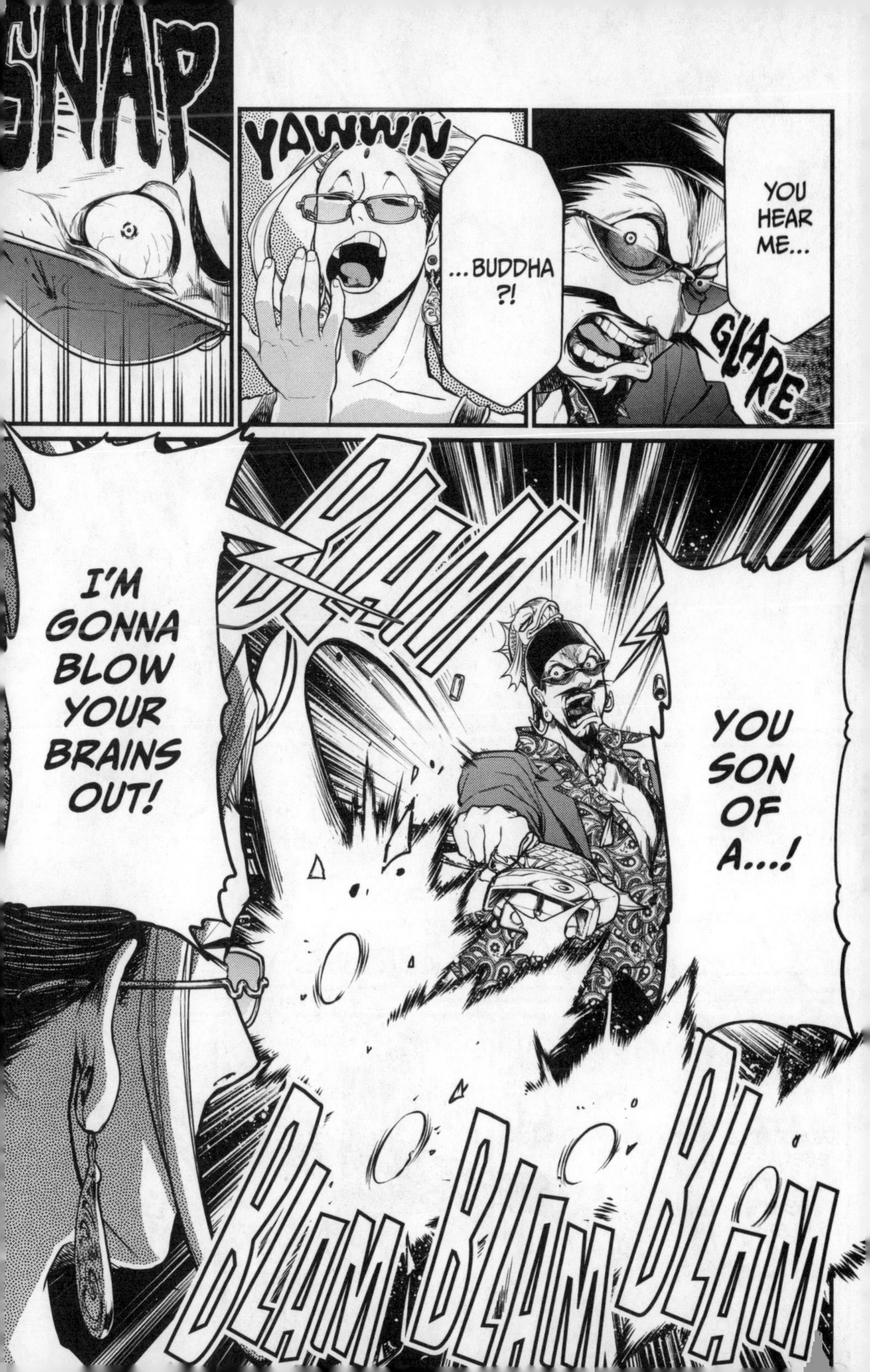
YOU HEAR ME...
GLARE
...BUDDHA ?!
YAWWN
SNAP
YOU SON OF A...!
I'M GONNA BLOW YOUR BRAINS OUT!
BLAM
BLAM BLAM BLAM

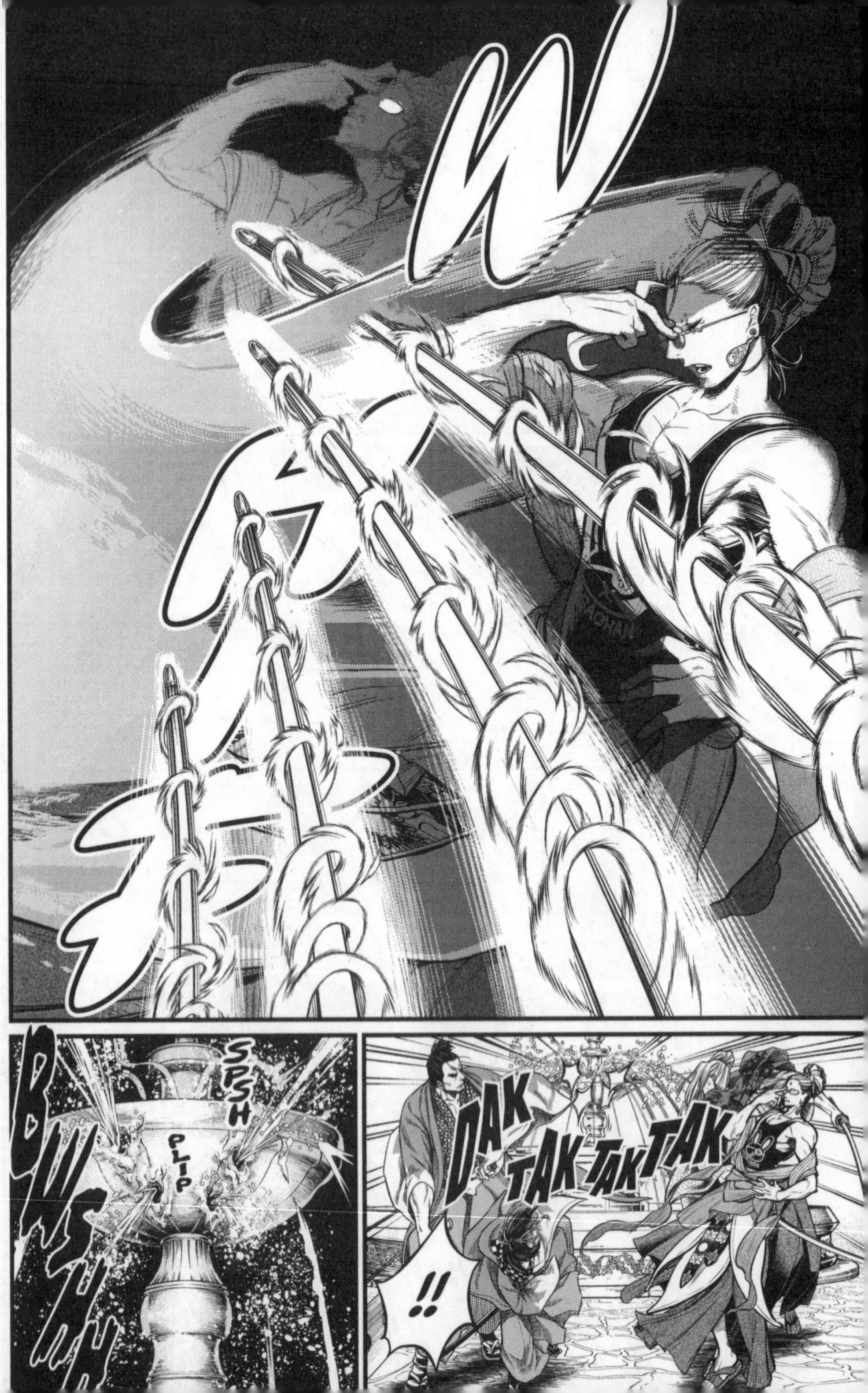
W
DAK TAK TAK TAK
!!
SPSH
PLIP

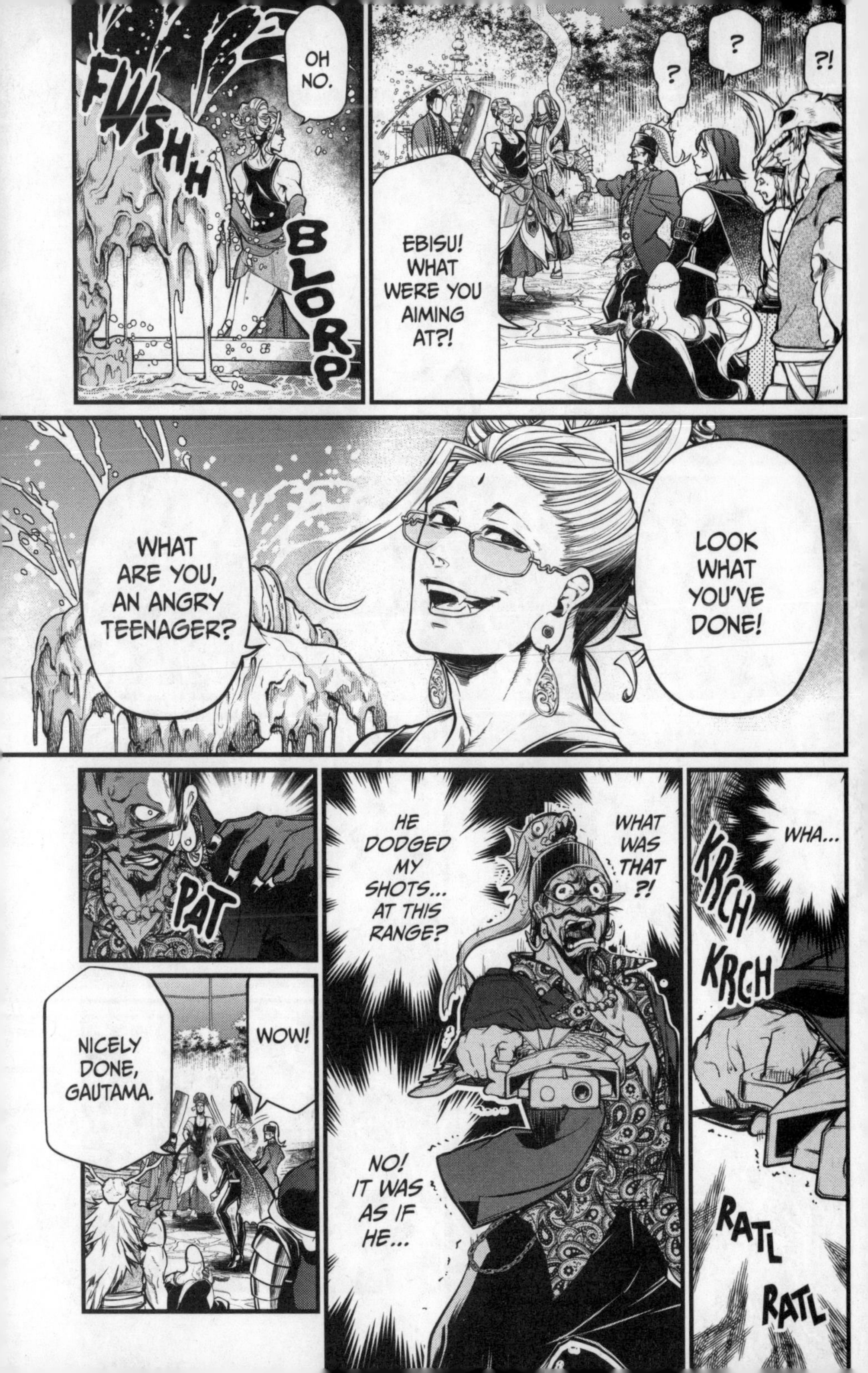
?
?
?!
EBISU! WHAT WERE YOU AIMING AT?!
OH NO.
FUSHHH
BLORP
LOOK WHAT YOU'VE DONE!
WHAT ARE YOU, AN ANGRY TEENAGER?
WHA...
KRCH
KRCH
RATL
RATL
WHAT WAS THAT?!
HE DODGED MY SHOTS... AT THIS RANGE?
NO! IT WAS AS IF HE...
PAT
WOW!
NICELY DONE, GAUTAMA.

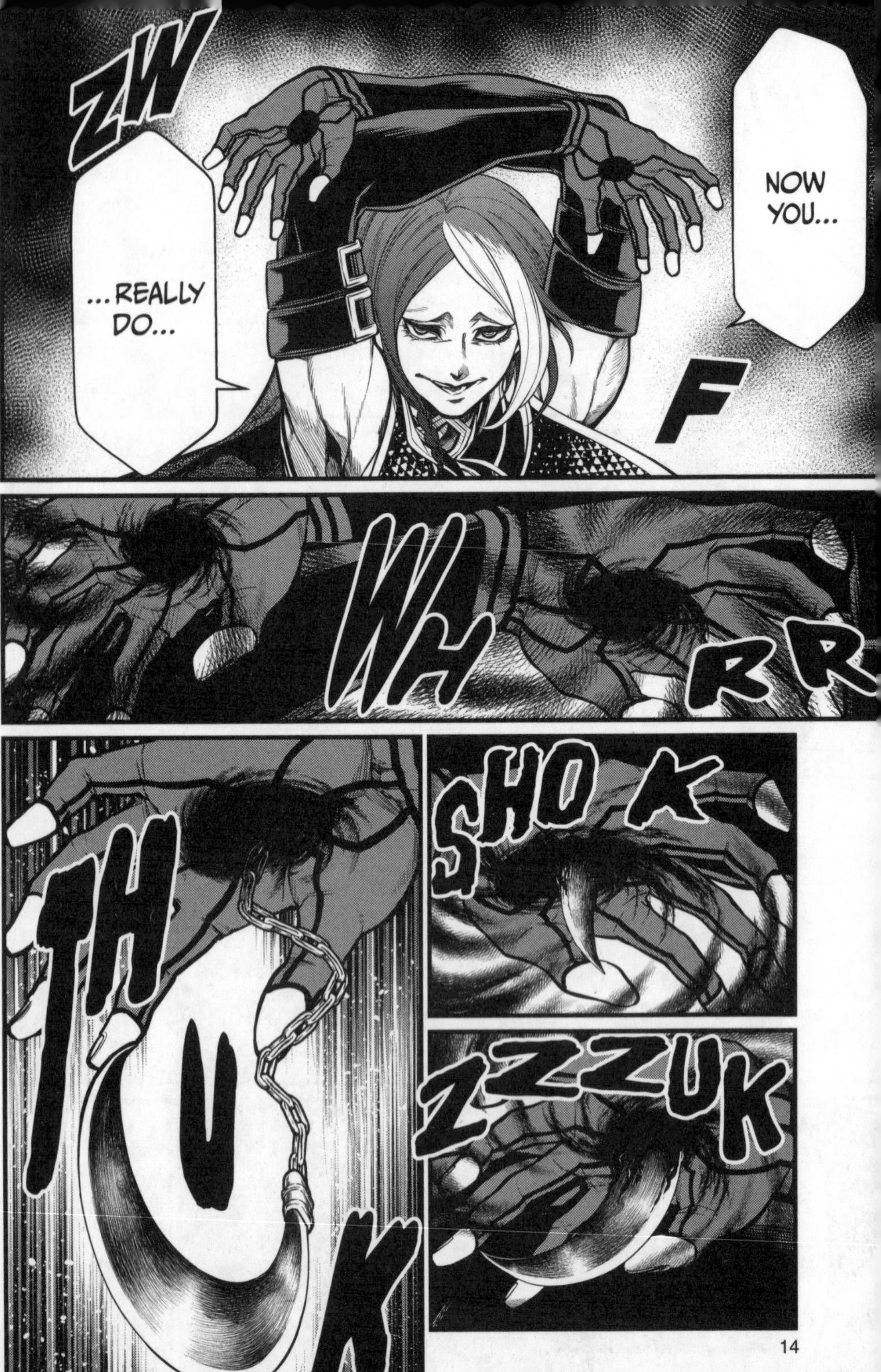

NOW YOU...
...REALLY DO...
ZW
F
WH
RRR
SHO K
ZZZZUK
TH
U
K

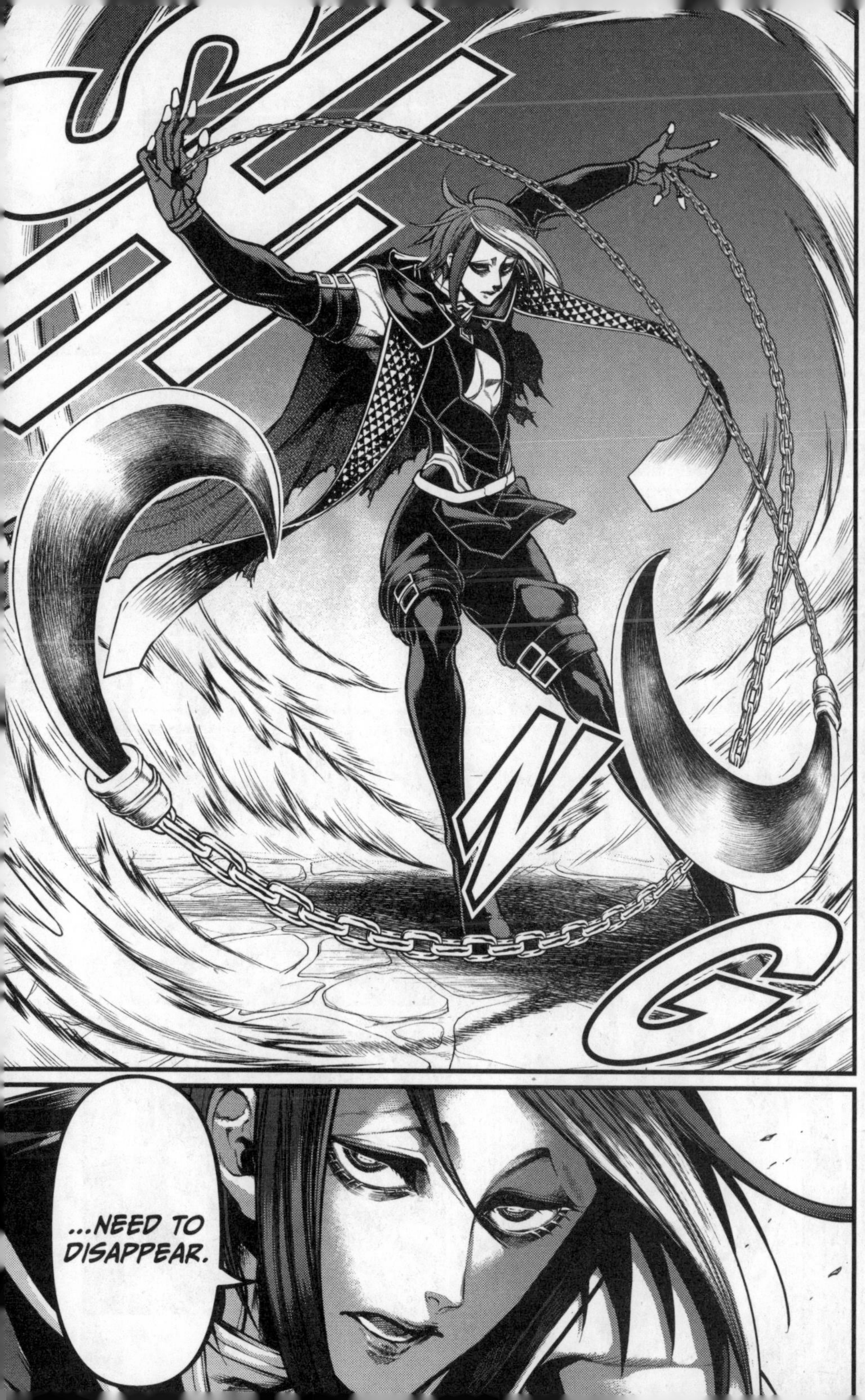
...NEED TO DISAPPEAR.

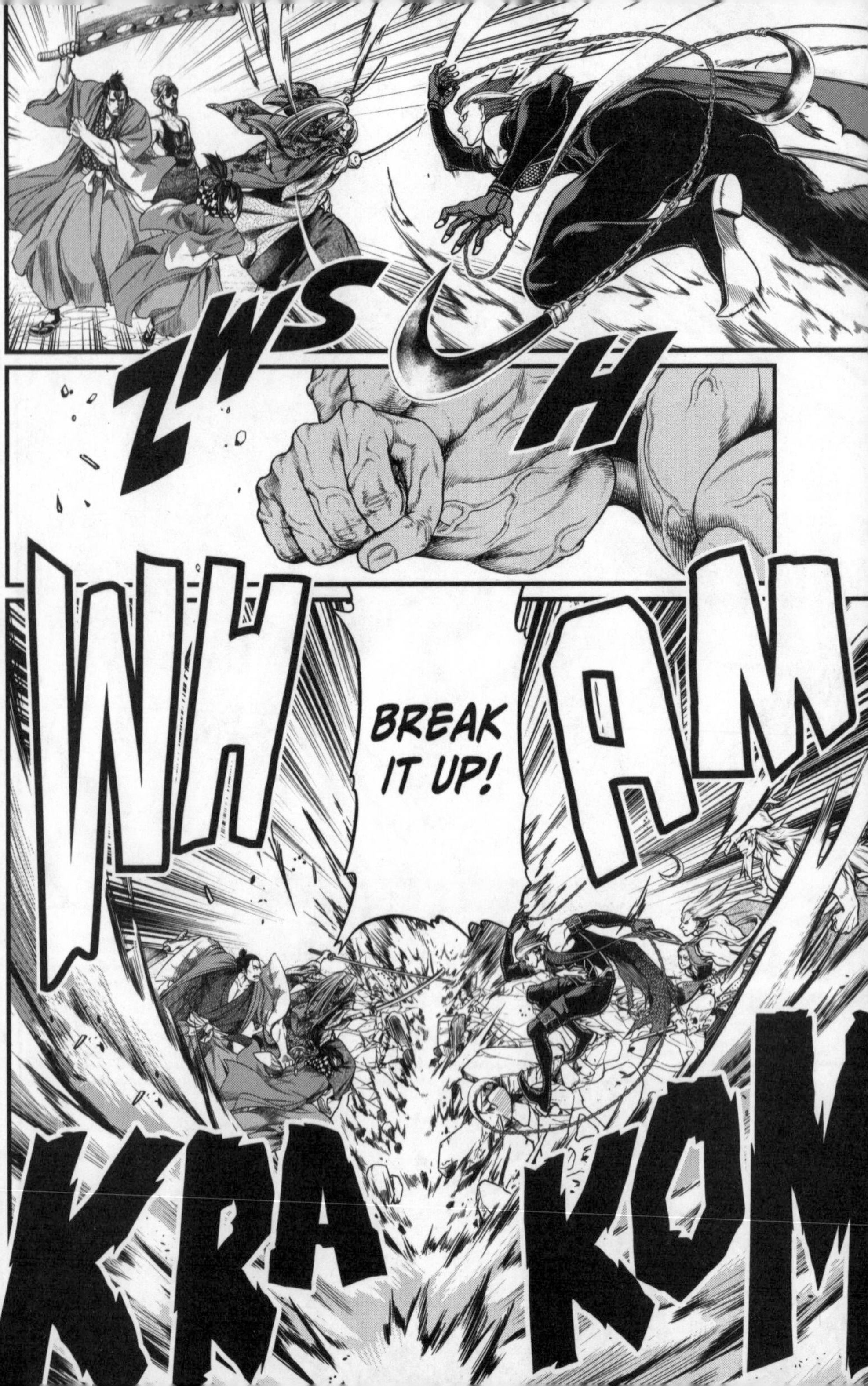
ZWSH
WHAM
BREAK IT UP!
KRA-KOM

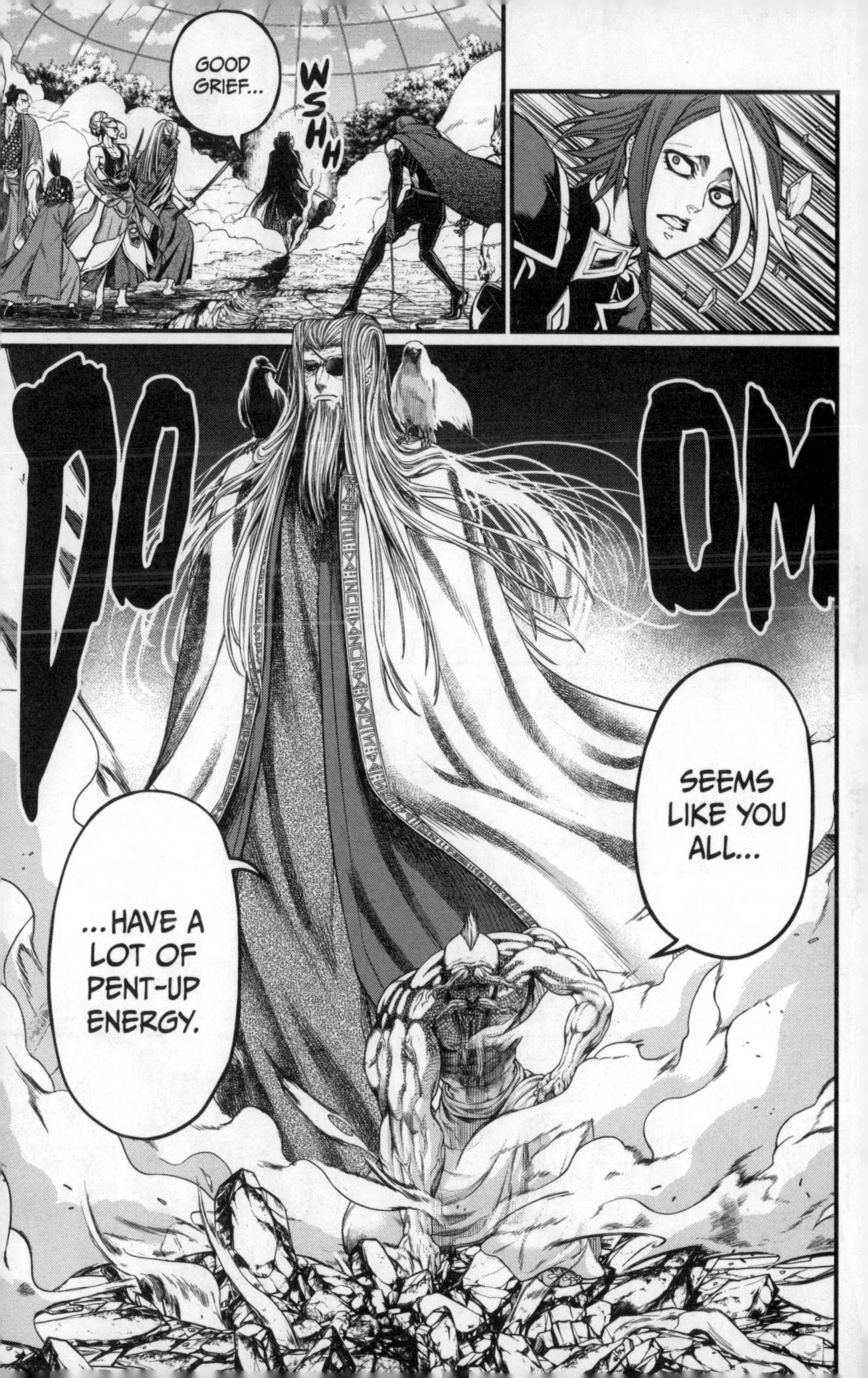
GOOD GRIEF...
WSHH
DOOM
SEEMS LIKE YOU ALL...
...HAVE A LOT OF PENT-UP ENERGY.

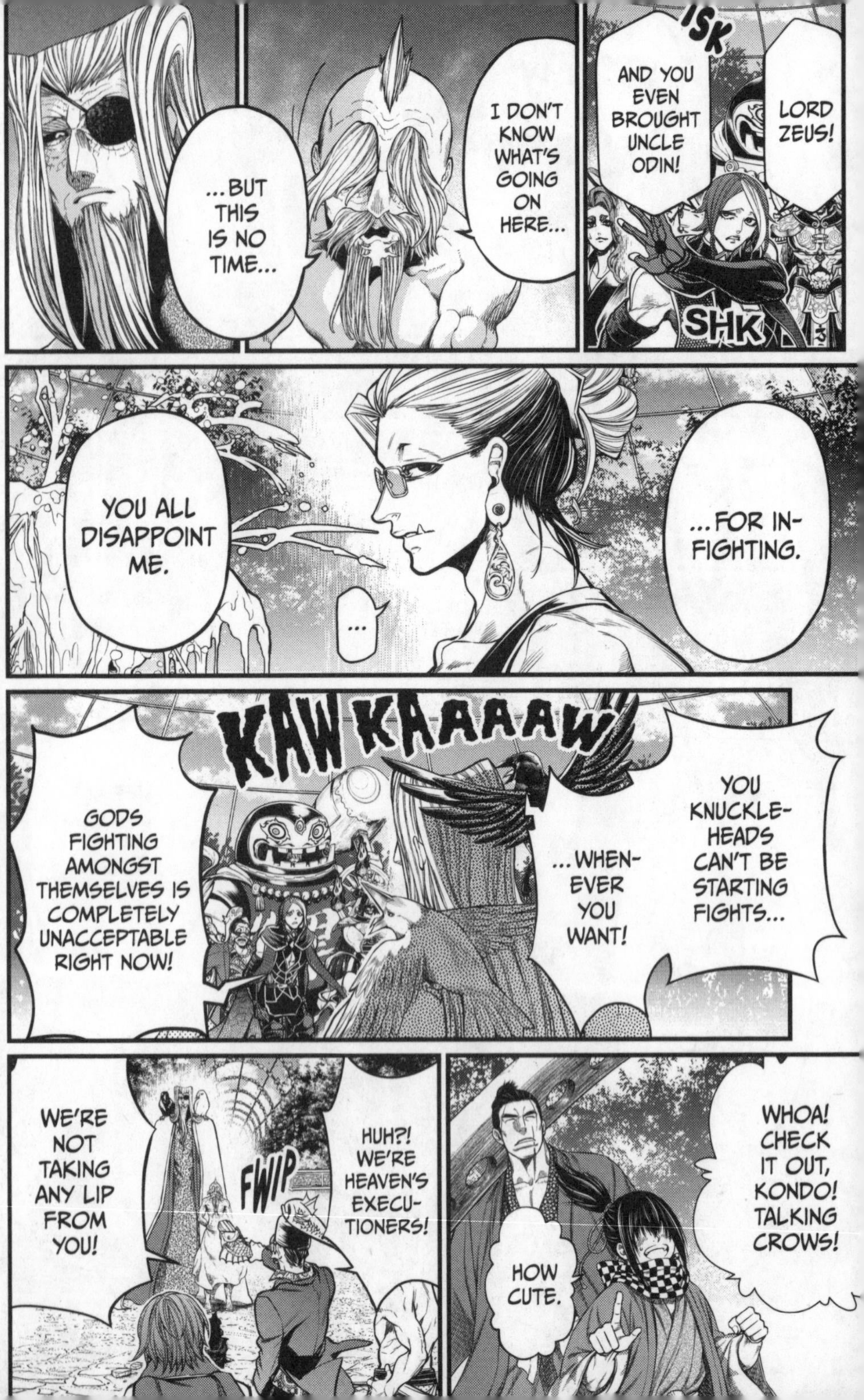
ISK
LORD ZEUS!
AND YOU EVEN BROUGHT UNCLE ODIN!
SHK
I DON'T KNOW WHAT'S GOING ON HERE...
...BUT THIS IS NO TIME...
...FOR IN-FIGHTING.
YOU ALL DISAPPOINT ME.
...
KAW KAAAAW!!
YOU KNUCKLE-HEADS CAN'T BE STARTING FIGHTS...
...WHEN-EVER YOU WANT!
GODS FIGHTING AMONGST THEMSELVES IS COMPLETELY UNACCEPTABLE RIGHT NOW!
WHOA! CHECK IT OUT, KONDO! TALKING CROWS!
HOW CUTE.
HUH?! WE'RE HEAVEN'S EXECU-TIONERS!
FWIP
WE'RE NOT TAKING ANY LIP FROM YOU!

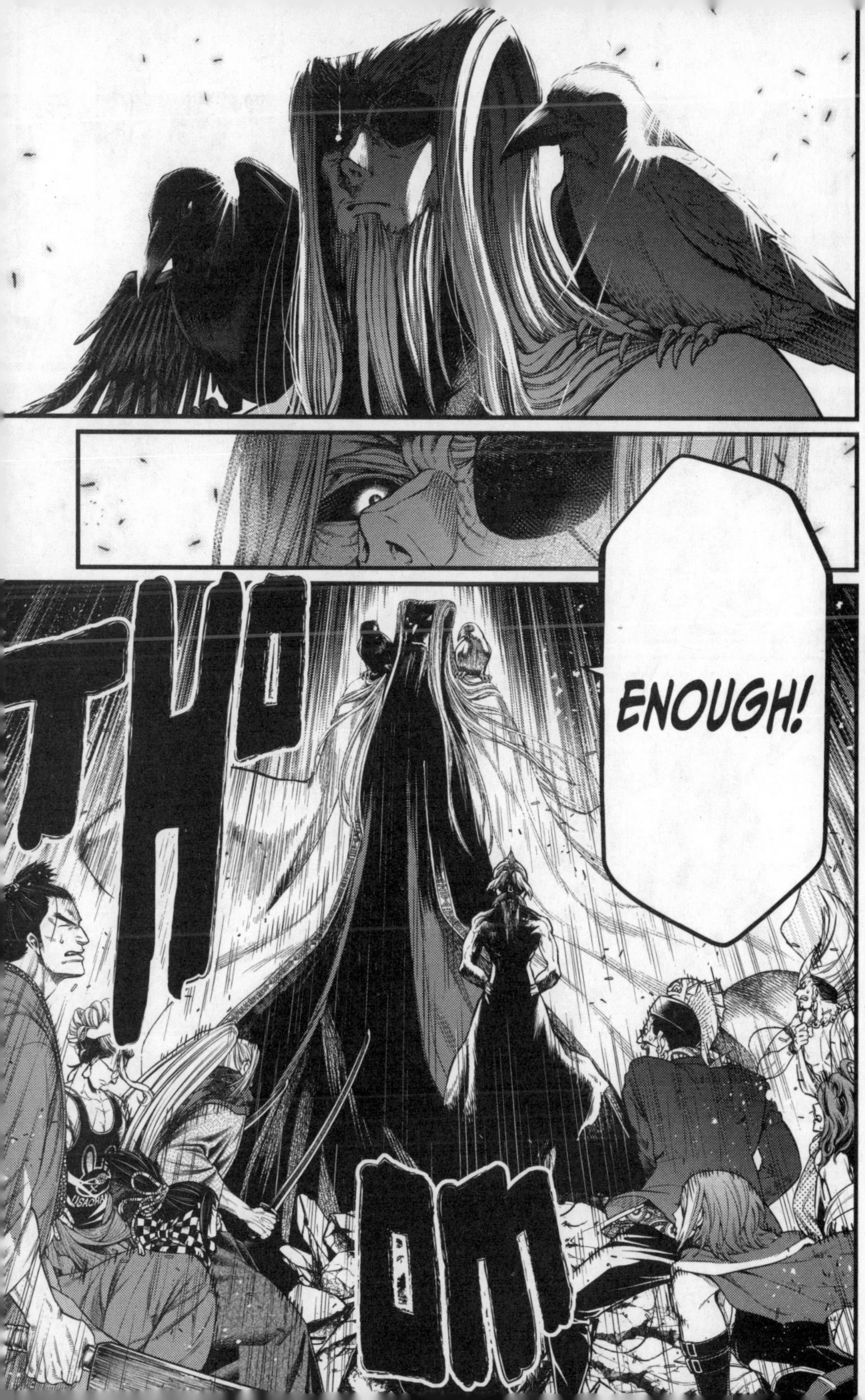
ENOUGH!
THOOM

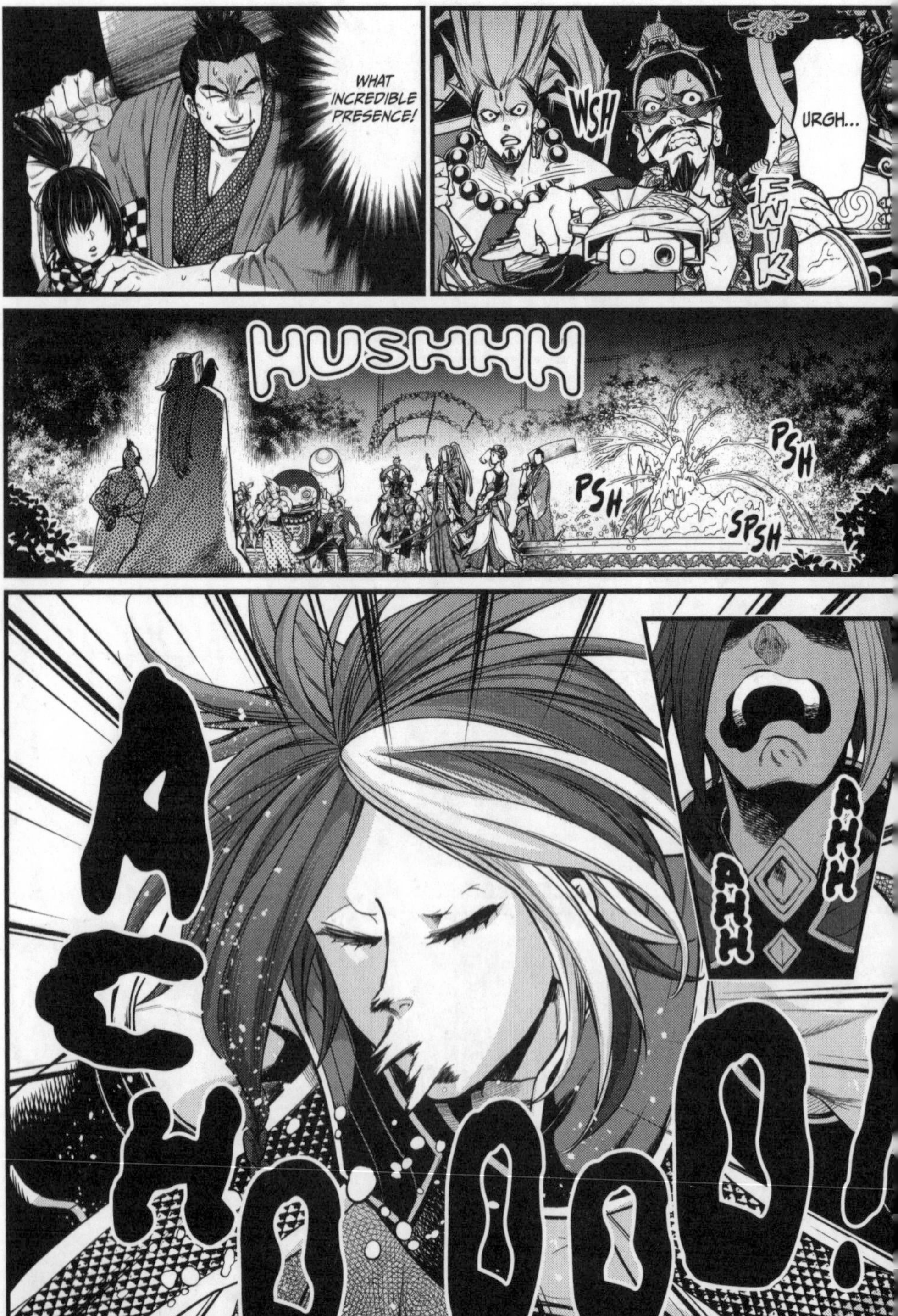
URGH...
FWIK
WSH
WHAT INCREDIBLE PRESENCE!
HUSHHH
PSH
SPSH
PSH
AHH
AHH
ACHOOOO!

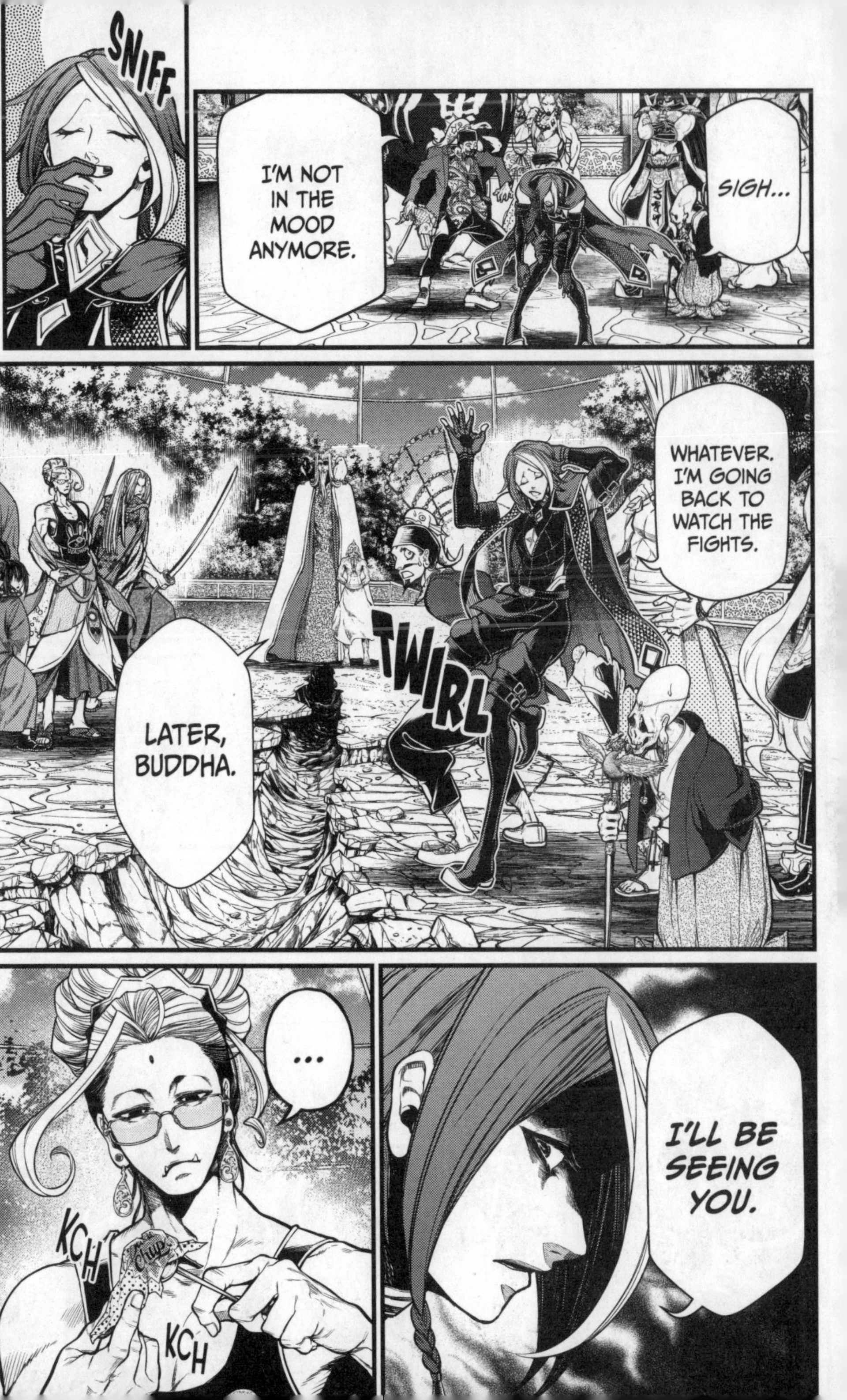
SIGH...
I'M NOT IN THE MOOD ANYMORE.
SNIFF
WHATEVER. I'M GOING BACK TO WATCH THE FIGHTS.
TWIRL
LATER, BUDDHA.
I'LL BE SEEING YOU.
...
KCH
Chup
KCH

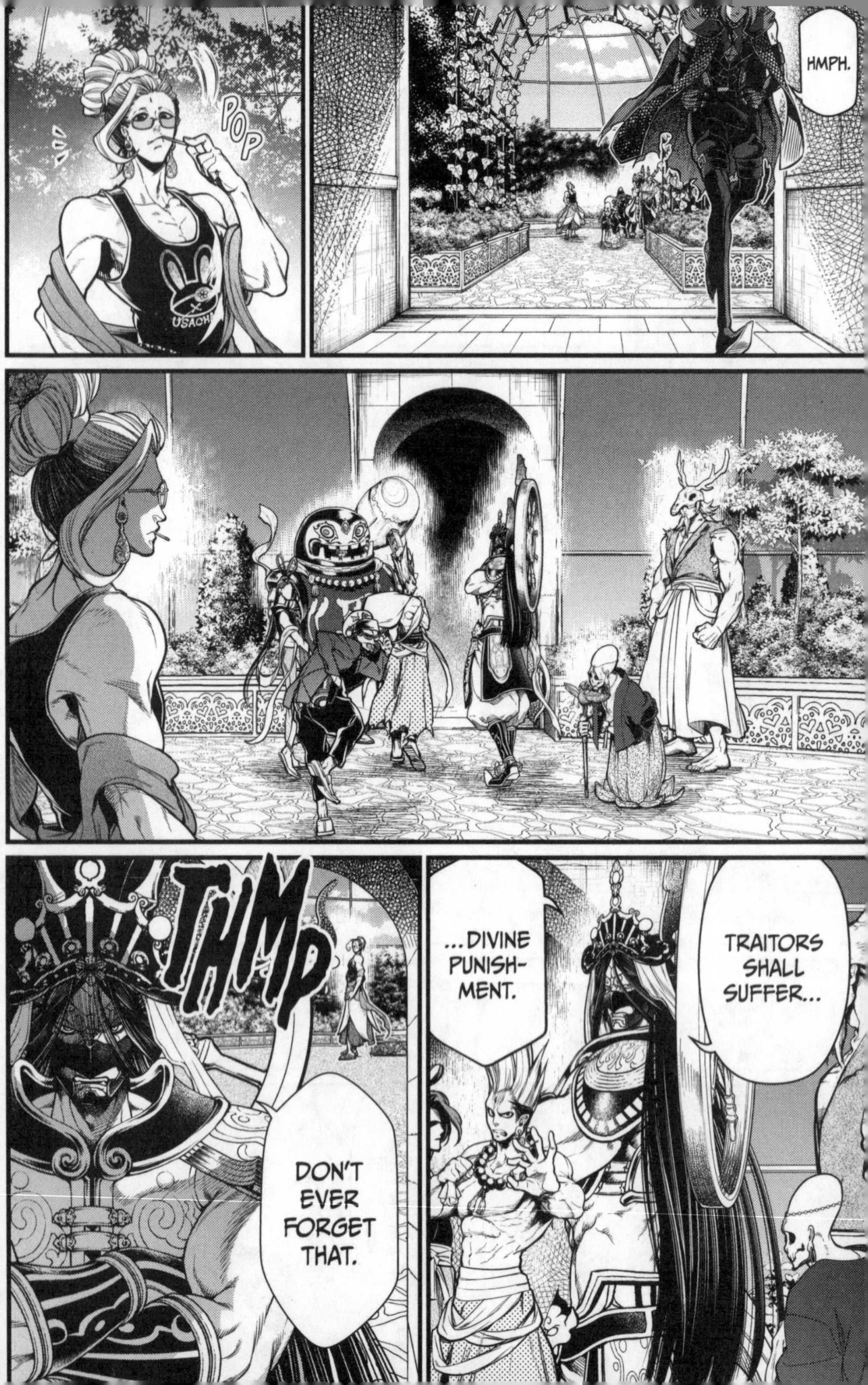
HMPH.
POP
TRAITORS SHALL SUFFER...
...DIVINE PUNISH-MENT.
THMP
DON'T EVER FORGET THAT.

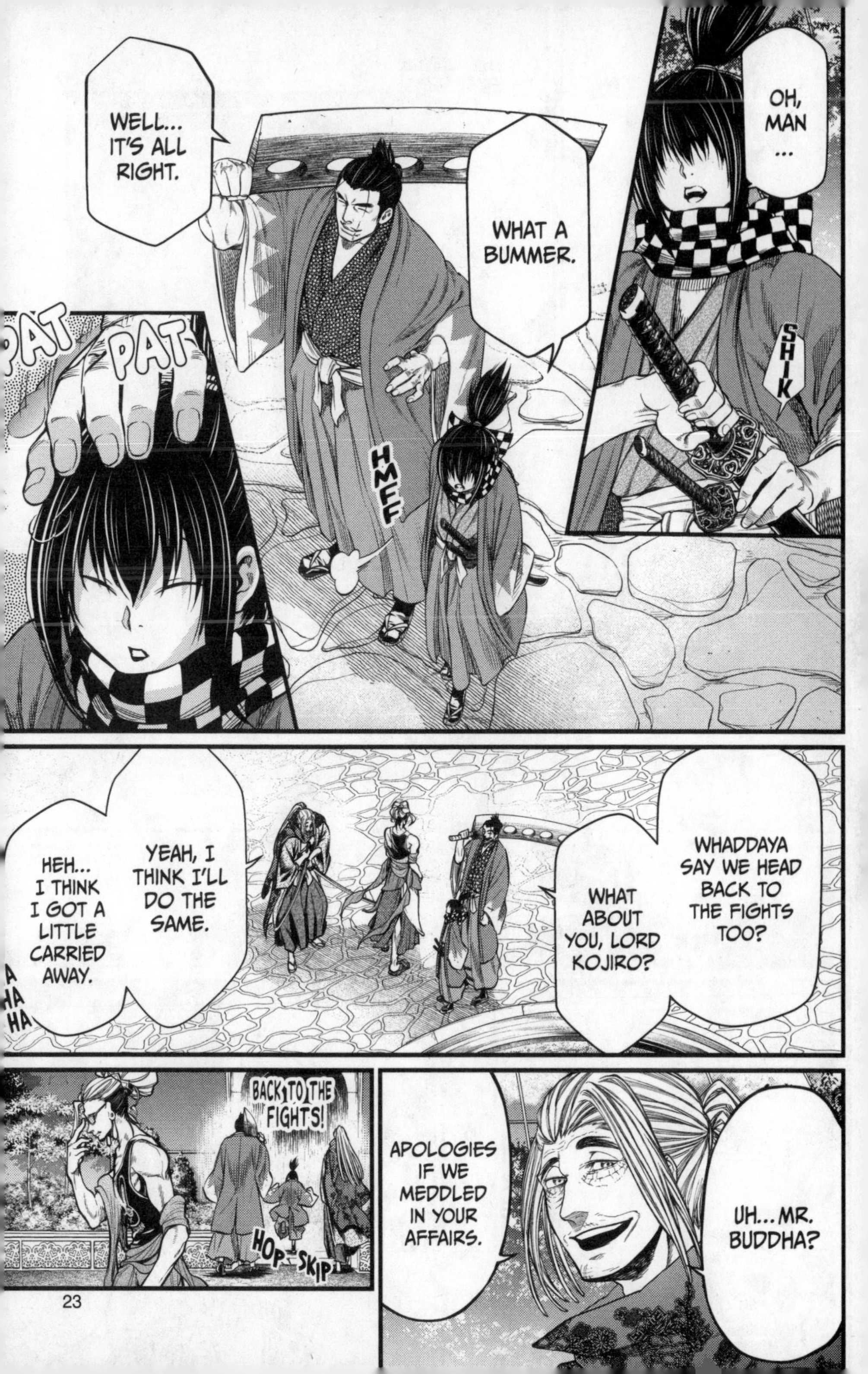
OH, MAN ...
SHIK
WHAT A BUMMER.
WELL... IT'S ALL RIGHT.
HMFF
PAT PAT
WHADDAYA SAY WE HEAD BACK TO THE FIGHTS TOO?
WHAT ABOUT YOU, LORD KOJIRO?
YEAH, I THINK I'LL DO THE SAME.
HEH... I THINK I GOT A LITTLE CARRIED AWAY.
A HA HA
UH...MR. BUDDHA?
APOLOGIES IF WE MEDDLED IN YOUR AFFAIRS.
BACK TO THE FIGHTS!
HOP SKIP

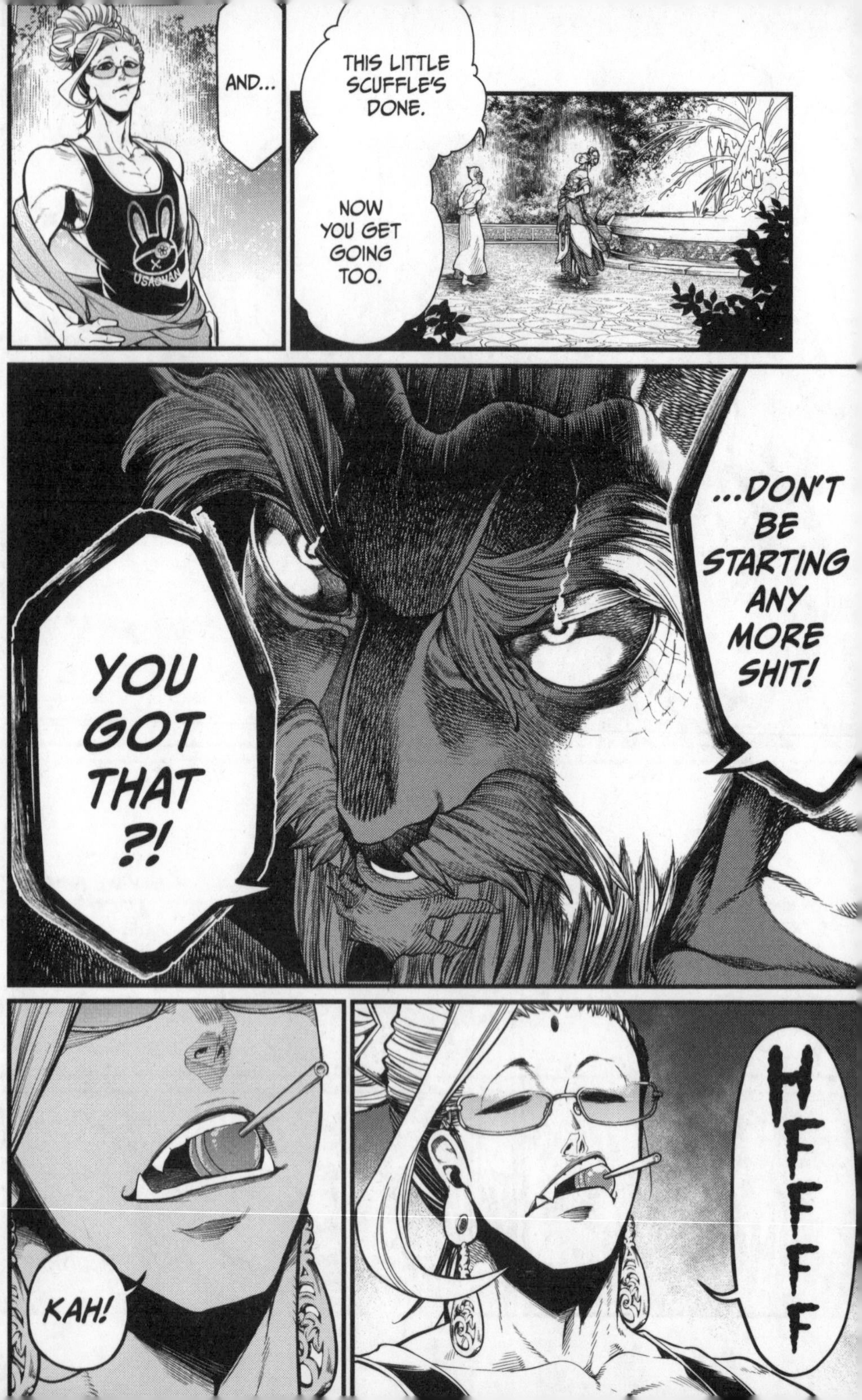
THIS LITTLE SCUFFLE'S DONE.
NOW YOU GET GOING TOO.
AND...
...DON'T BE STARTING ANY MORE SHIT!
YOU GOT THAT?!
HFFFF
KAH!
USAGHAN

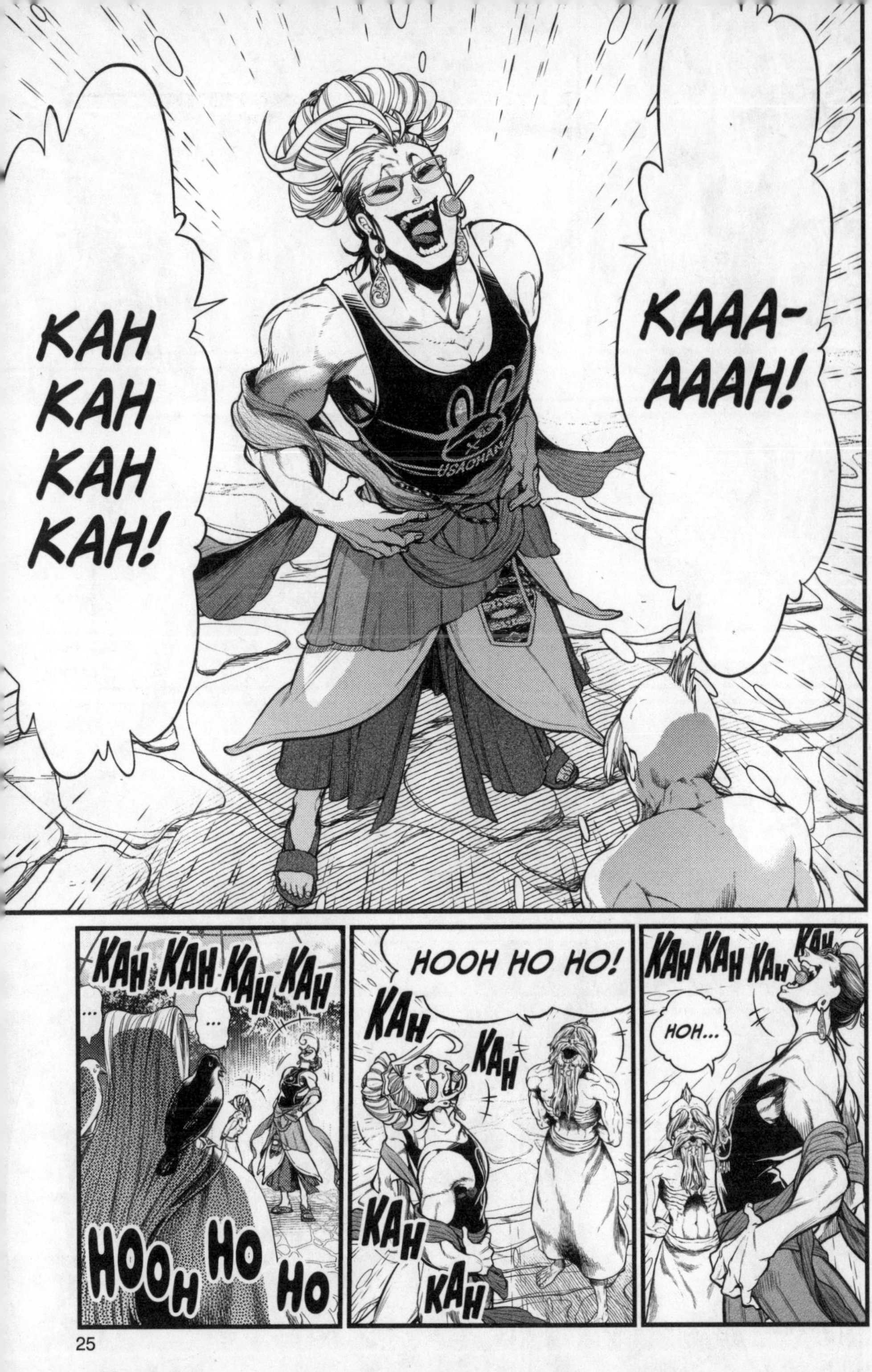
KAAAA-AAAH!
KAH KAH KAH KAH!
KAH KAH KAH KAH
HOH...
HOOH HO HO!
KAH KAH
KAH KAH
KAH KAH KAH KAH
...
...
HOOH HO HO

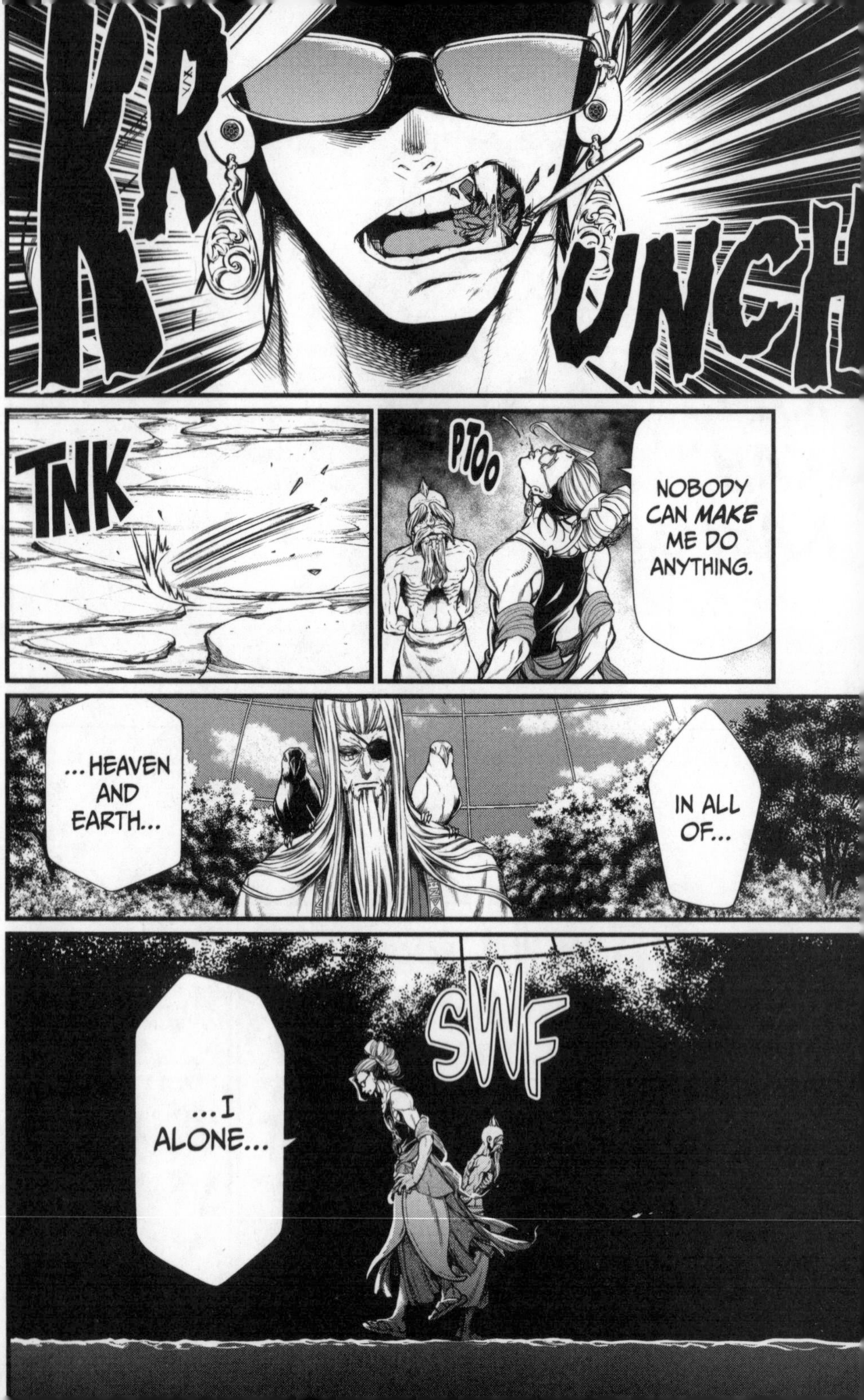
KRUNCH
PTOO
NOBODY CAN MAKE ME DO ANYTHING.
TNK
IN ALL OF...
...HEAVEN AND EARTH...
SWF
...I ALONE...

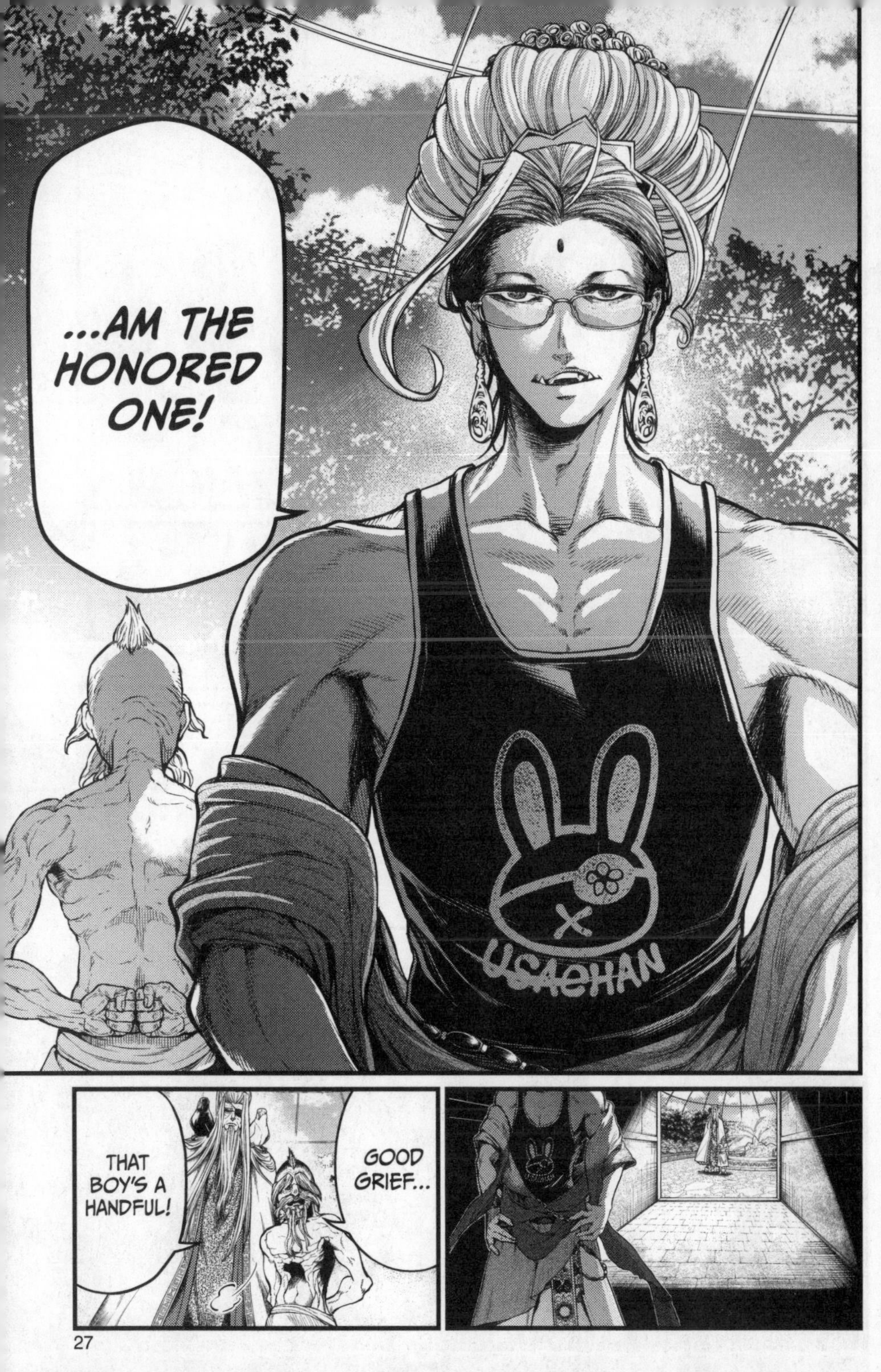
...AM THE HONORED ONE!
USACHAN
GOOD GRIEF...
THAT BOY'S A HANDFUL!

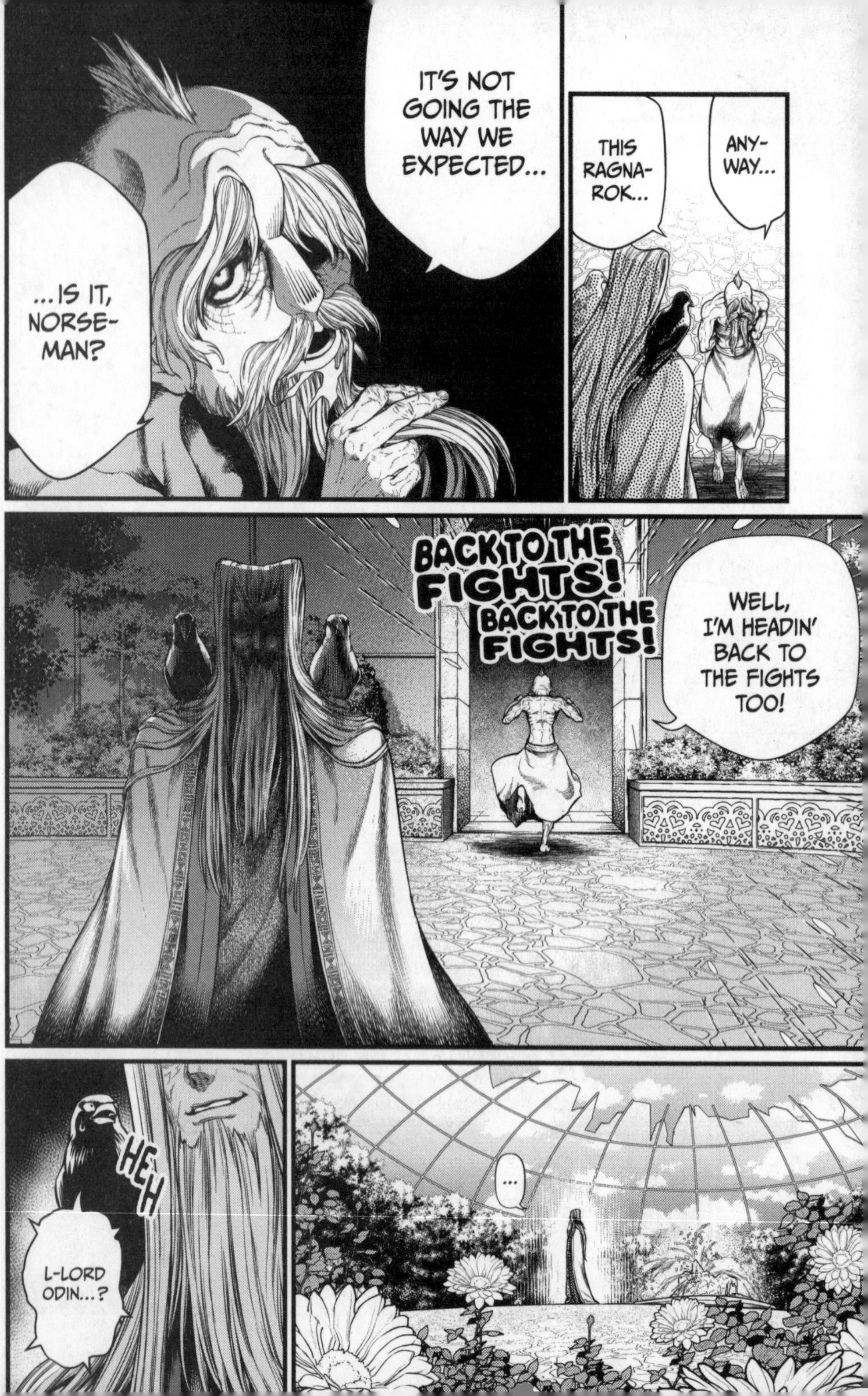
ANY-WAY...
THIS RAGNA-ROK...
IT'S NOT GOING THE WAY WE EXPECTED...
...IS IT, NORSE-MAN?
WELL, I'M HEADIN' BACK TO THE FIGHTS TOO!
BACK TO THE FIGHTS!
BACK TO THE FIGHTS!
...
HEH
L-LORD ODIN...?

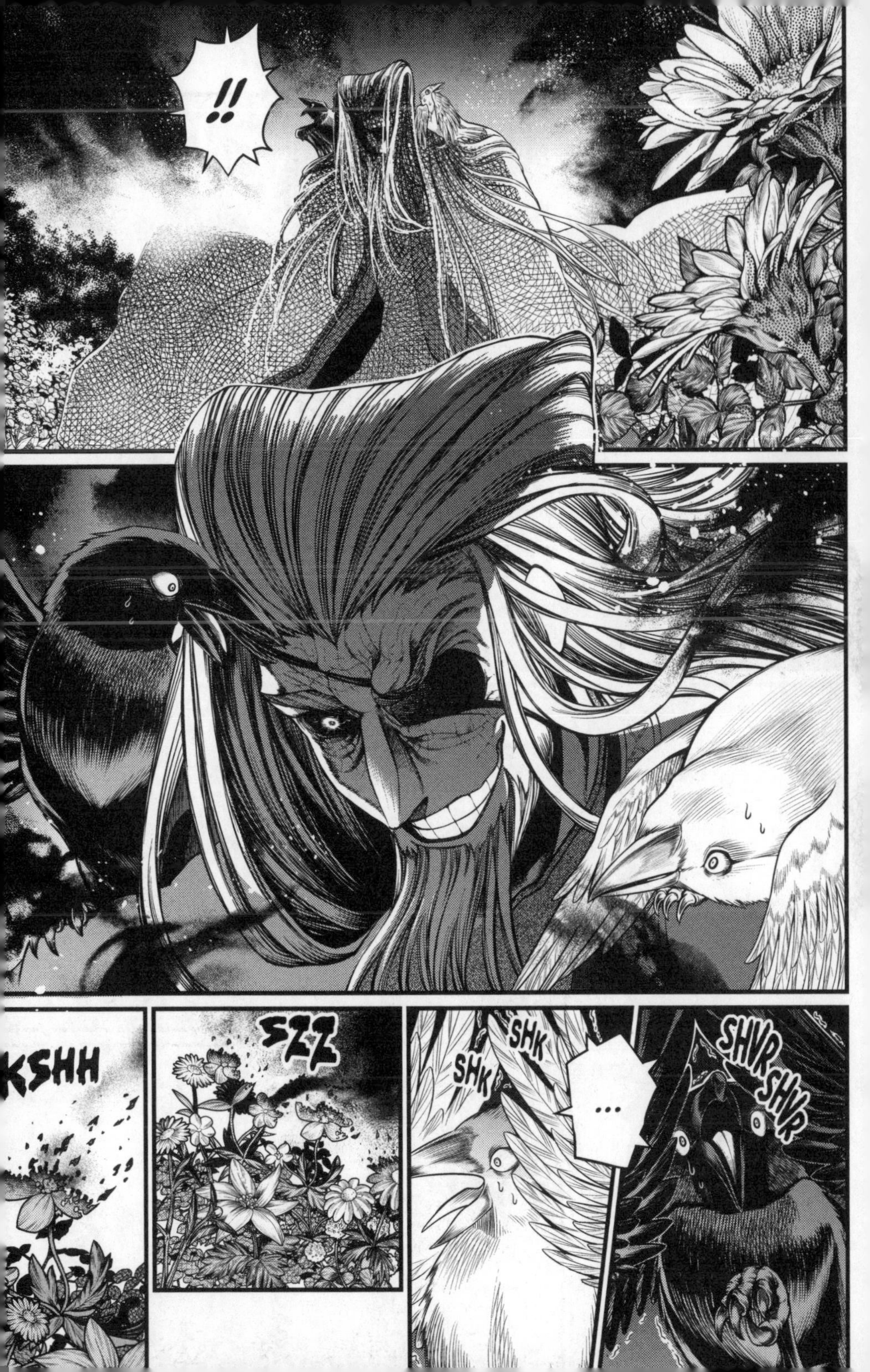
!!
SHVR SHVR
SHK
SHK
...
SZZ
KSHH

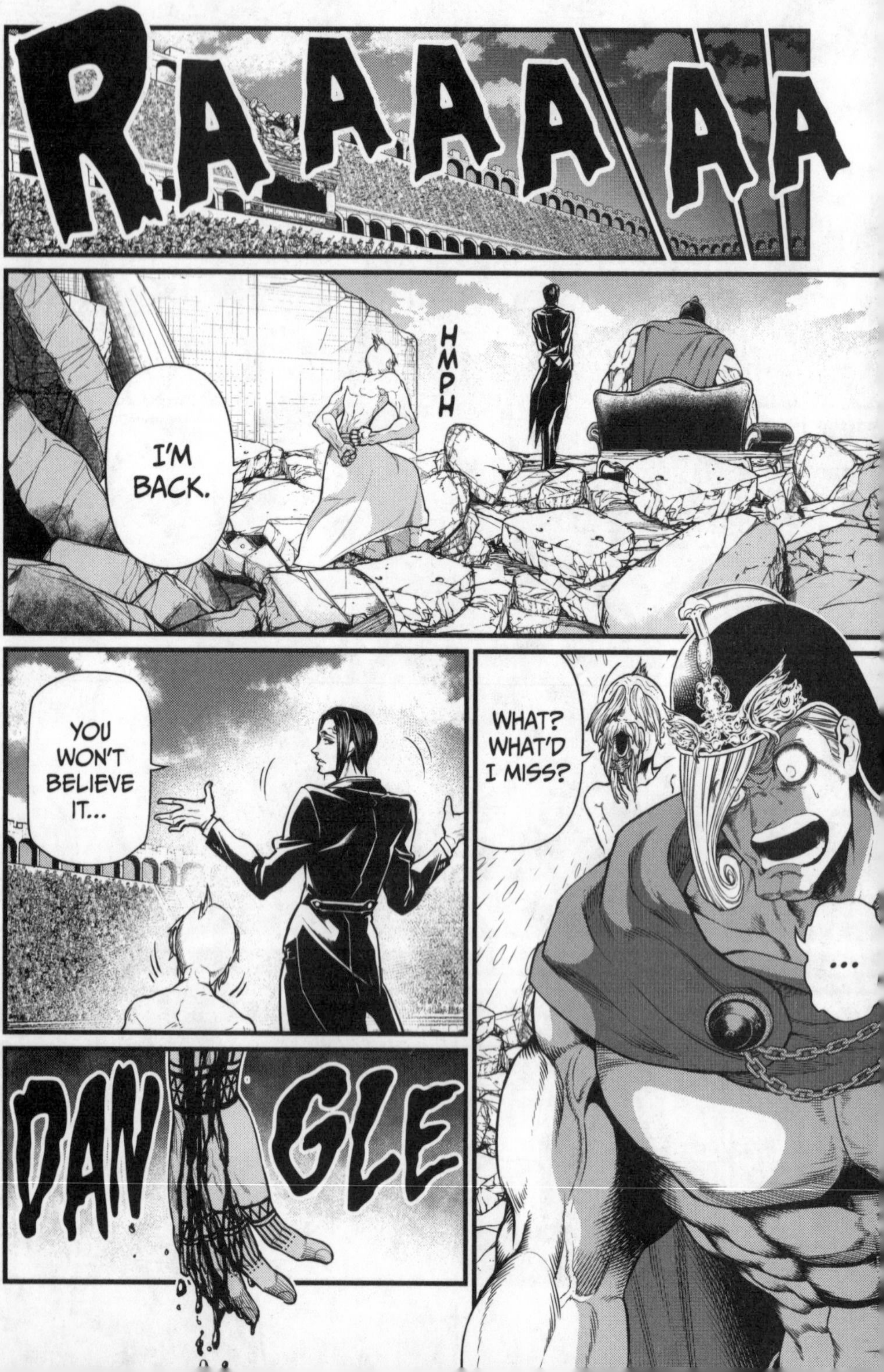
RAAAAAA
HMPH
I'M BACK.
WHAT? WHAT'D I MISS?
...
YOU WON'T BELIEVE IT...
DANGLE

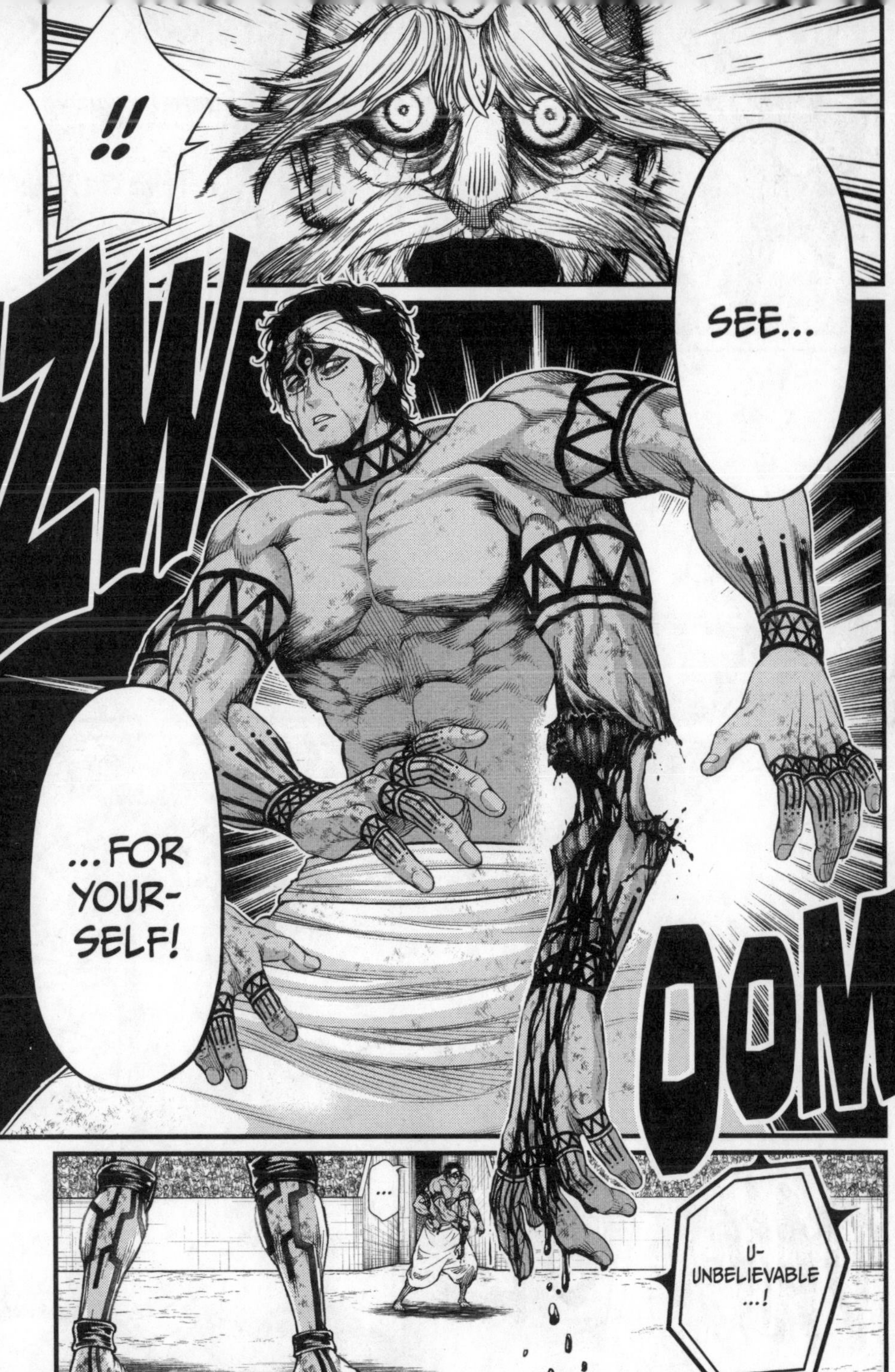
!!
SEE...
ZW
...FOR YOUR-SELF!
OOM
U-UNBELIEVABLE...!
...

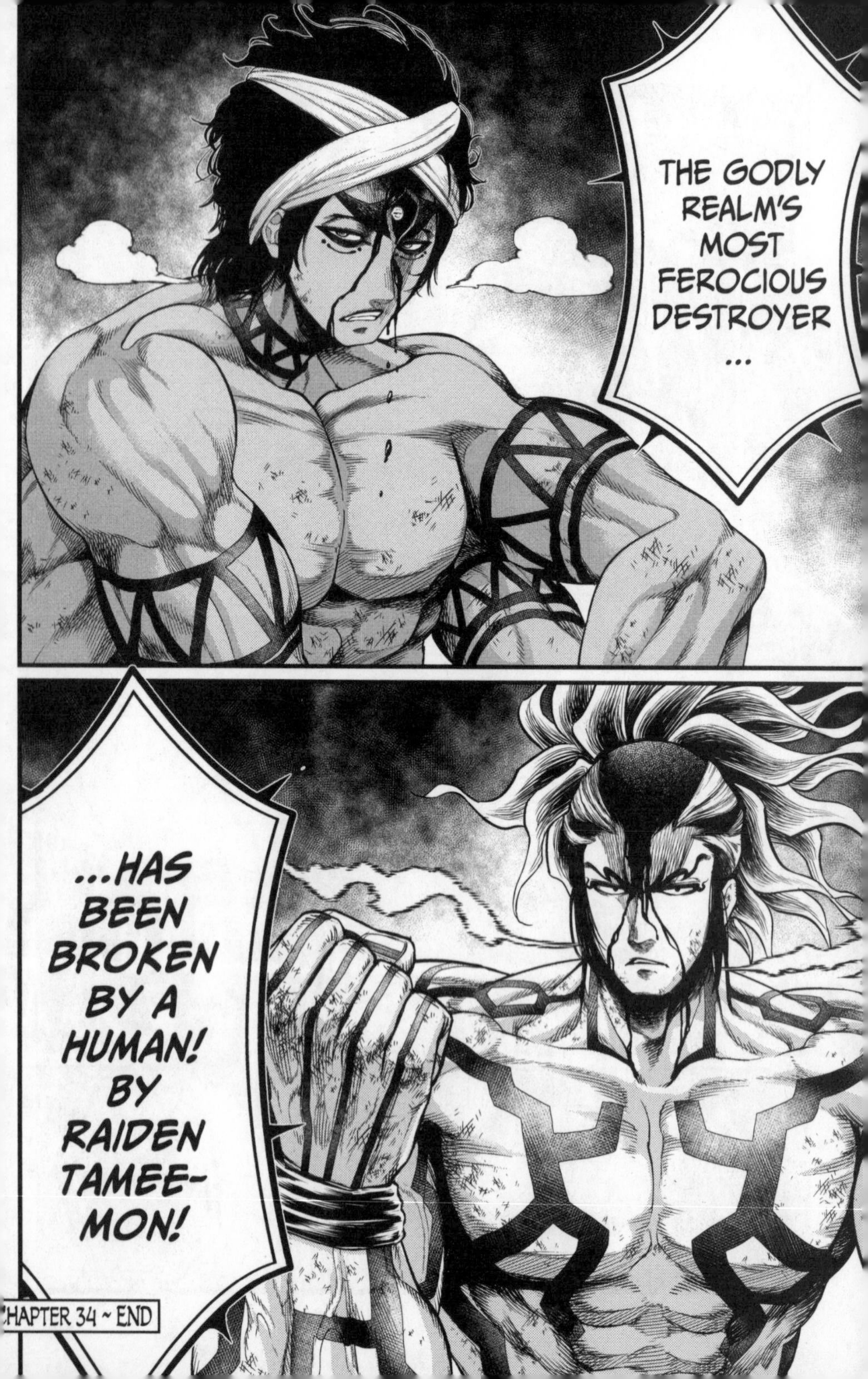
THE GODLY REALM'S MOST FEROCIOUS DESTROYER ...
...HAS BEEN BROKEN BY A HUMAN! BY RAIDEN TAMEE-MON!
CHAPTER 34 ~ END

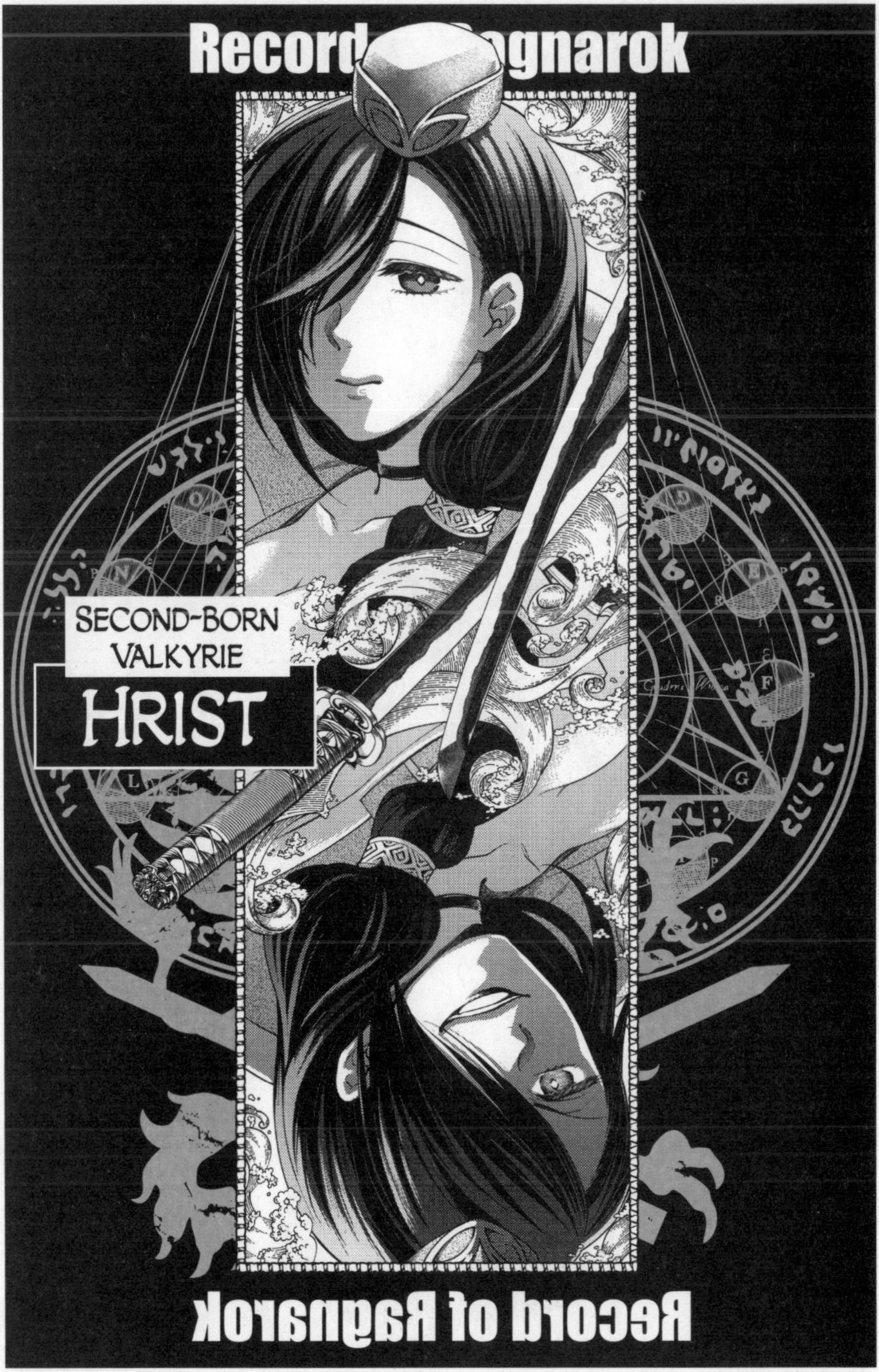
SECOND-BORN VALKYRIE
HRIST
Record of Ragnarok

RECORD OF

RAGNAROK

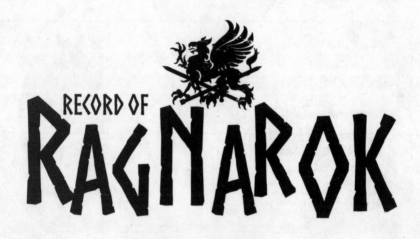

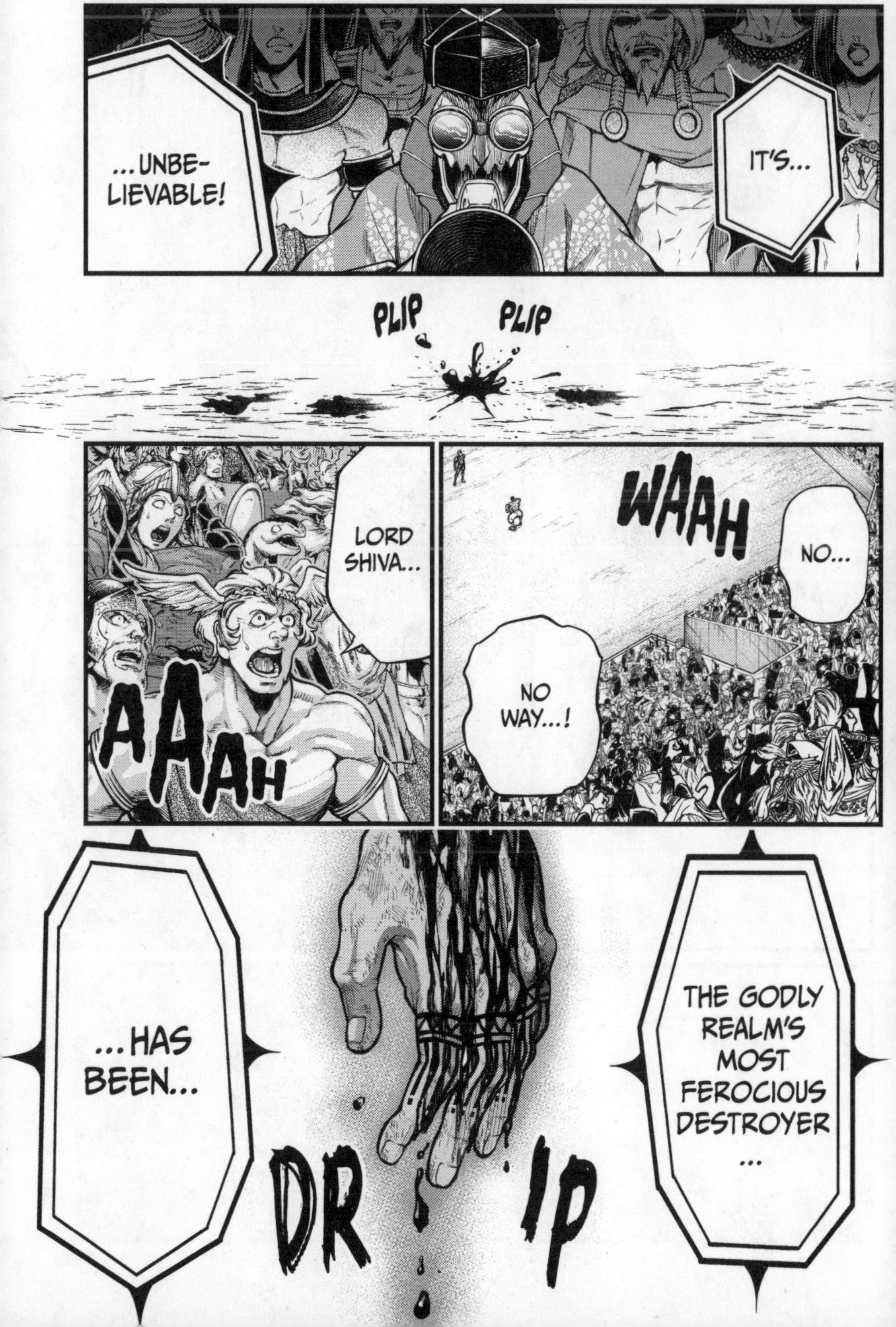
IT'S...
...UNBE-LIEVABLE!
PLIP
PLIP
WAAH
NO...
NO WAY...!
LORD SHIVA...
AAAH
THE GODLY REALM'S MOST FEROCIOUS DESTROYER ...
...HAS BEEN...
DR IP

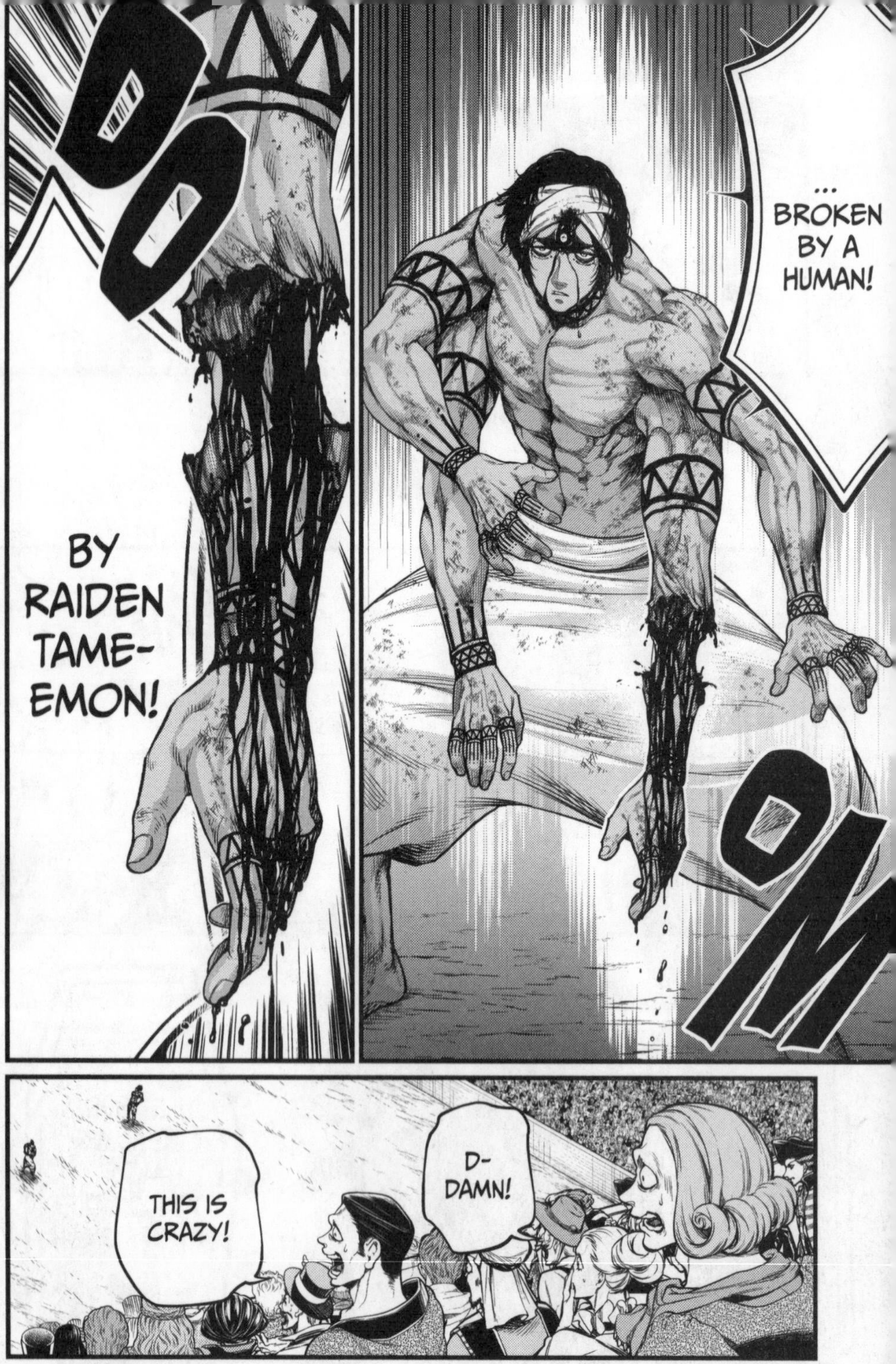
... BROKEN BY A HUMAN!
BY RAIDEN TAME-EMON!
D-DAMN!
THIS IS CRAZY!

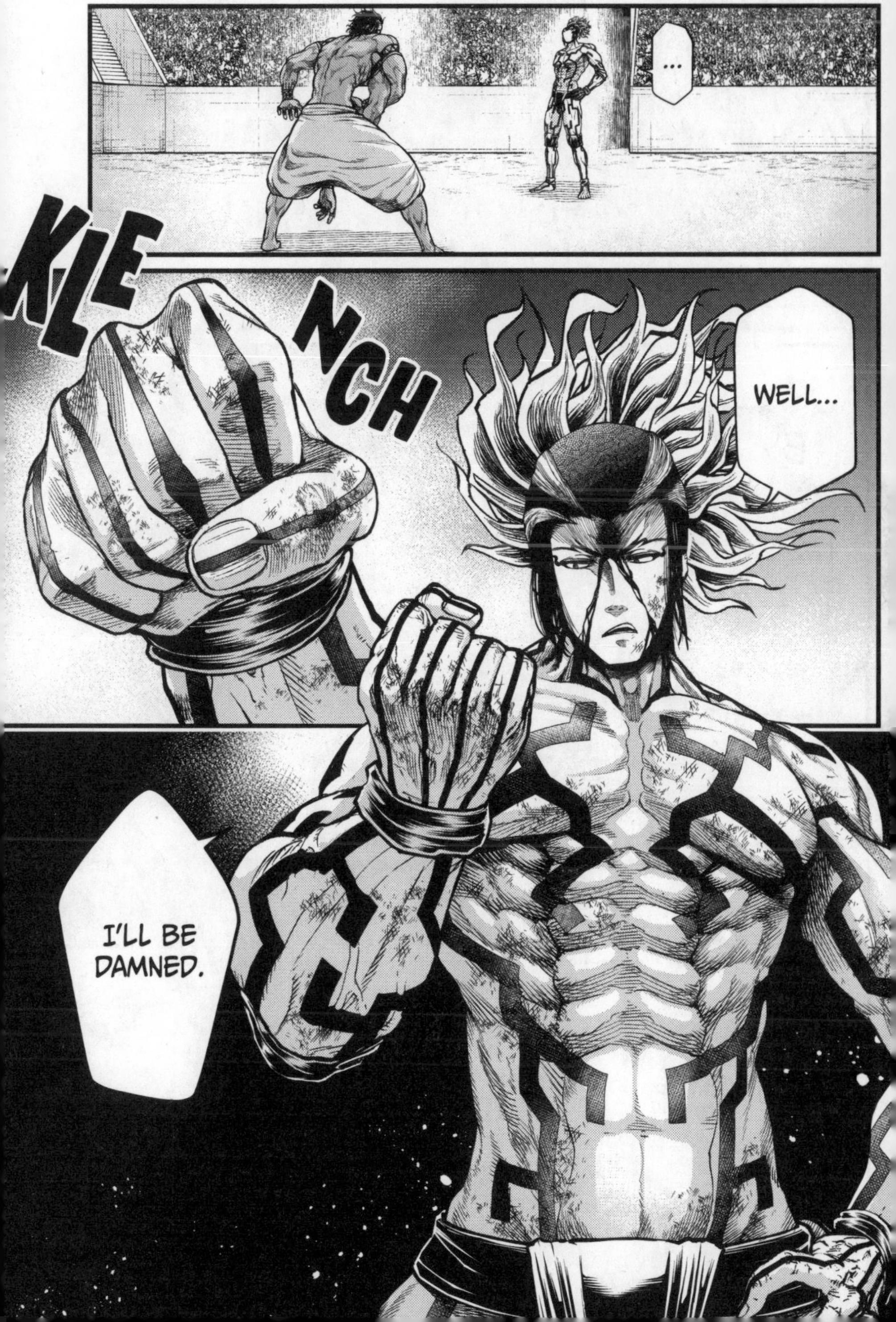
...
WELL...
KLENCH
I'LL BE DAMNED.

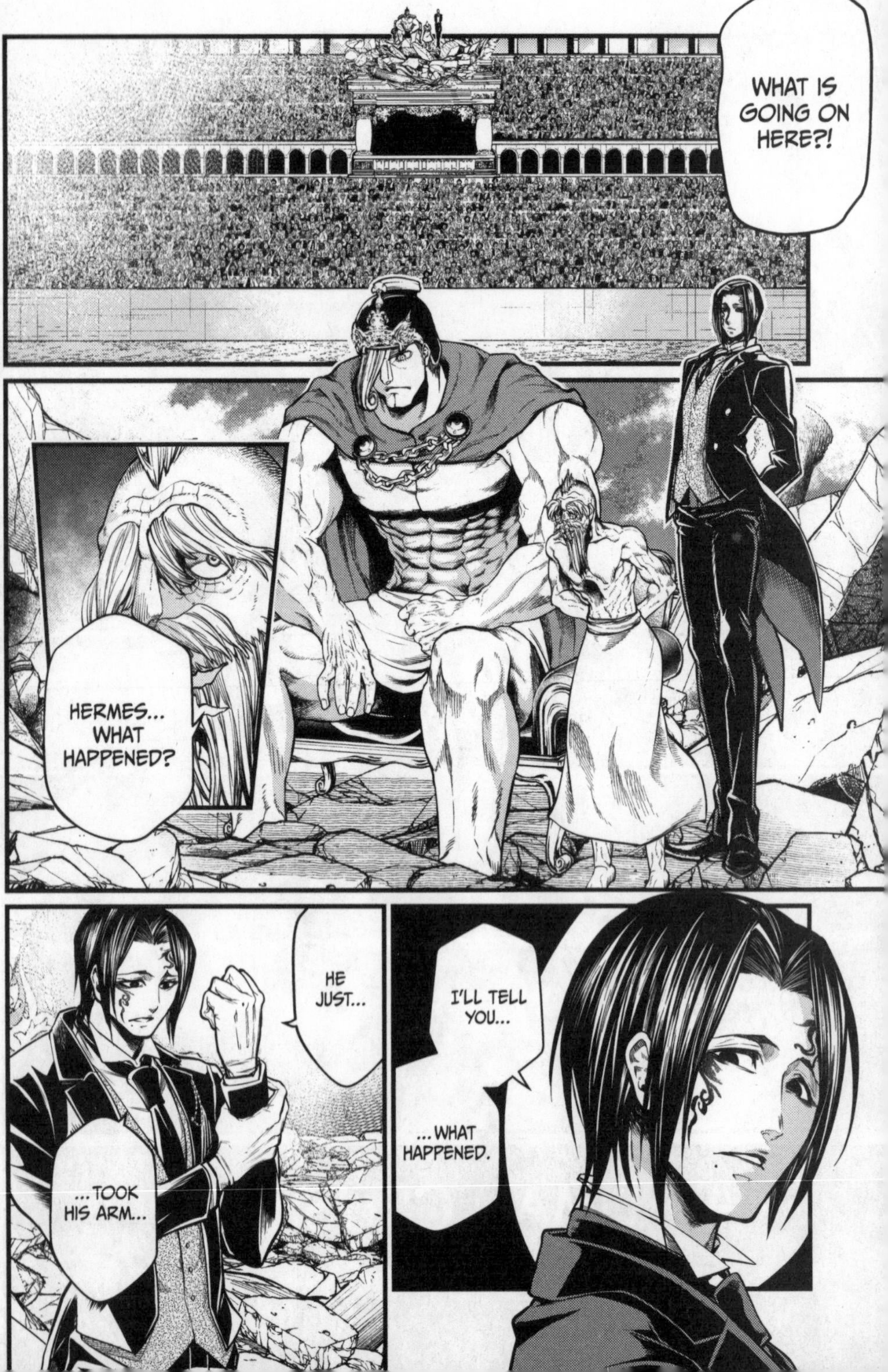
WHAT IS GOING ON HERE?!
HERMES... WHAT HAPPENED?
I'LL TELL YOU...
...WHAT HAPPENED.
HE JUST...
...TOOK HIS ARM...

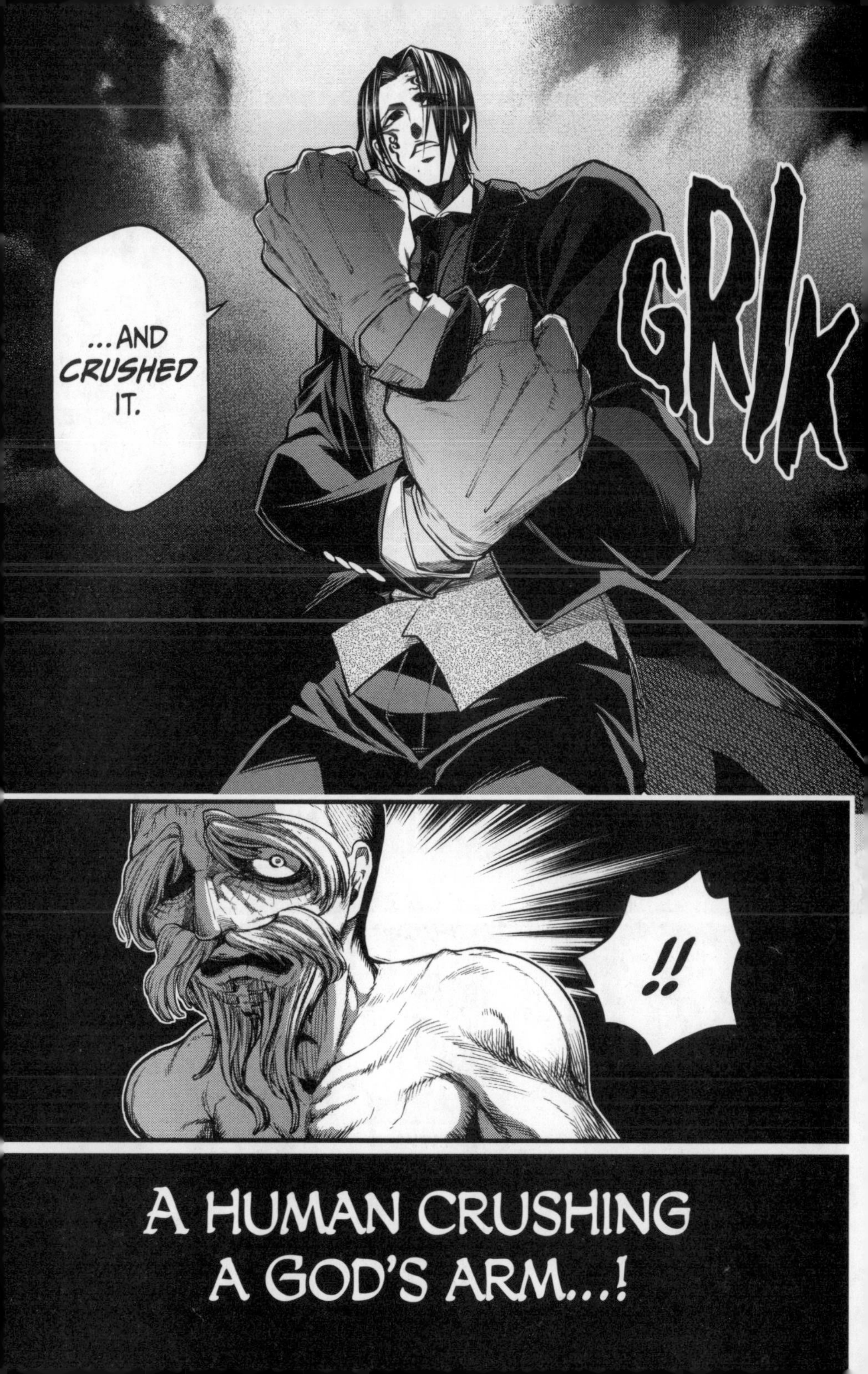
GRIK
...AND CRUSHED IT.
!!
A HUMAN CRUSHING A GOD'S ARM...!

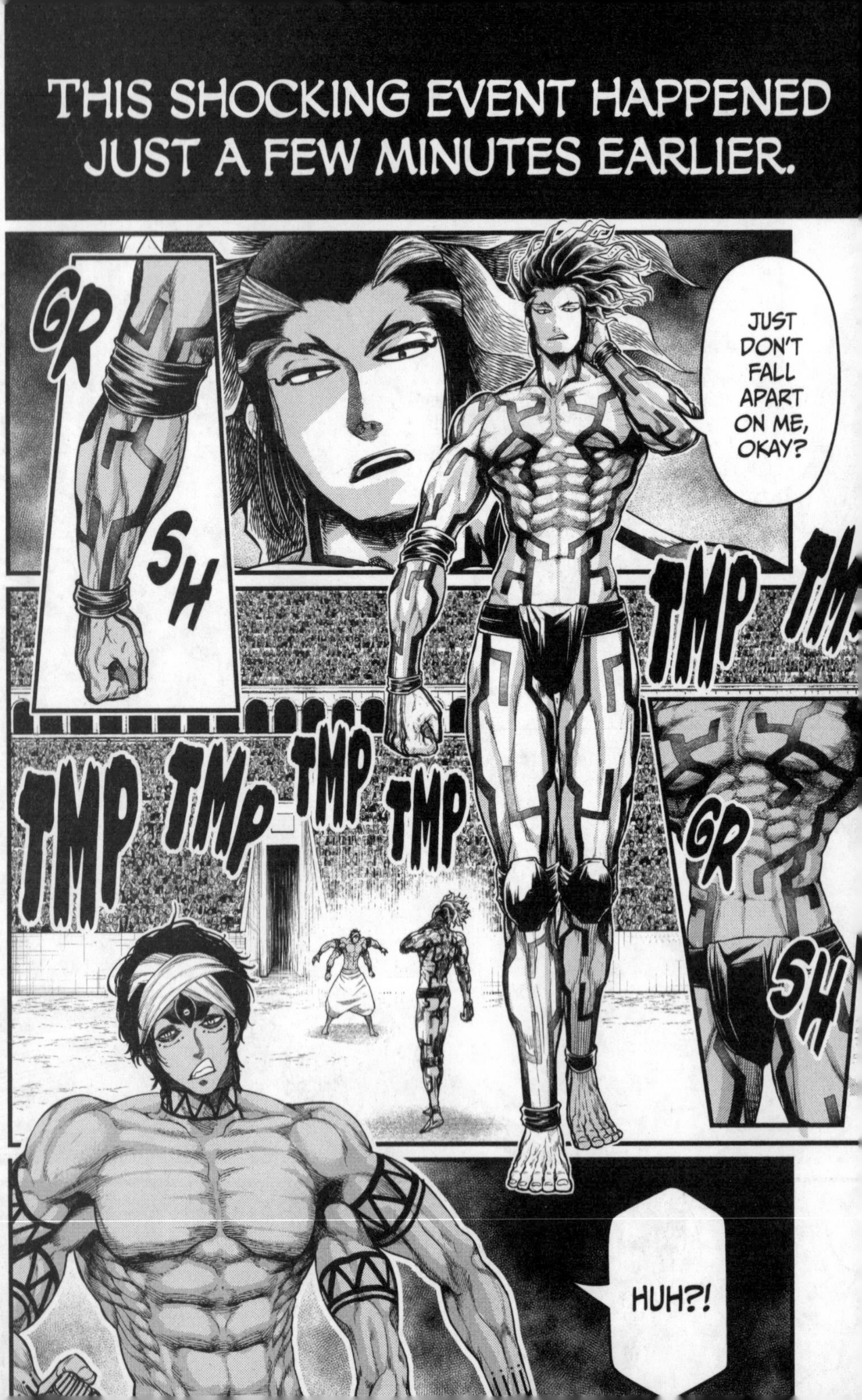
THIS SHOCKING EVENT HAPPENED JUST A FEW MINUTES EARLIER.
JUST DON'T FALL APART ON ME, OKAY?
TMP
GR
SH
TMP TMP TMP TMP
GR
SH
HUH?!

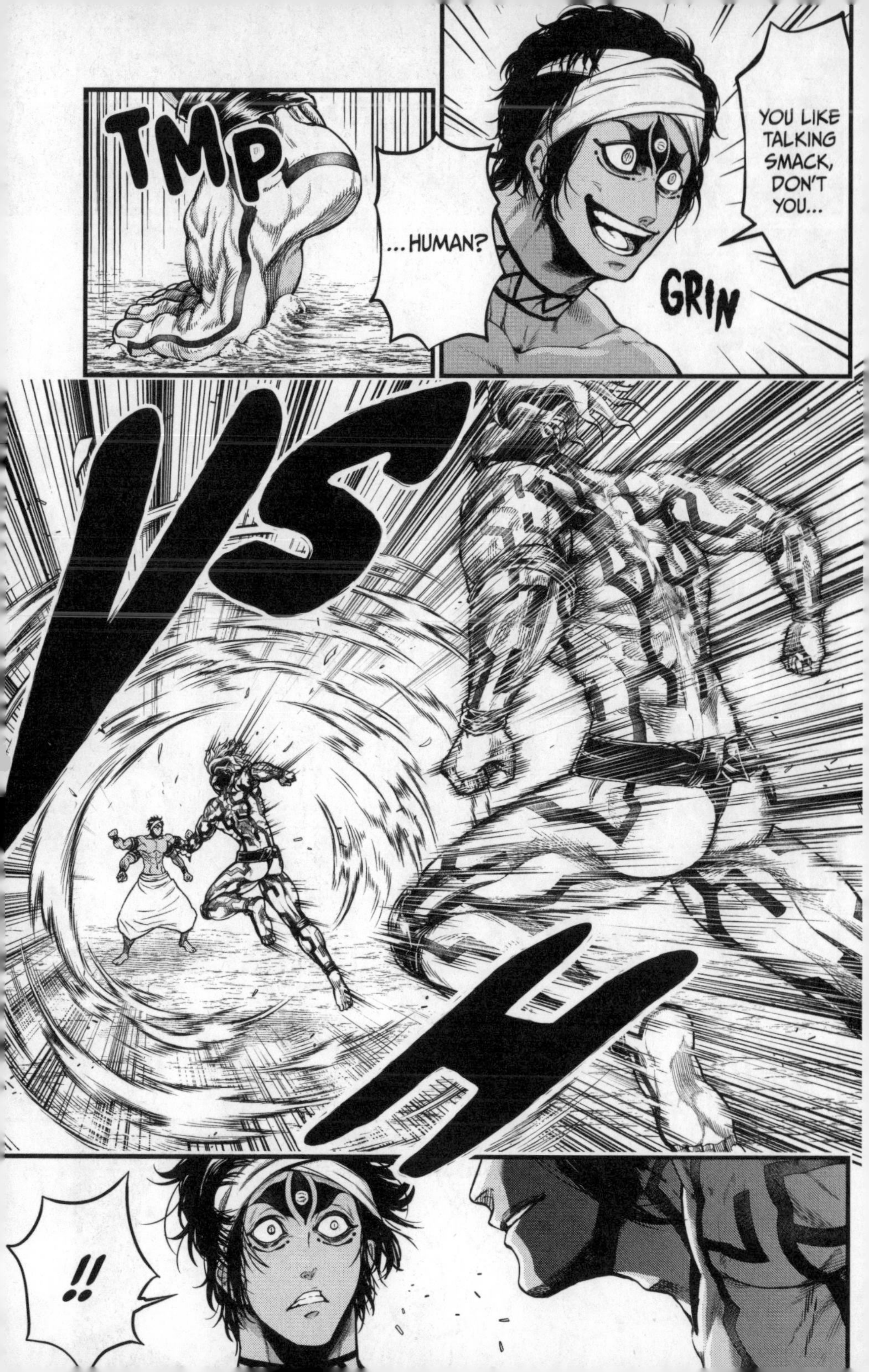
YOU LIKE TALKING SMACK, DON'T YOU...
GRIN
...HUMAN?
TMP
VSH
!!

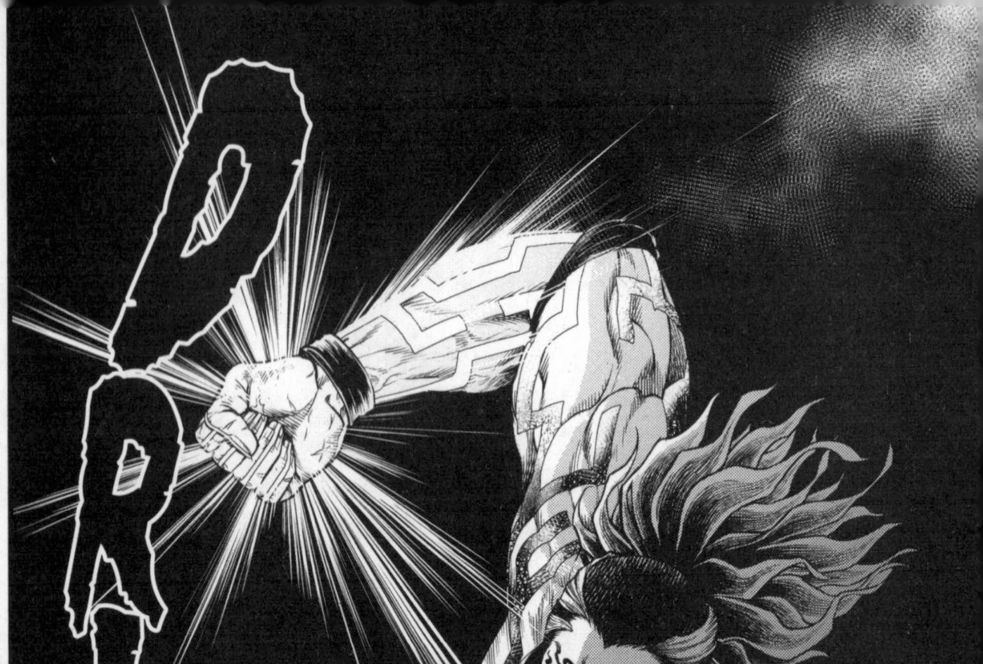
DR

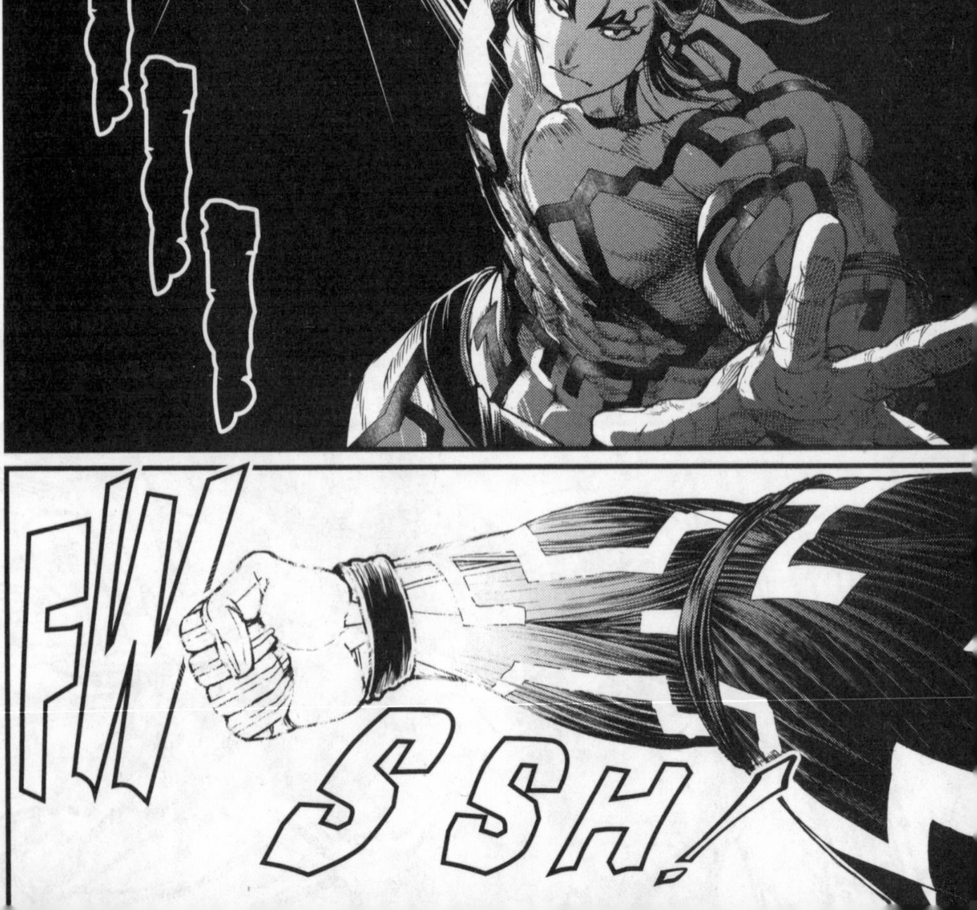
FWSSH!

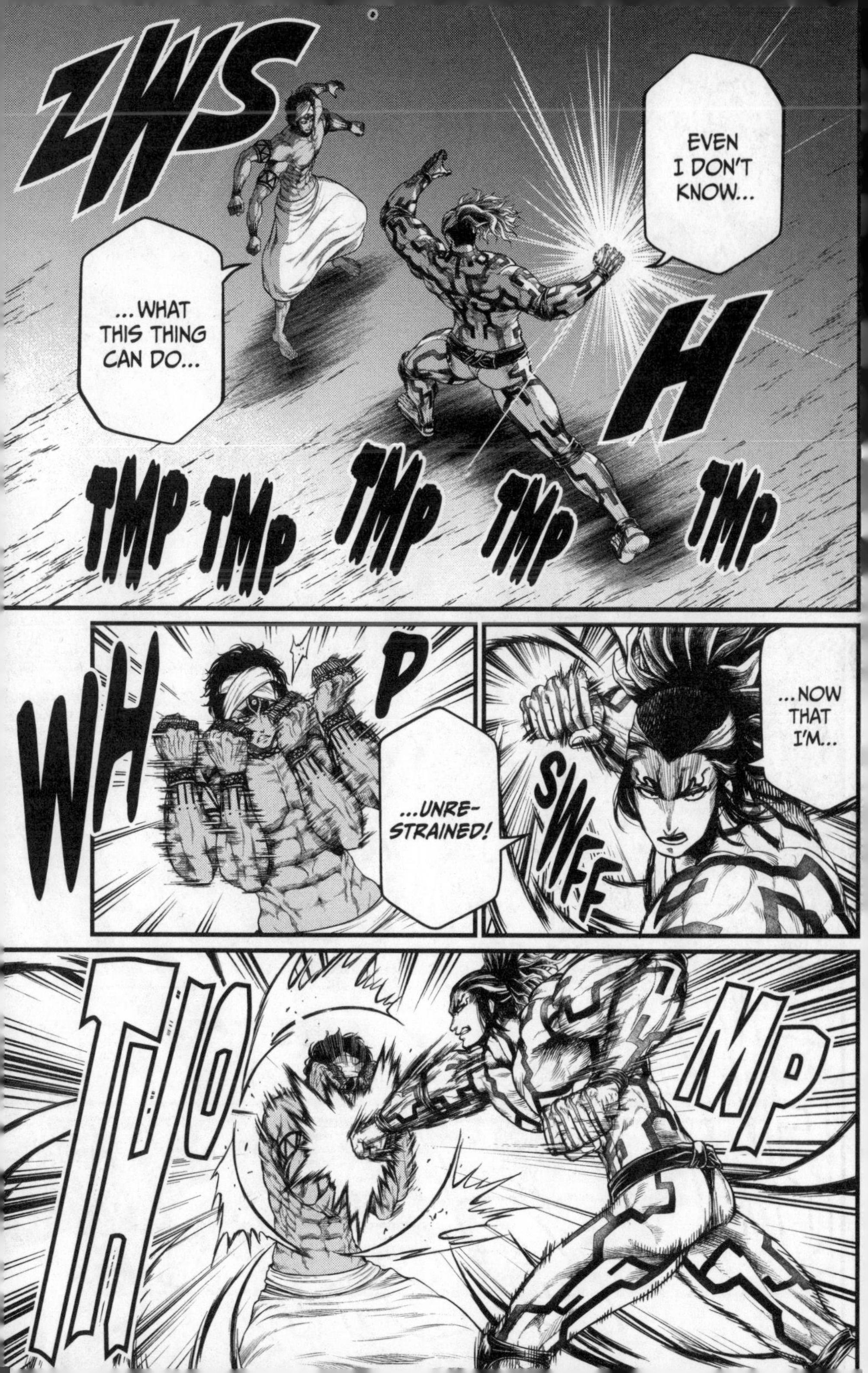
ZWS
EVEN I DON'T KNOW...
...WHAT THIS THING CAN DO...
H
TMP TMP TMP TMP TMP
...NOW THAT I'M...
SWFF
WH
P
...UNRE-STRAINED!
THO
MP

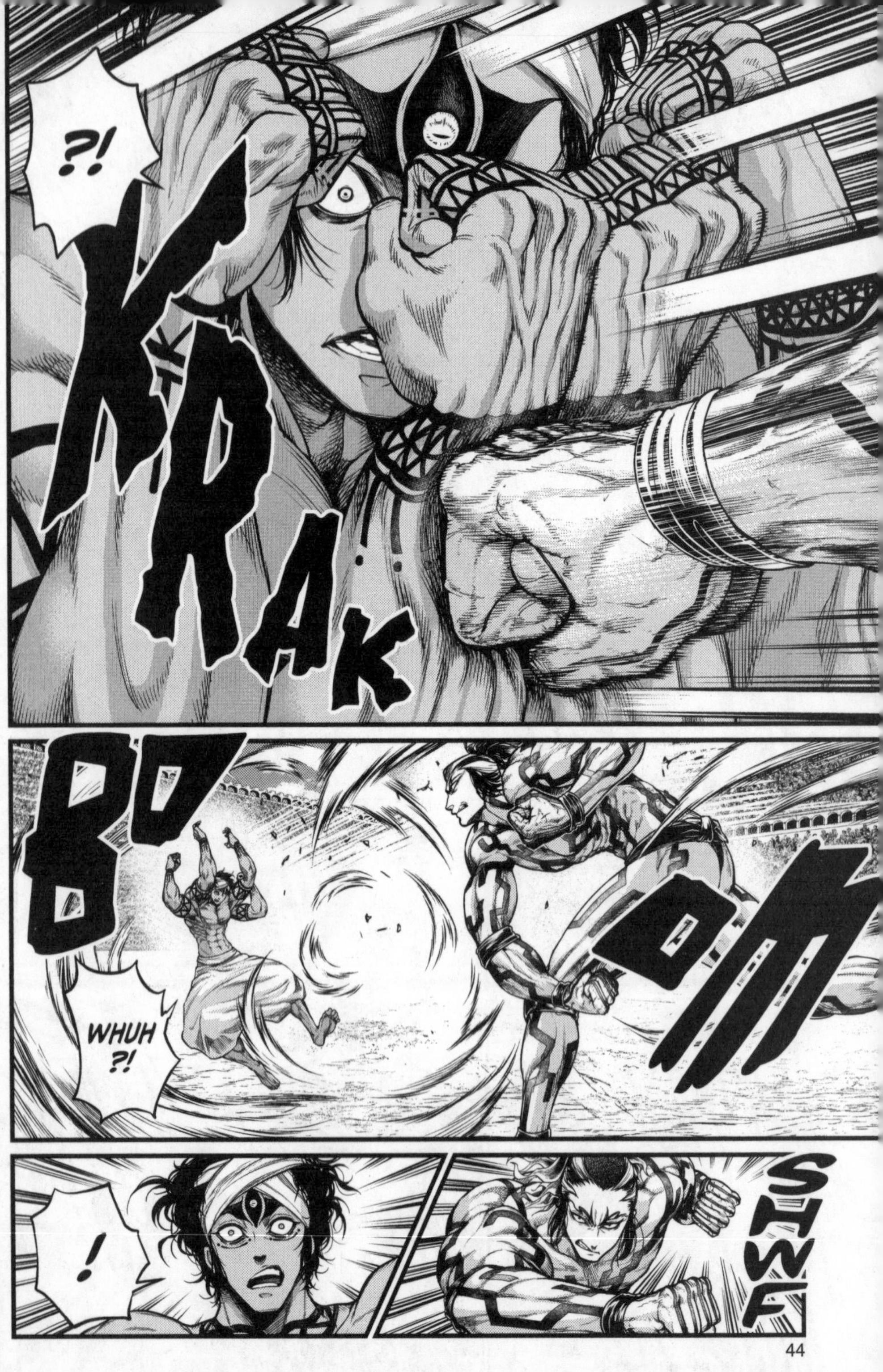
?!
KRAK
WHUH ?!
SHWF
!

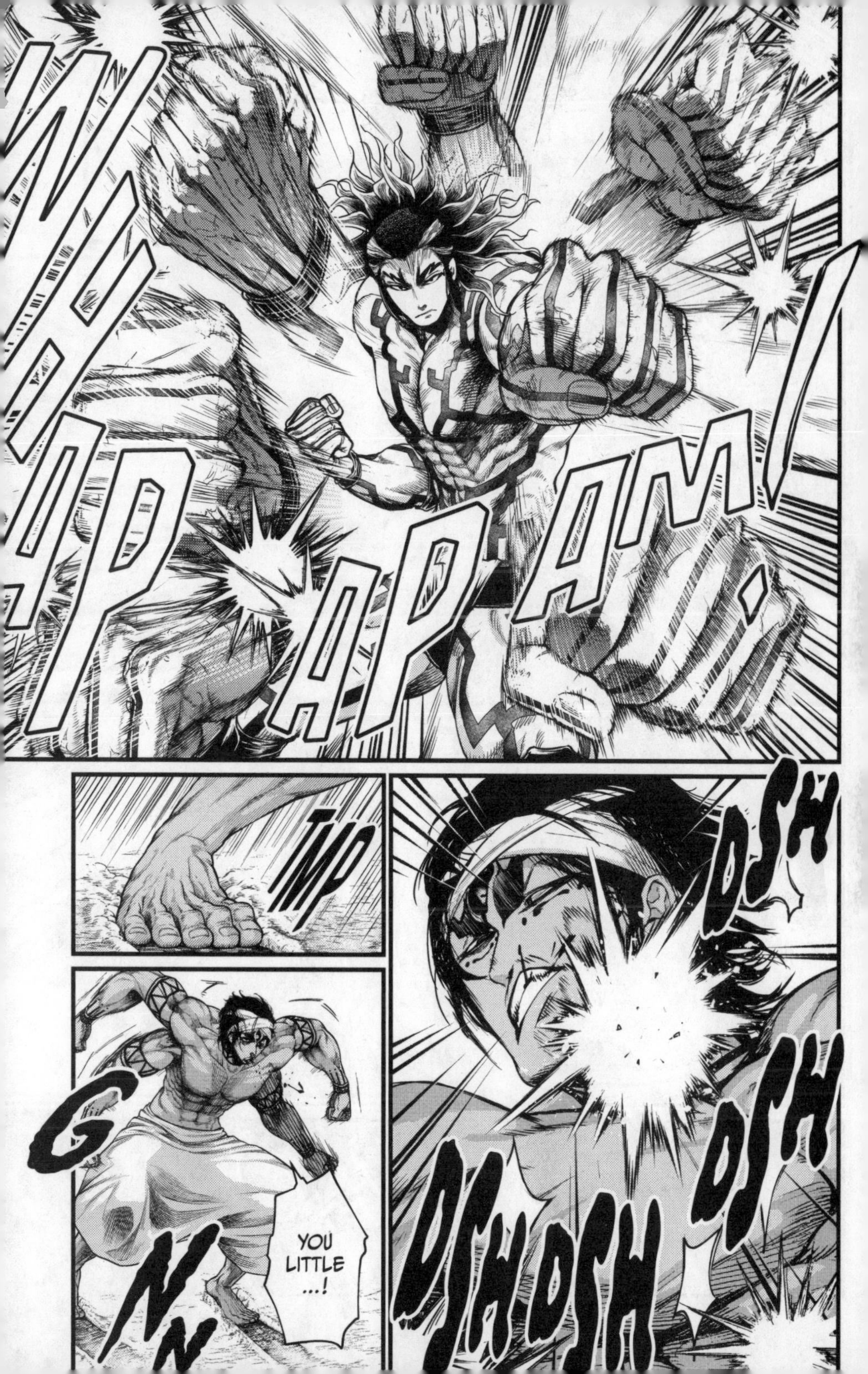
WHAP PAP PAM!
DOSH
DOSH
DOSH
DOSH
TMP
GNN
YOU LITTLE ...!

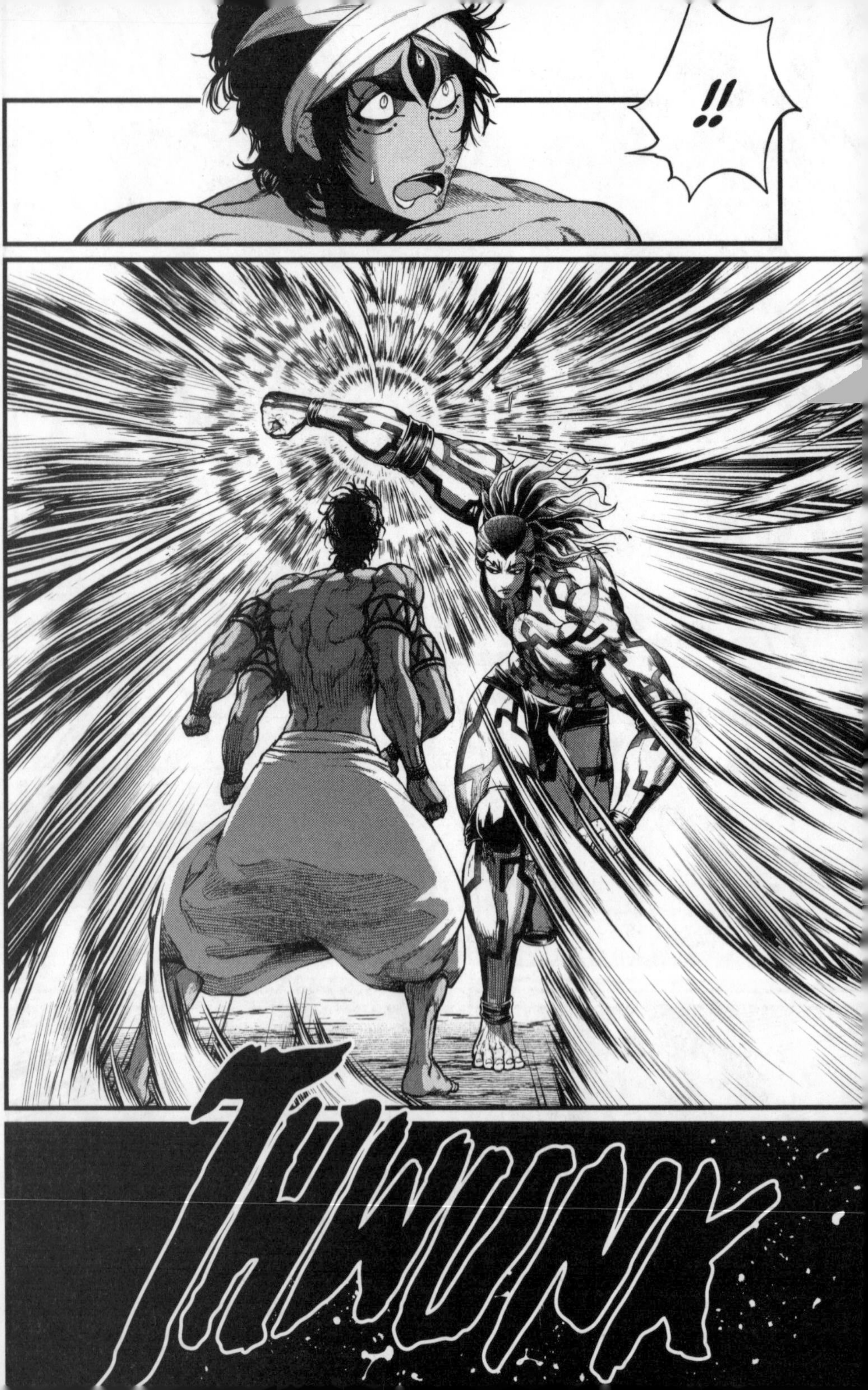
!!
THWUNK

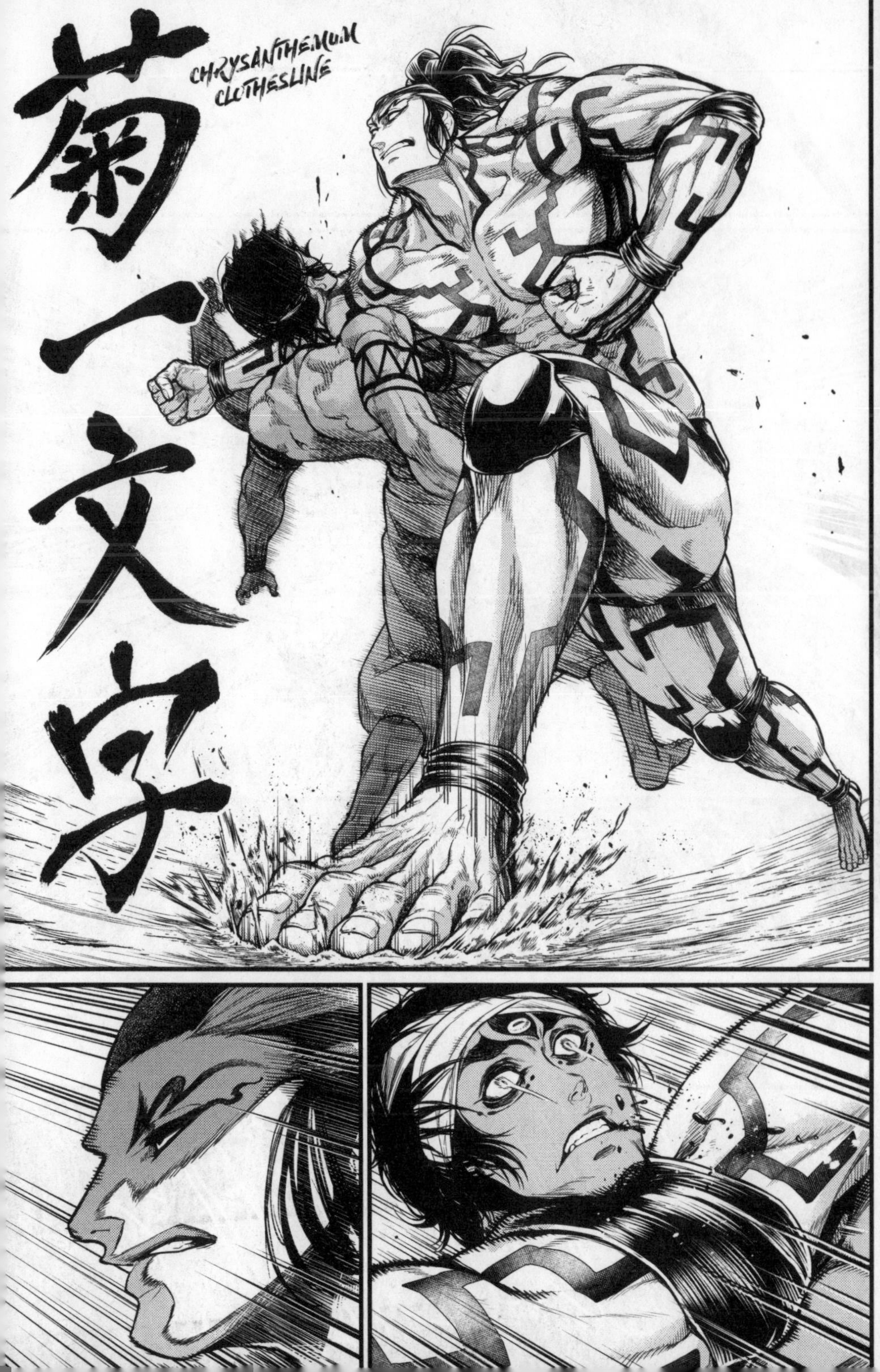

菊一文字
CHRYSANTHEMUM CLOTHESLINE

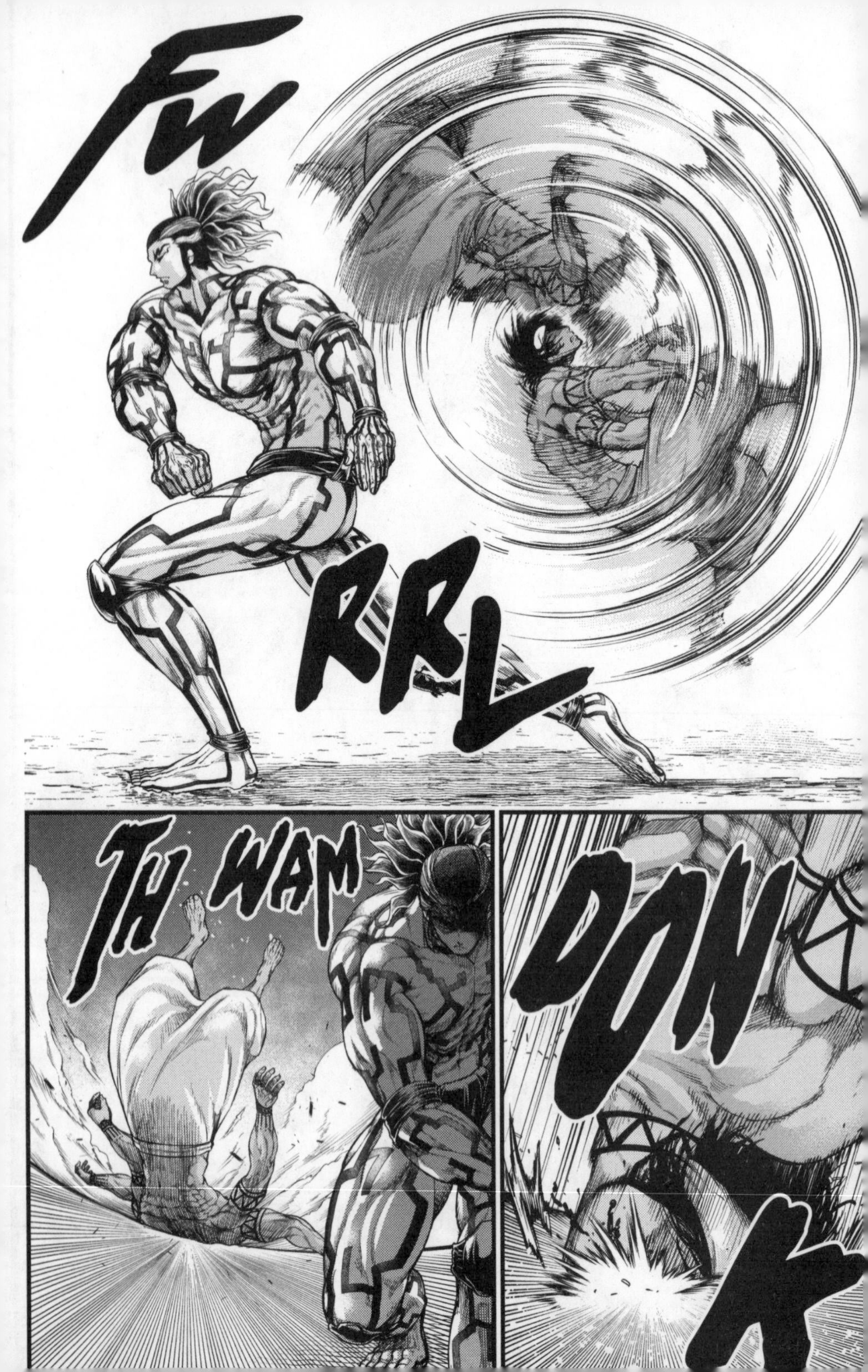
FW
RRL
DON
K
TH WAM

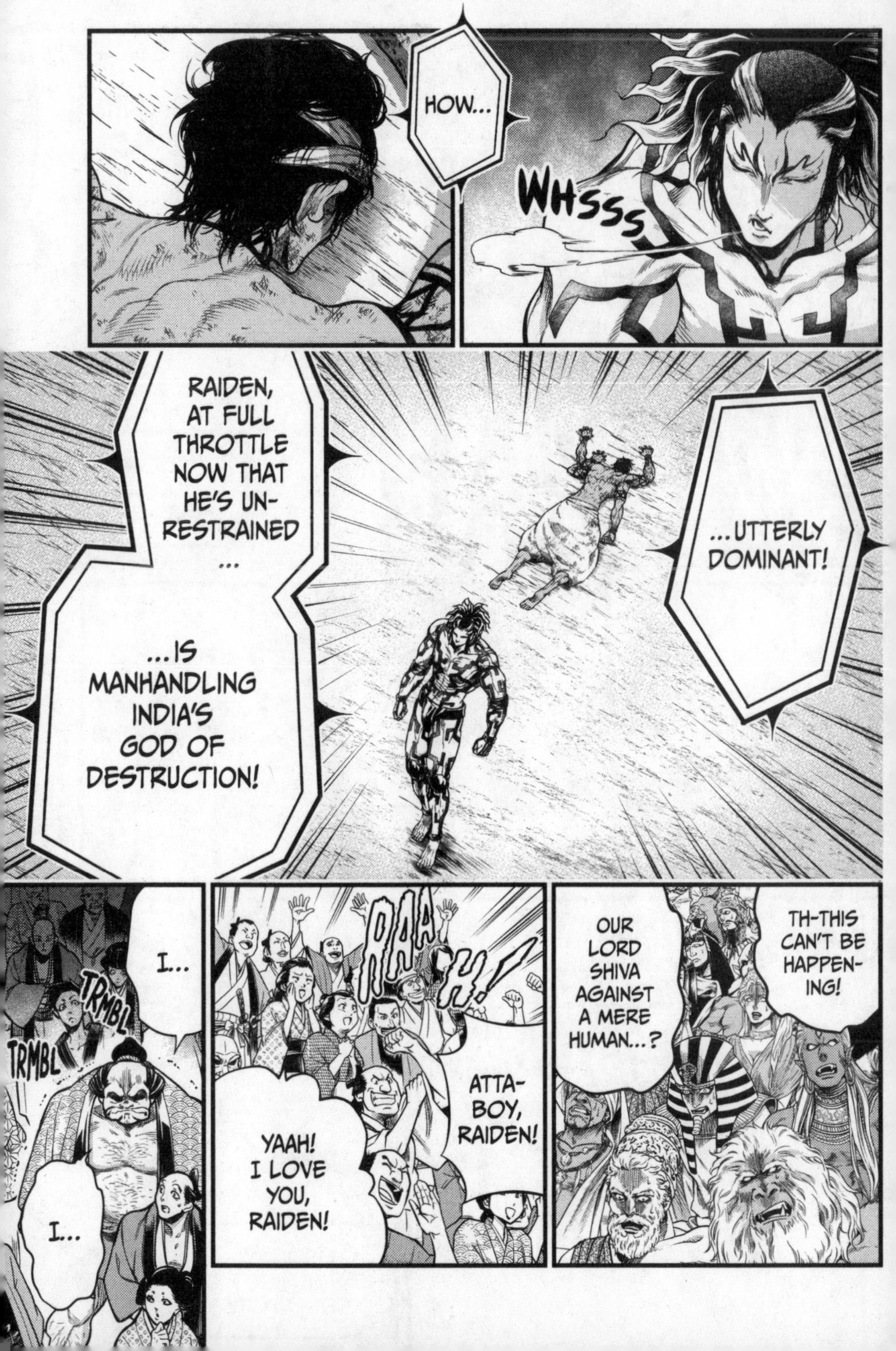
WHSSS
HOW...
...UTTERLY DOMINANT!
RAIDEN, AT FULL THROTTLE NOW THAT HE'S UN-RESTRAINED ...
...IS MANHANDLING INDIA'S GOD OF DESTRUCTION!
TH-THIS CAN'T BE HAPPEN-ING!
OUR LORD SHIVA AGAINST A MERE HUMAN...?
RAAAH!!
ATTA-BOY, RAIDEN!
YAAH! I LOVE YOU, RAIDEN!
I...
TRMBL
TRMBL
I...

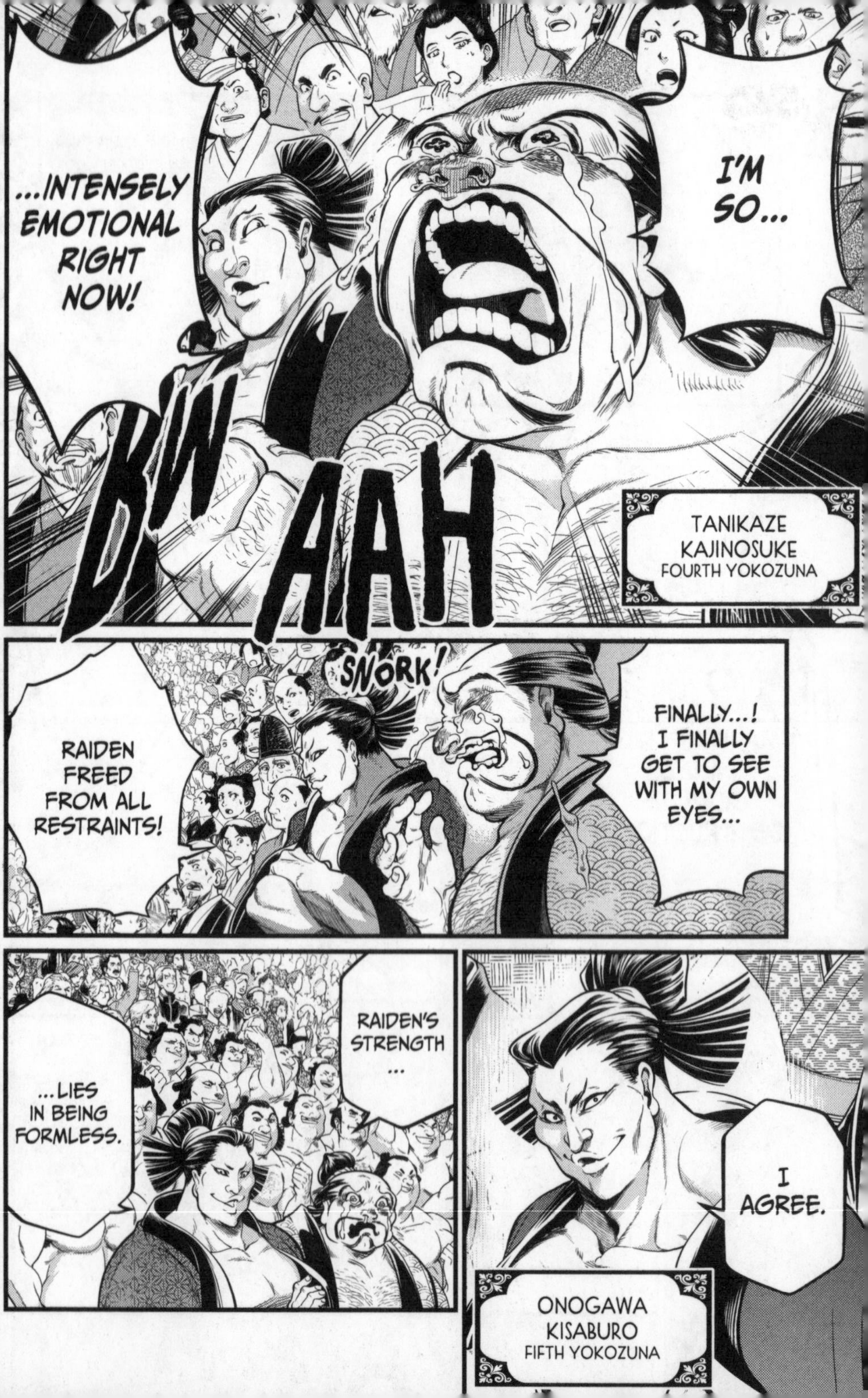
I'M SO...
...INTENSELY EMOTIONAL RIGHT NOW!
BWAAH
TANIKAZE KAJINOSUKE
FOURTH YOKOZUNA
SNORK!
FINALLY...! I FINALLY GET TO SEE WITH MY OWN EYES...
RAIDEN FREED FROM ALL RESTRAINTS!
I AGREE.
ONOGAWA KISABURO
FIFTH YOKOZUNA
RAIDEN'S STRENGTH ...
...LIES IN BEING FORMLESS.

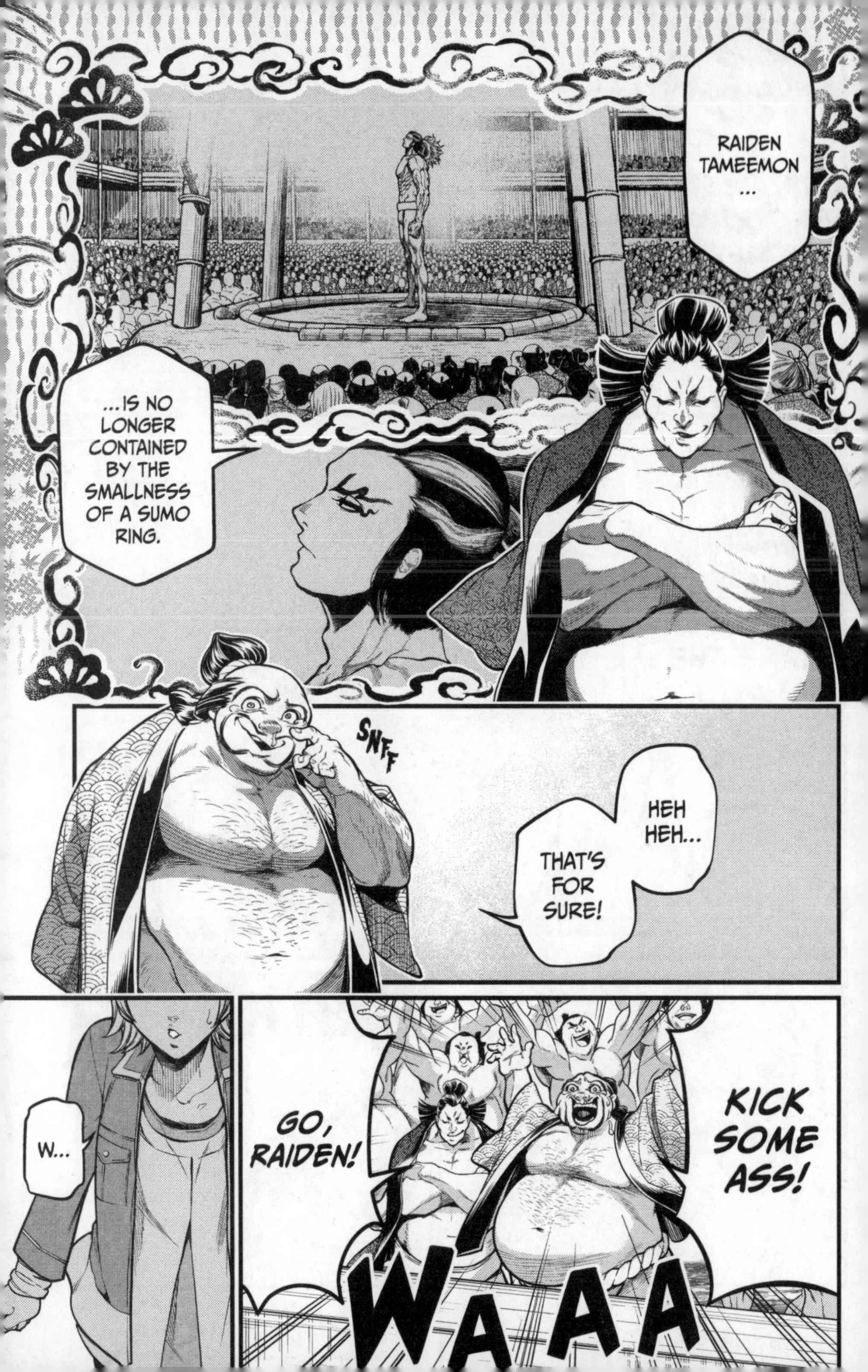
RAIDEN TAMEEMON ...
...IS NO LONGER CONTAINED BY THE SMALLNESS OF A SUMO RING.
SNFF
HEH HEH...
THAT'S FOR SURE!
KICK SOME ASS!
GO, RAIDEN!
WAAA
W...

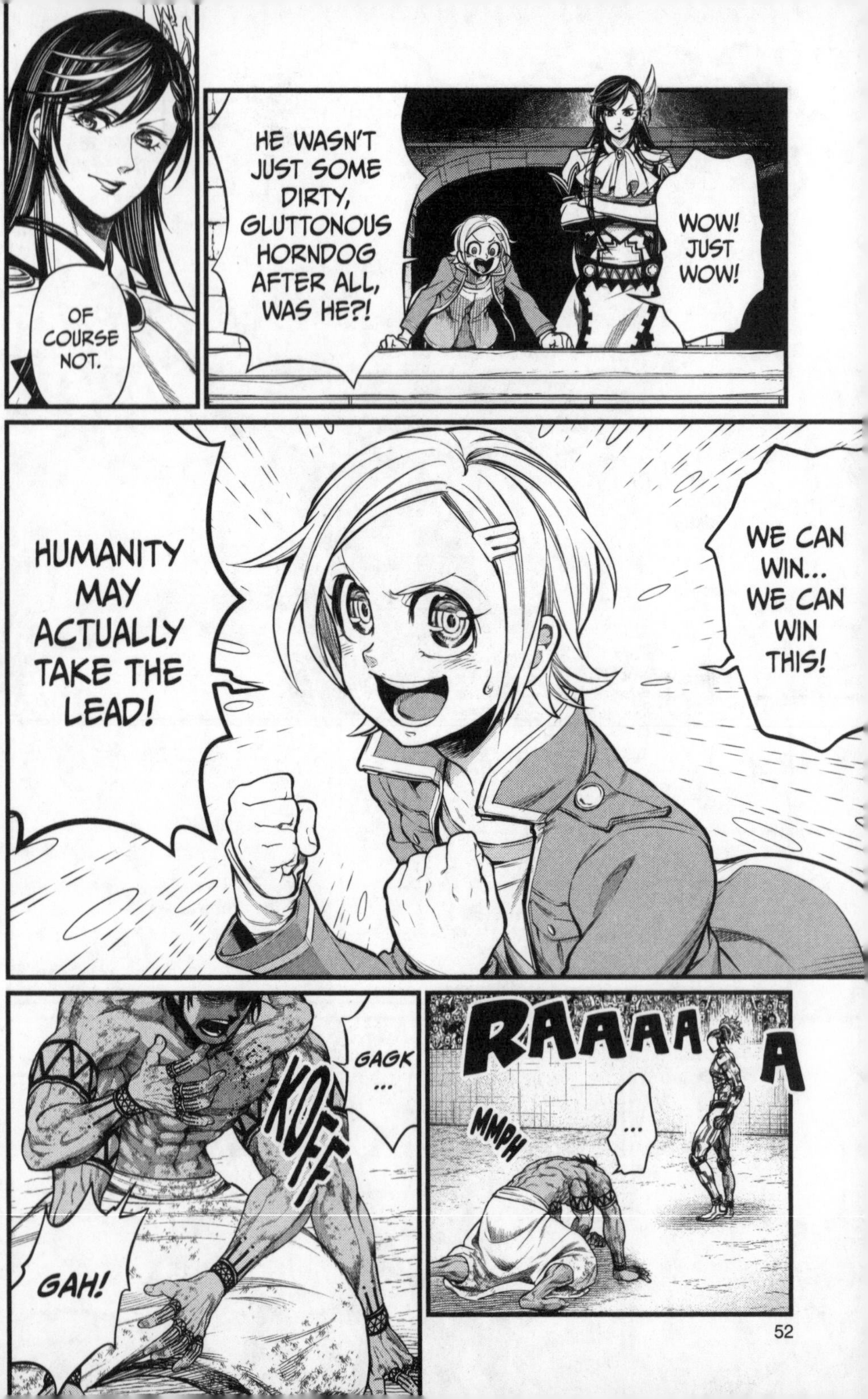
WOW! JUST WOW!
HE WASN'T JUST SOME DIRTY, GLUTTONOUS HORNDOG AFTER ALL, WAS HE?!
OF COURSE NOT.
WE CAN WIN... WE CAN WIN THIS!
HUMANITY MAY ACTUALLY TAKE THE LEAD!
RAAAAA
...
MMPH
GAGK ...
KOFF
GAH!

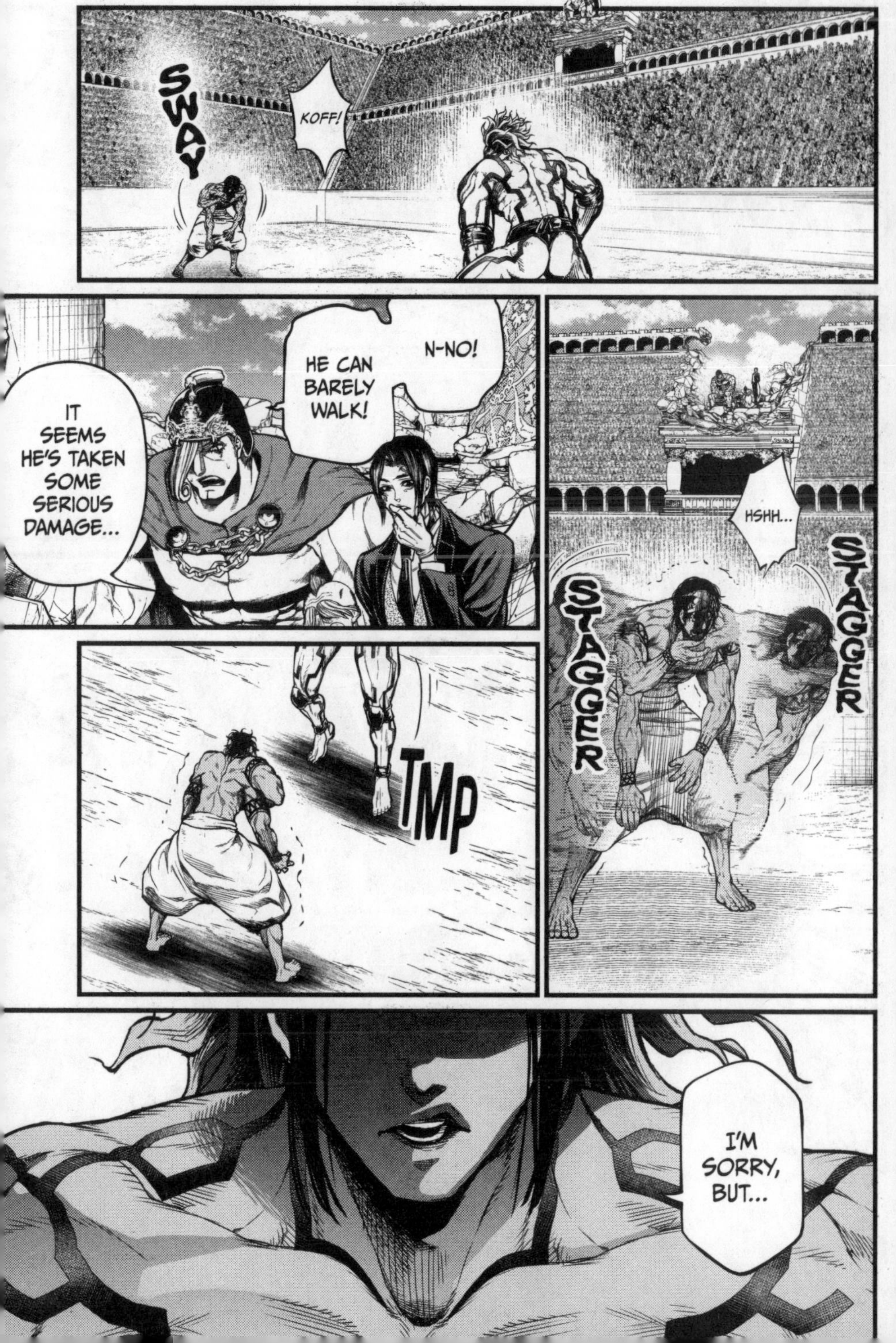
KOFF!
SWAY
HSHH...
STAGGER
STAGGER
N-NO!
HE CAN BARELY WALK!
IT SEEMS HE'S TAKEN SOME SERIOUS DAMAGE...
TMP
I'M SORRY, BUT...

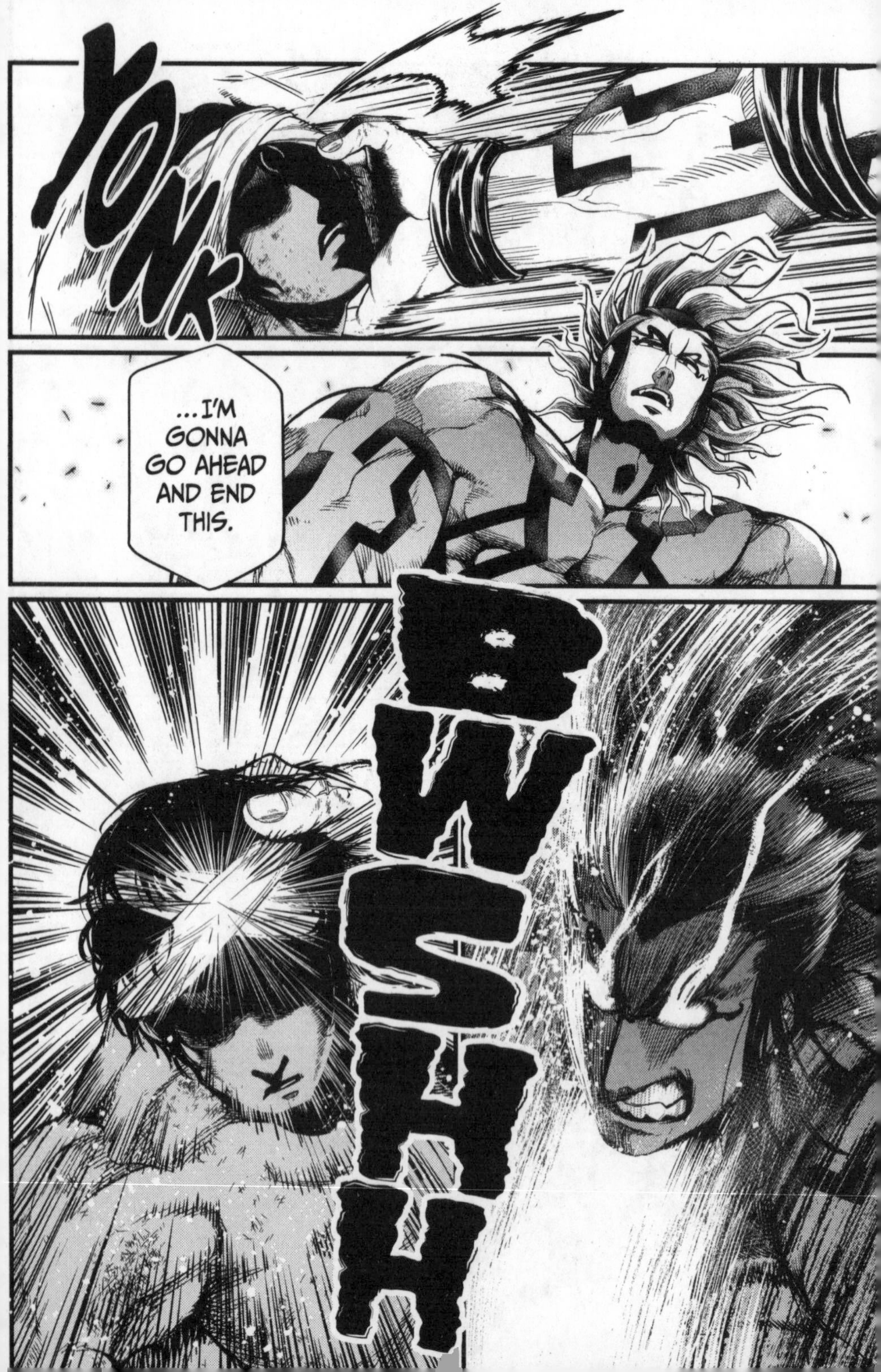
YOINK
...I'M GONNA GO AHEAD AND END THIS.
BWSHH

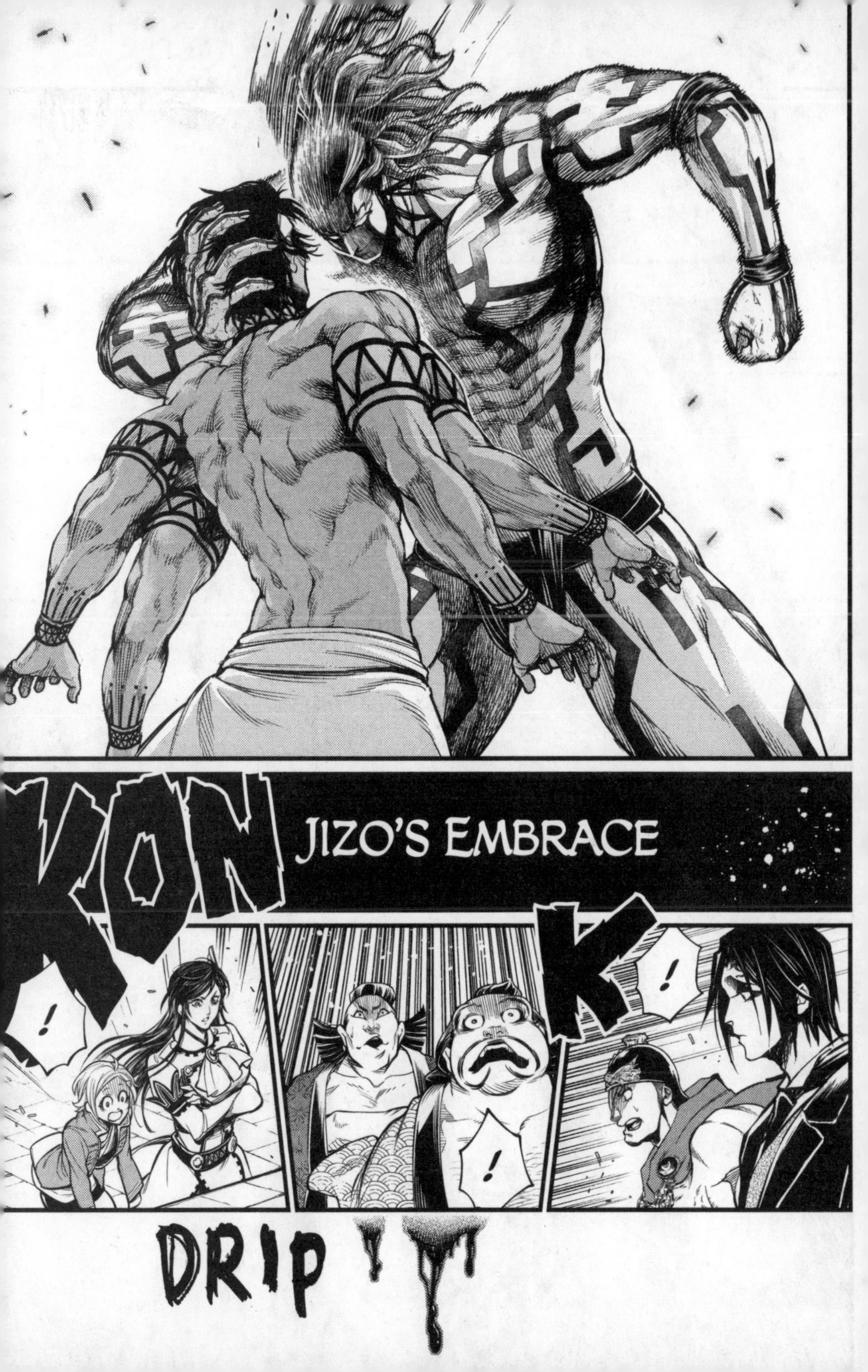
JIZO'S EMBRACE
KON
!
!
!
DRIP

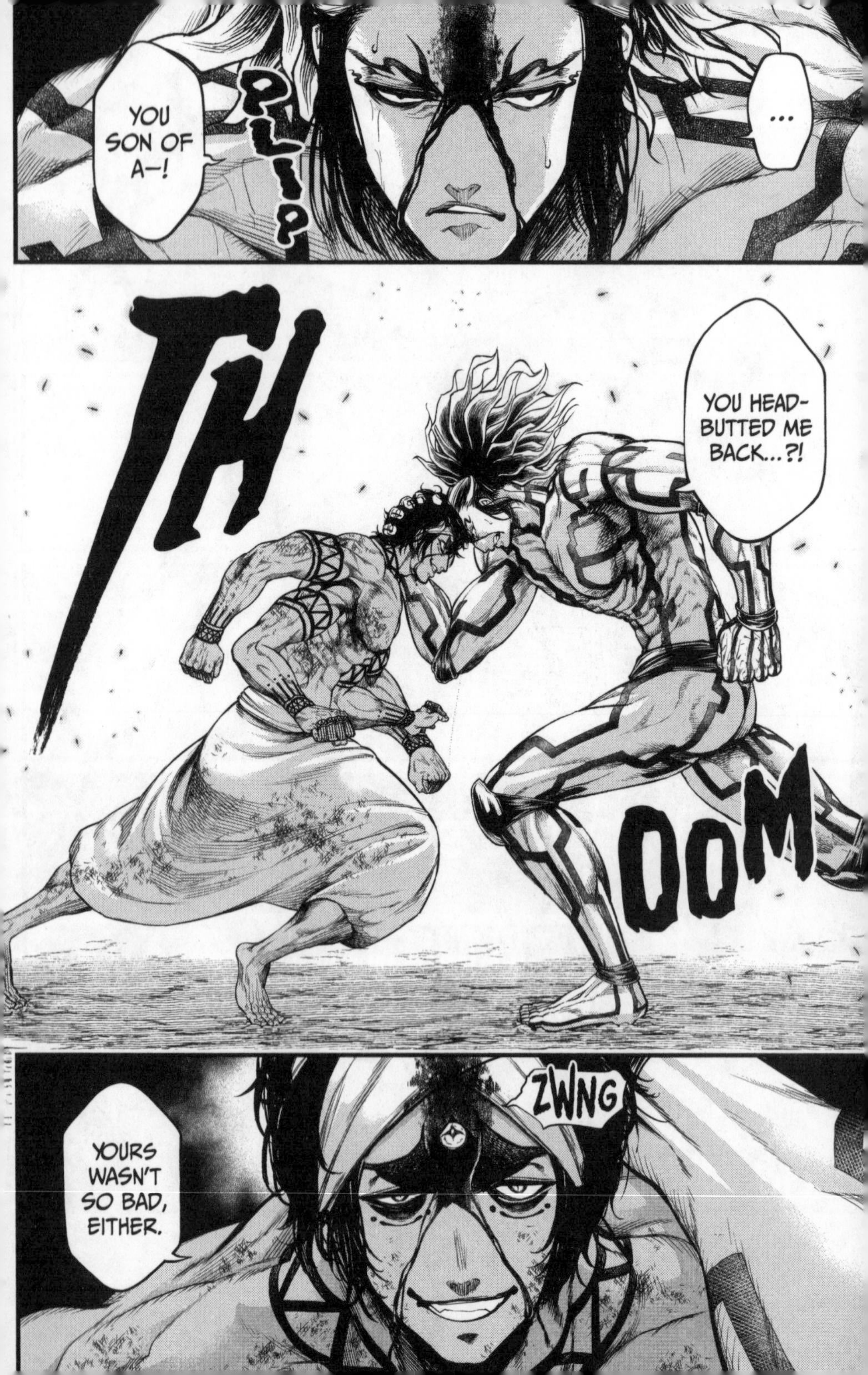
...
PLIP
YOU SON OF A—!
YOU HEAD-BUTTED ME BACK...?!
THOOM
ZWNG
YOURS WASN'T SO BAD, EITHER.

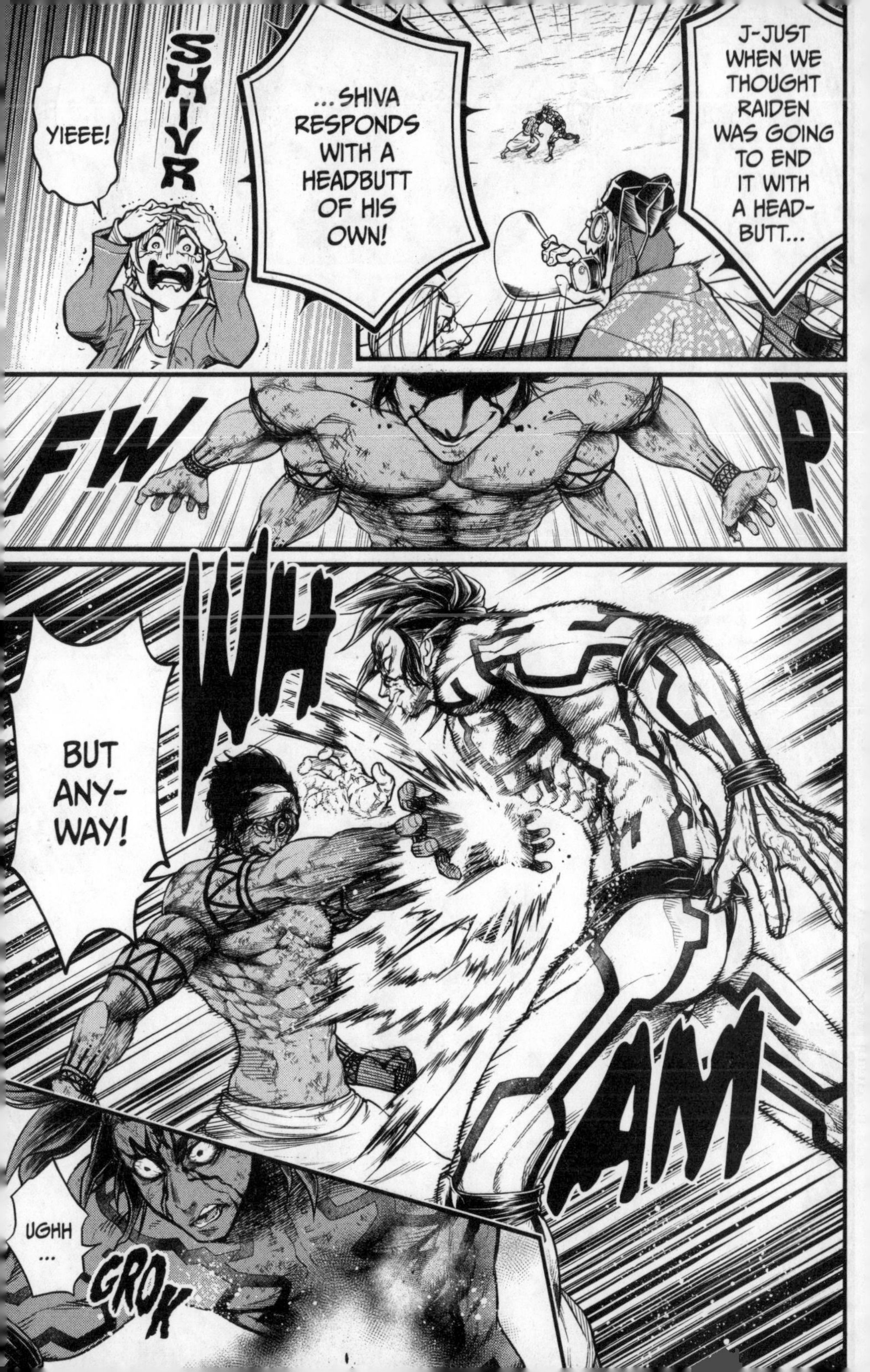
J-JUST WHEN WE THOUGHT RAIDEN WAS GOING TO END IT WITH A HEAD-BUTT...
...SHIVA RESPONDS WITH A HEADBUTT OF HIS OWN!
SHIVR
YIEEE!
FW P
WH AM
BUT ANY-WAY!
UGHH ...
GROK

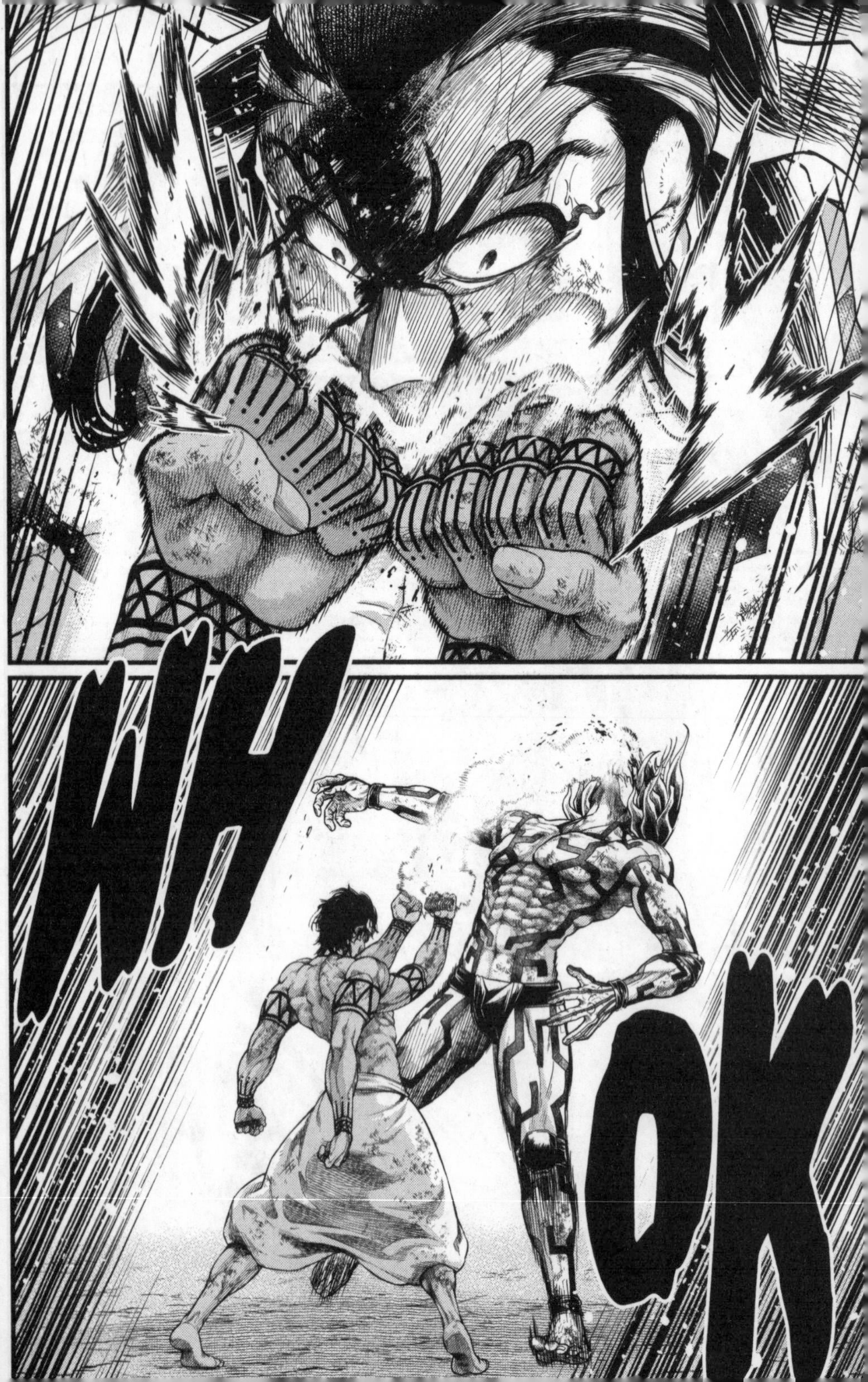
WH
OK

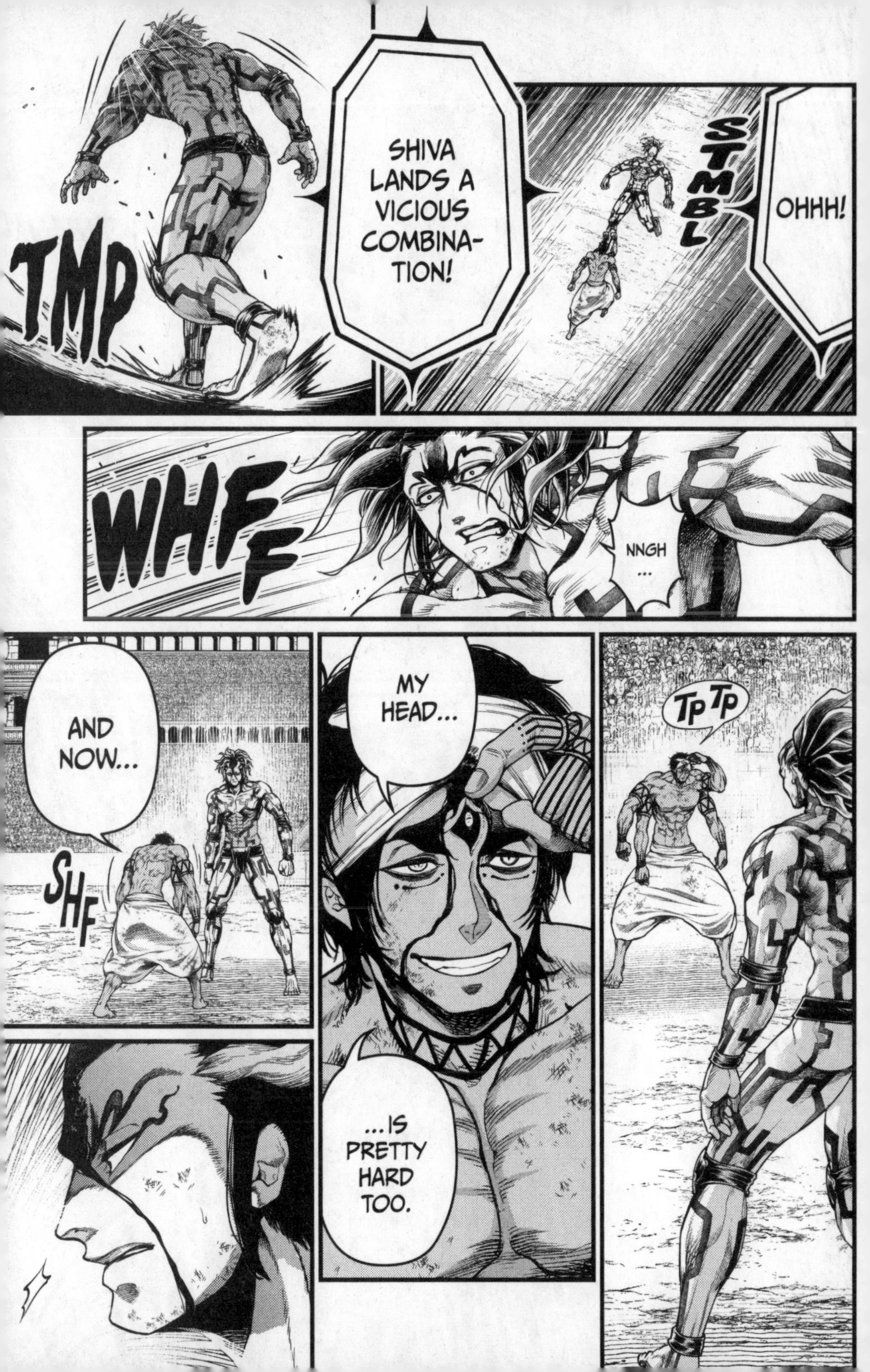
OHHH!
STMBL
SHIVA LANDS A VICIOUS COMBINATION!
TMP
NNGH ...
WHFF
Tp Tp
MY HEAD...
...IS PRETTY HARD TOO.
AND NOW...
SHF

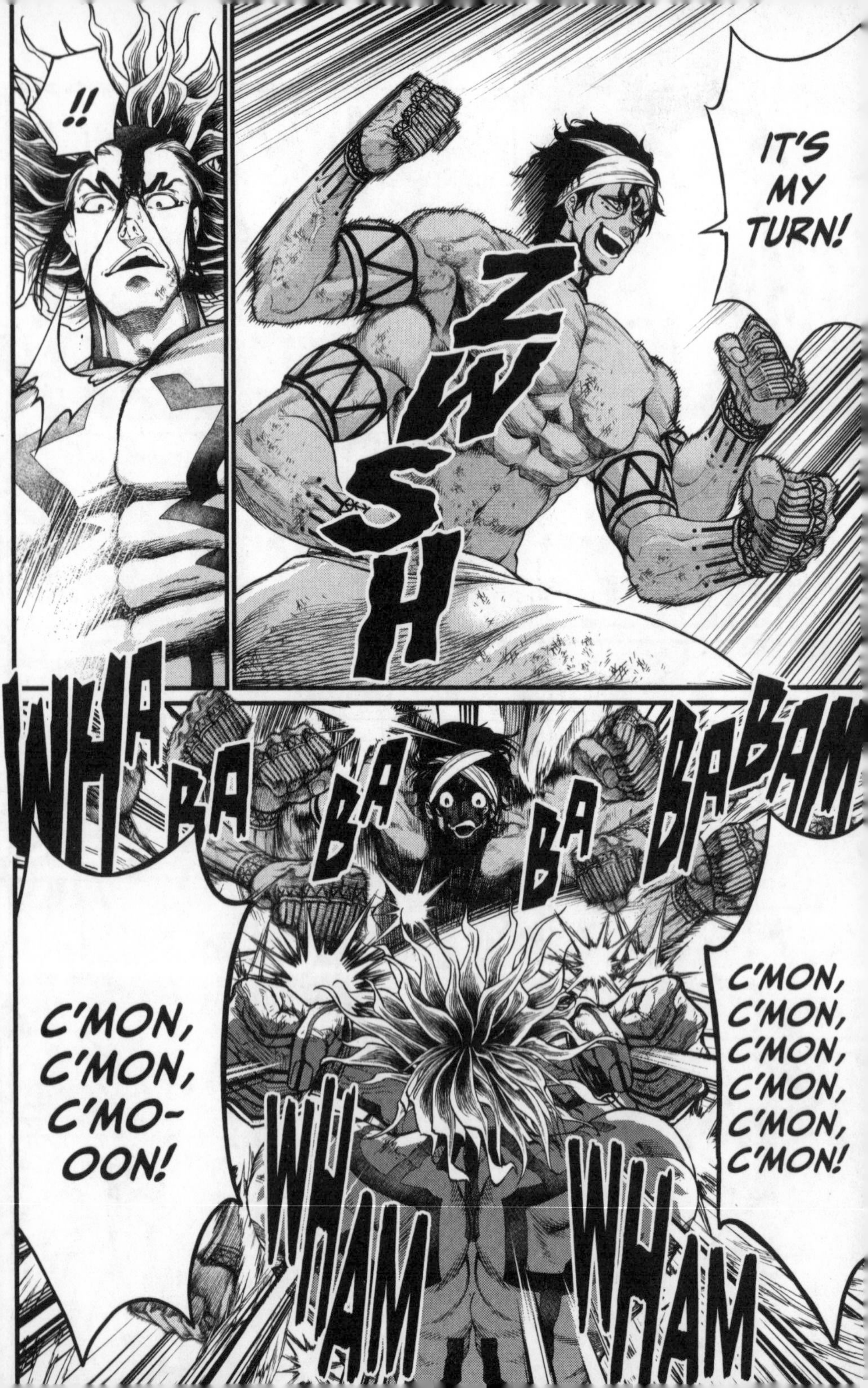
IT'S MY TURN!
ZWSH
!!
WHA BA BA BA BA BABAM
C'MON, C'MON, C'MON, C'MON, C'MON, C'MON!
C'MON, C'MON, C'MO-OON!
WHAM
WHAM

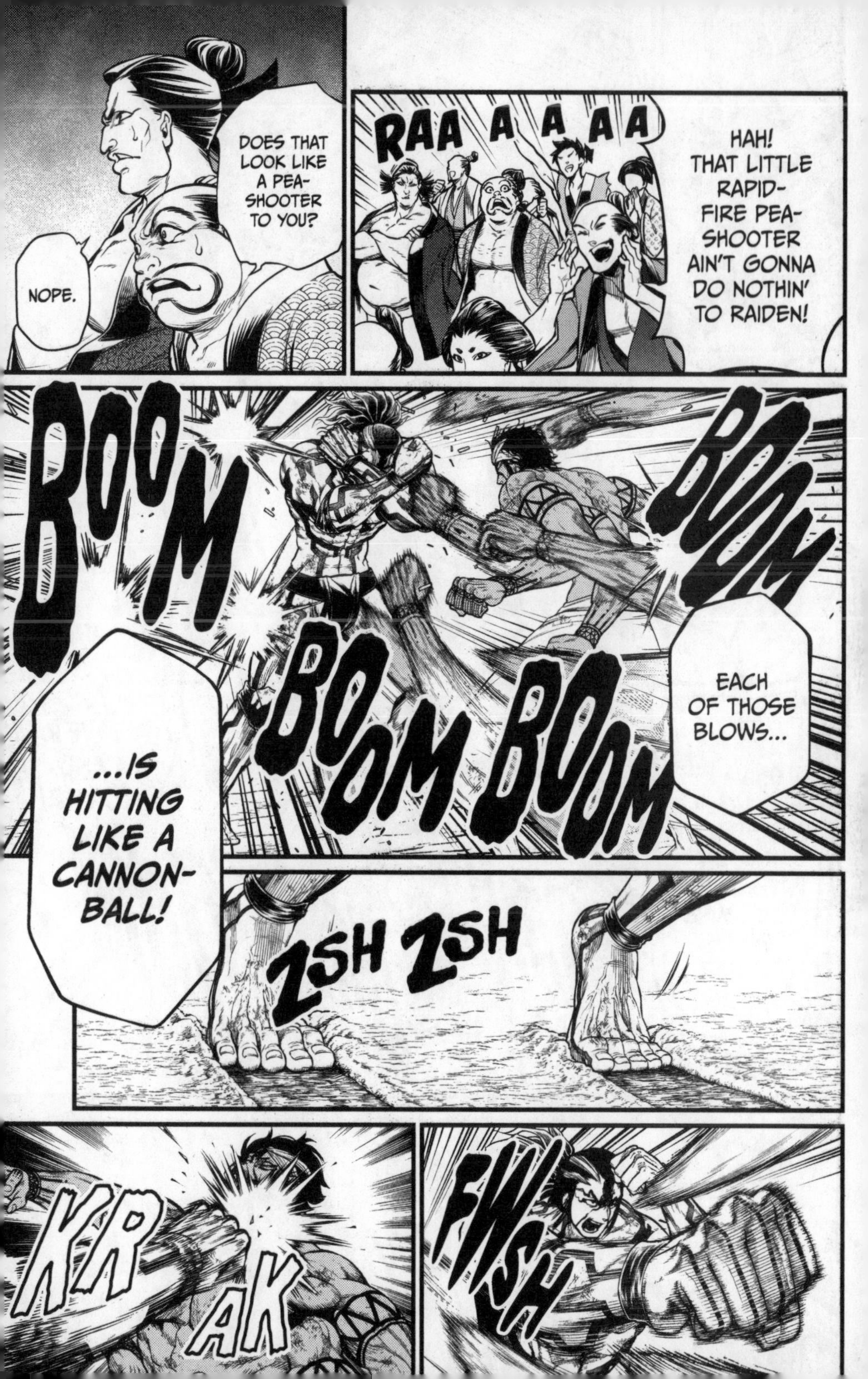
RAA A A A
HAH! THAT LITTLE RAPID-FIRE PEA-SHOOTER AIN'T GONNA DO NOTHIN' TO RAIDEN!
DOES THAT LOOK LIKE A PEA-SHOOTER TO YOU?
NOPE.
BOOM
BOOM
EACH OF THOSE BLOWS...
BOOM BOOM
...IS HITTING LIKE A CANNON-BALL!
ZSH ZSH
FWSH
KRAK

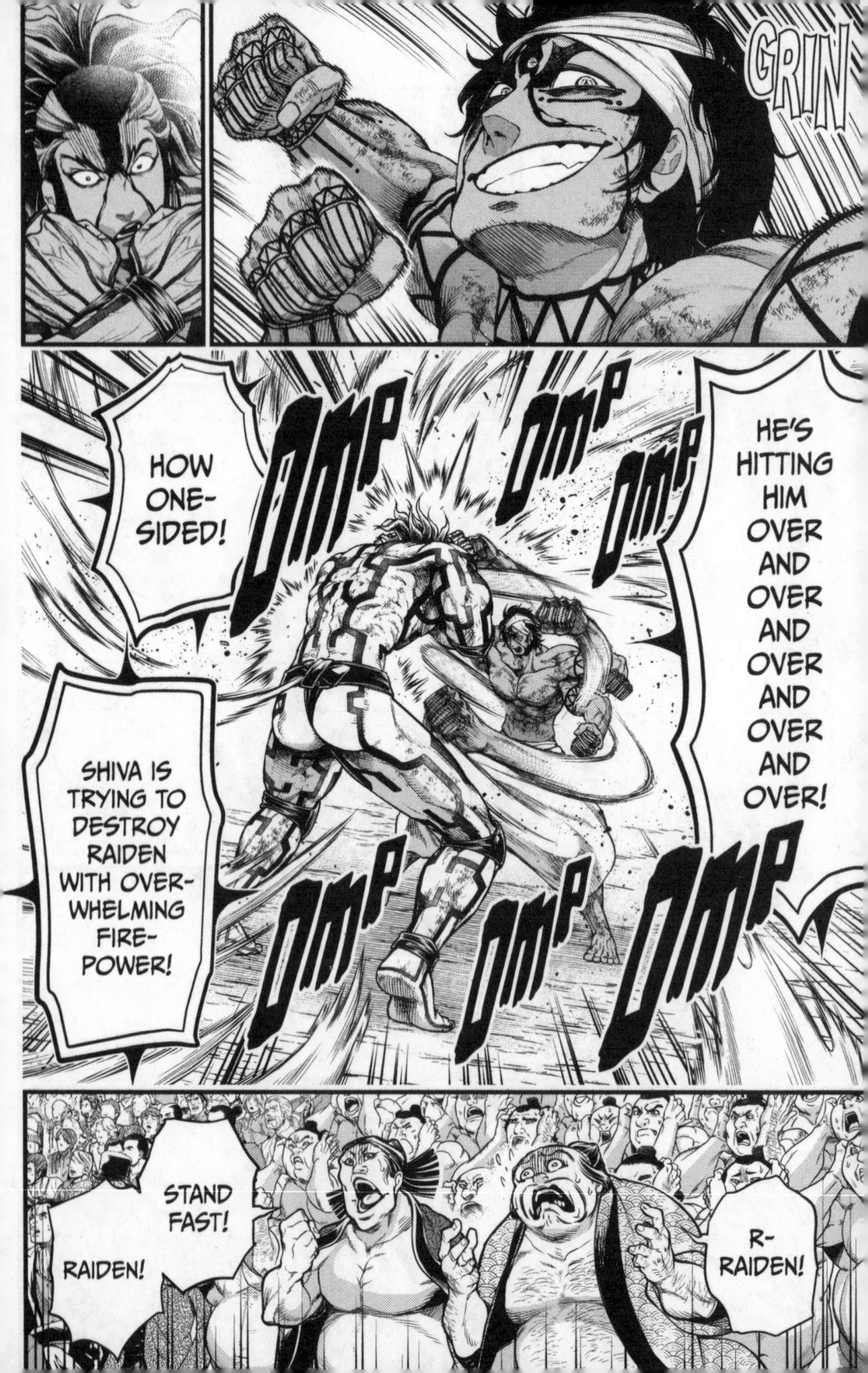
GRIN
DMP
HE'S HITTING HIM OVER AND OVER AND OVER AND OVER AND OVER!
DMP
DMP
HOW ONE-SIDED!
DMP
DMP
DMP
SHIVA IS TRYING TO DESTROY RAIDEN WITH OVER-WHELMING FIRE-POWER!
R-RAIDEN!
STAND FAST!
RAIDEN!

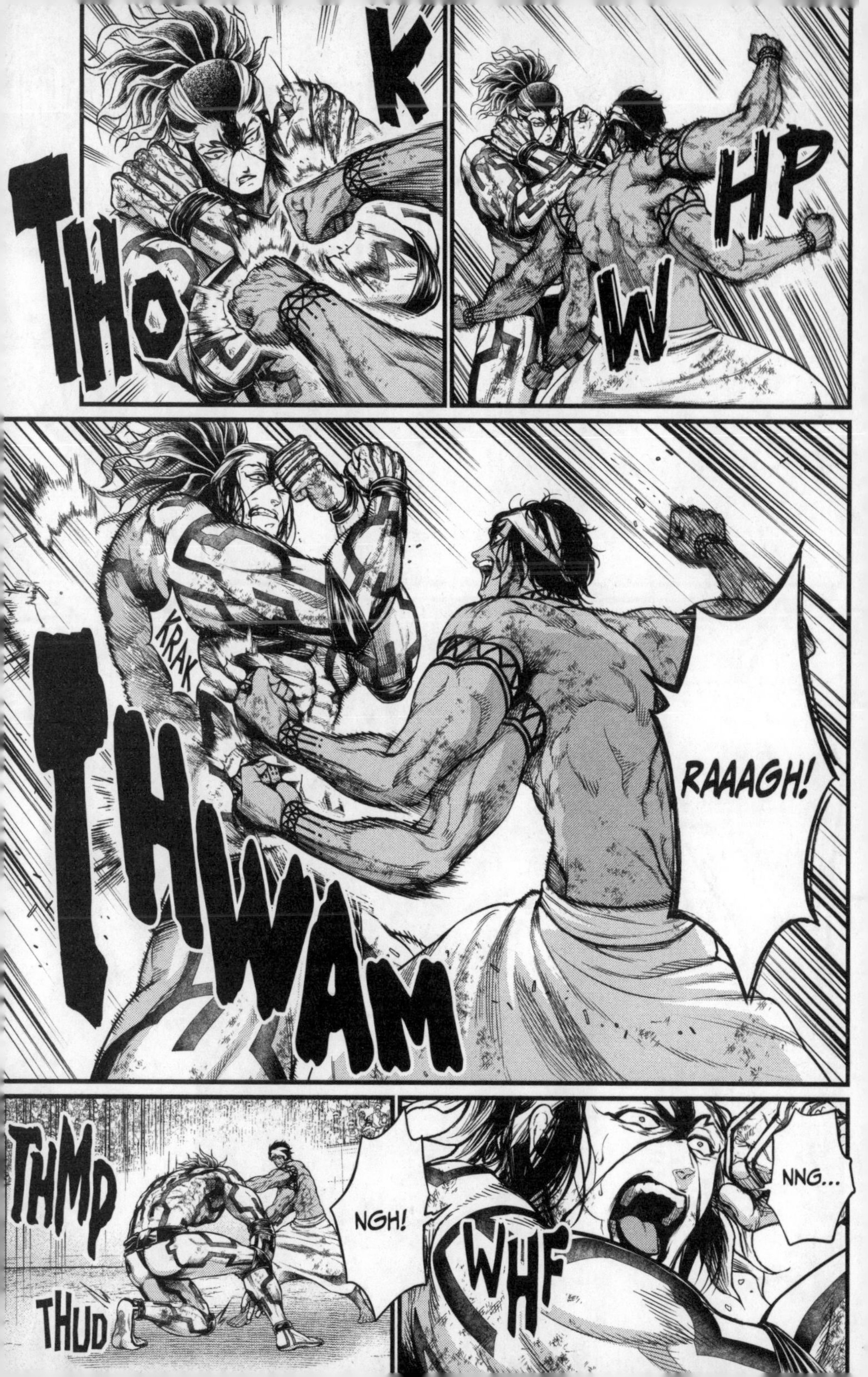
HP
W
K
THO
RAAAGH!
KRAK
THWAM
NNG...
NGH!
WHF
THMP
THUD

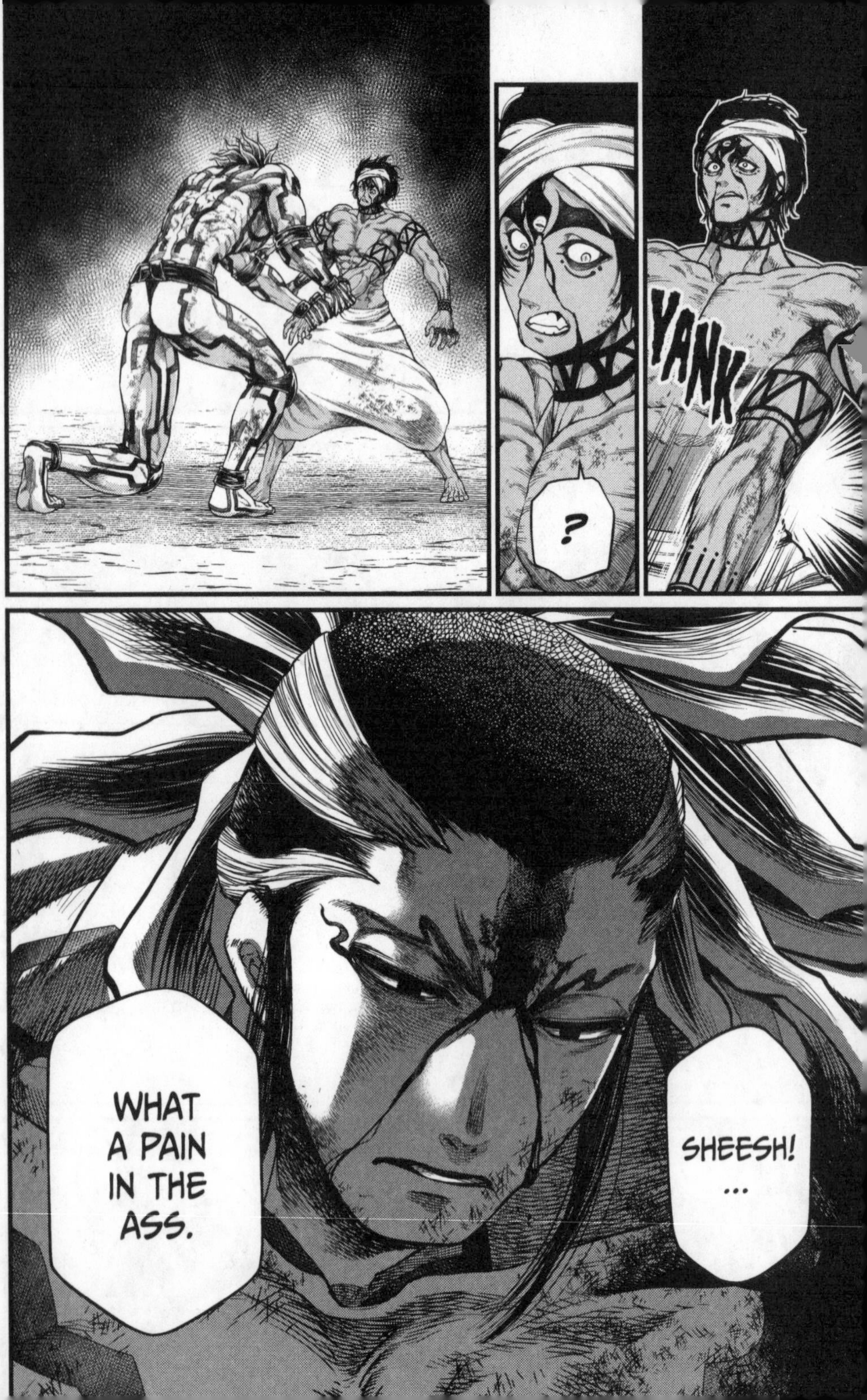
YANK
?
SHEESH! ...
WHAT A PAIN IN THE ASS.

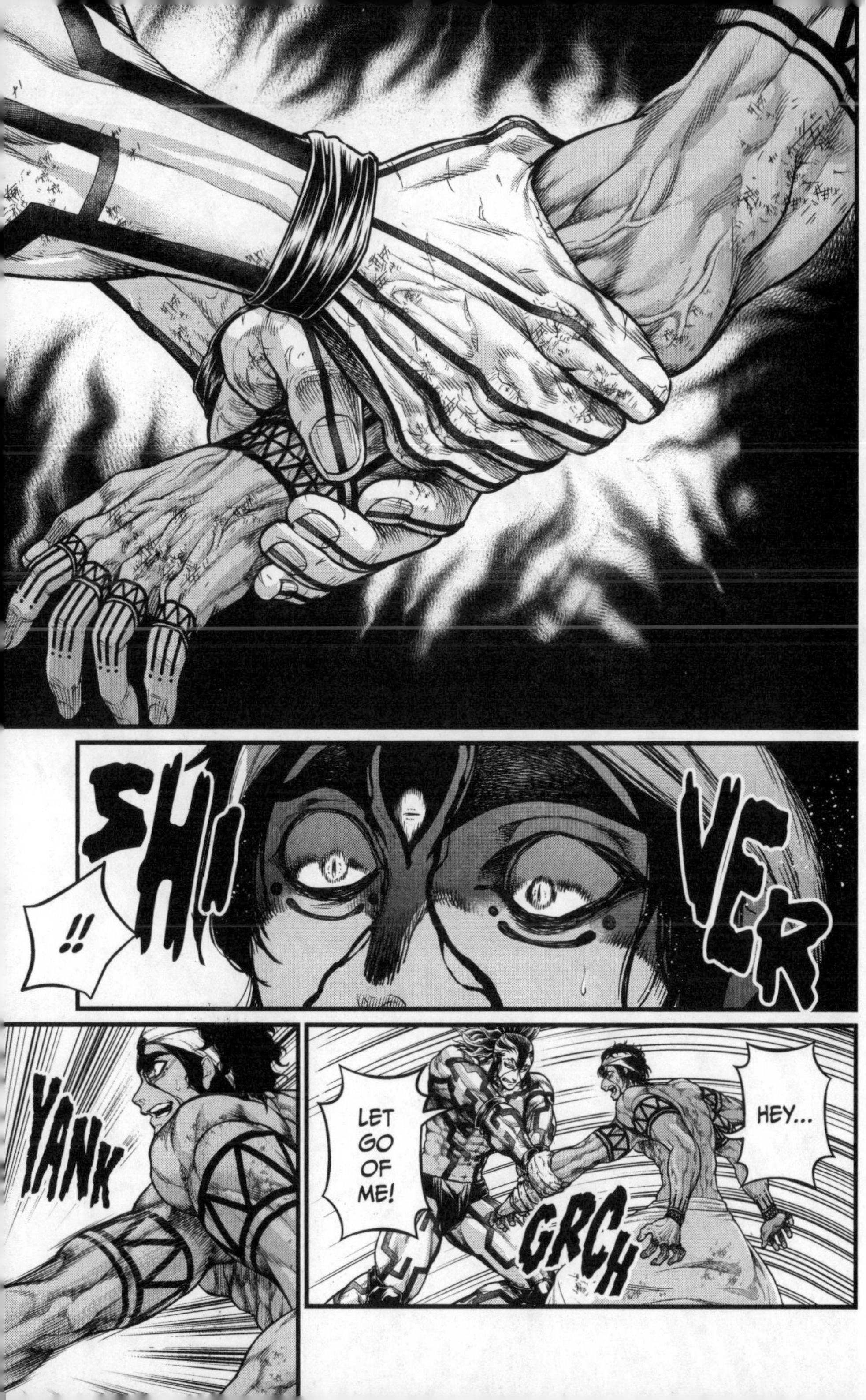
SHIVER
!!
HEY...
LET GO OF ME!
GRCH
YANK

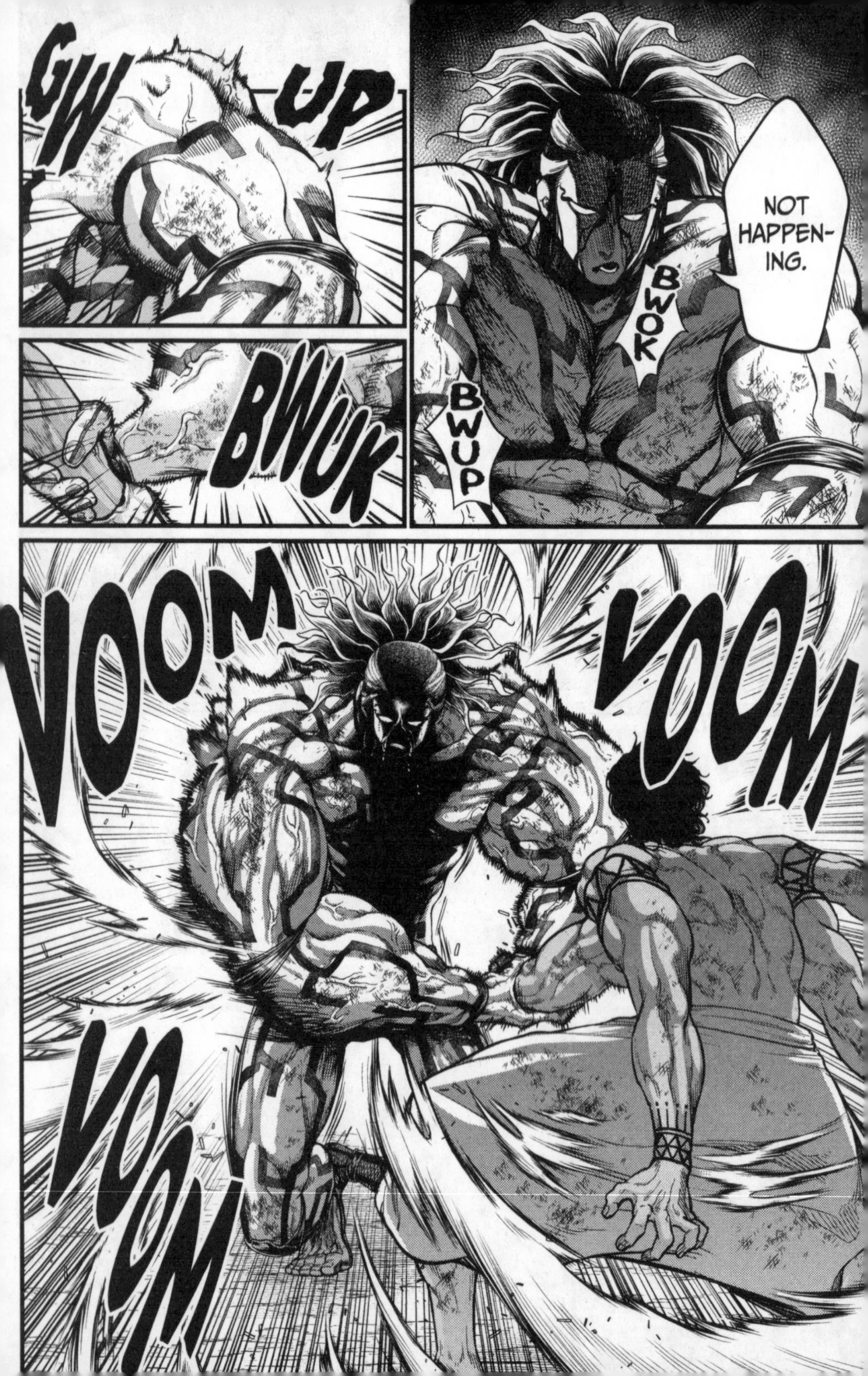
NOT HAPPEN-ING.
BWOK
BWUP
GW UP
BWUK
VOOM
VOOM
VOOM

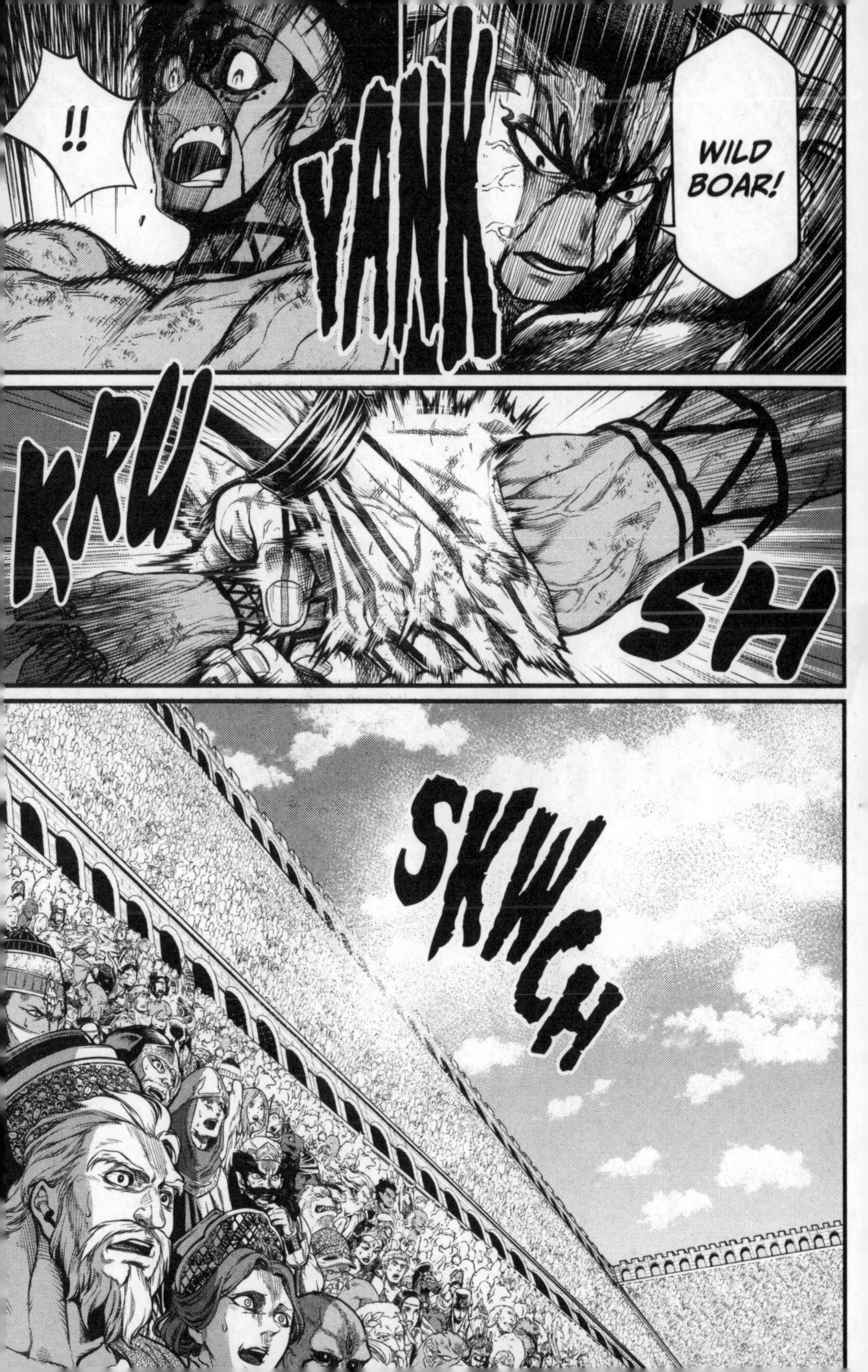
WILD BOAR!
YANK
!!
KRU
SH
SKWCH

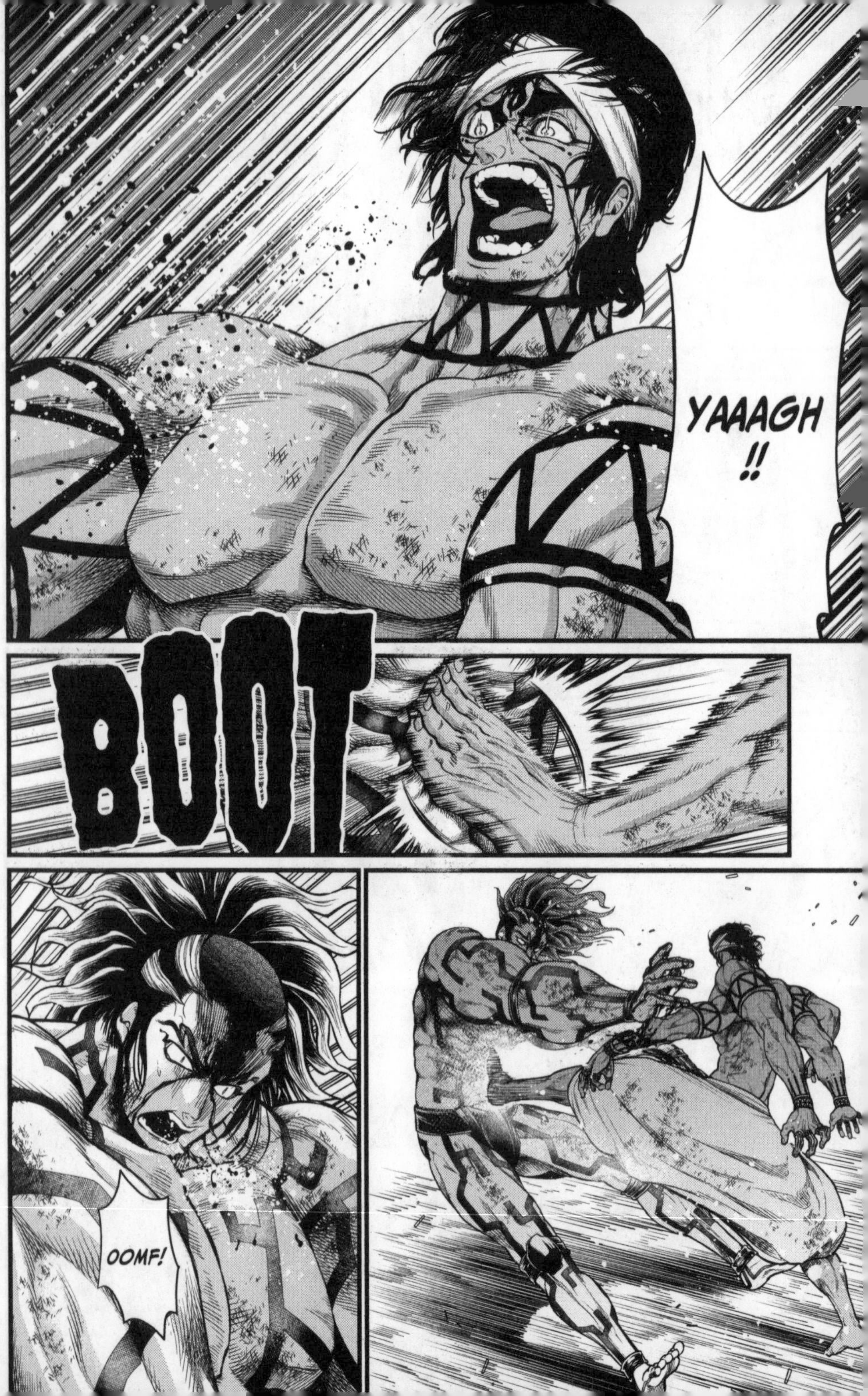
YAAAGH!!
BOOT
OOMF!

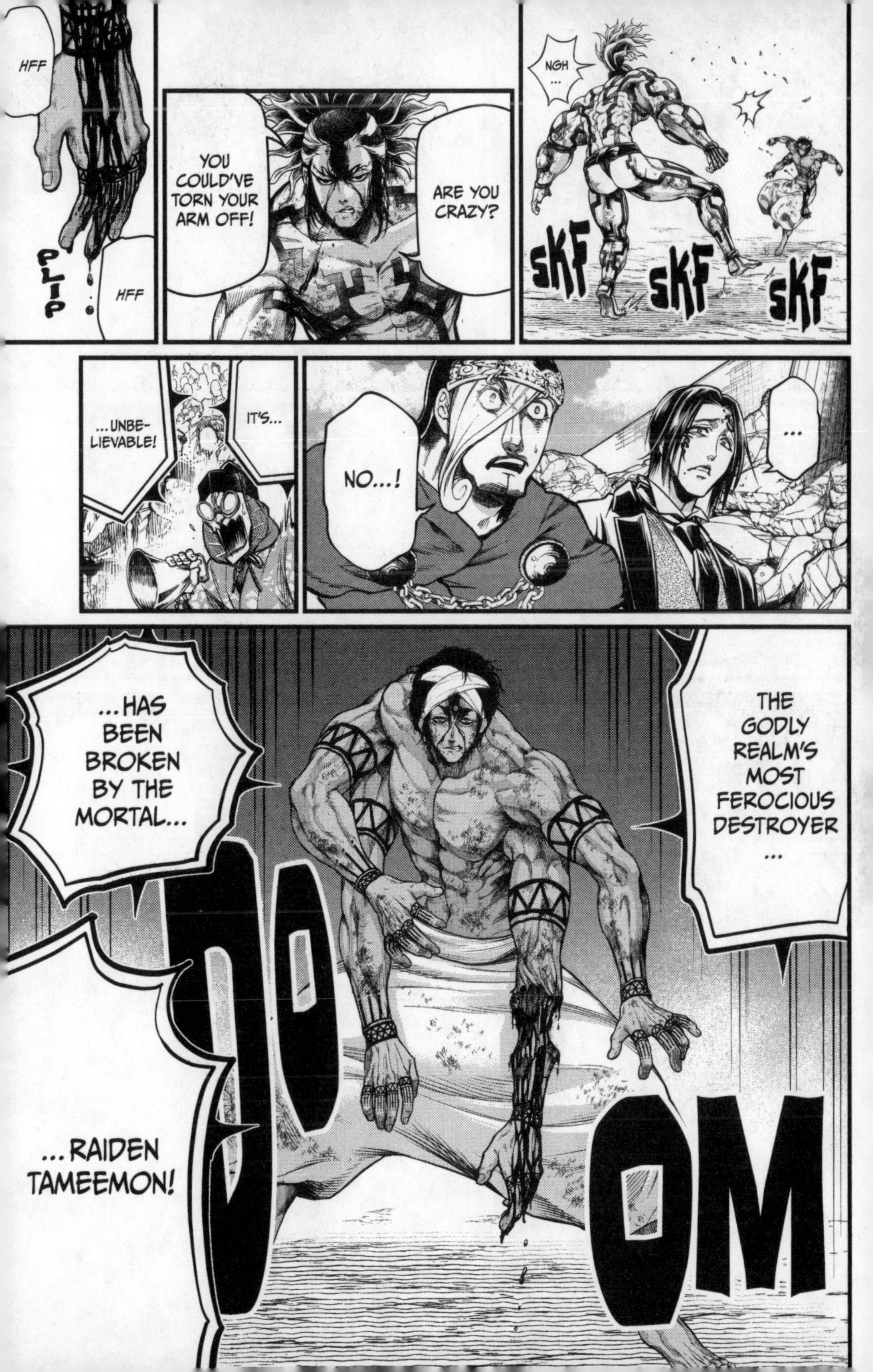
NGH ...
SKF
SKF
SKF
ARE YOU CRAZY?
YOU COULD'VE TORN YOUR ARM OFF!
HFF
PLIP
HFF
...
NO...!
IT'S...
...UNBE-LIEVABLE!
THE GODLY REALM'S MOST FEROCIOUS DESTROYER ...
...HAS BEEN BROKEN BY THE MORTAL...
...RAIDEN TAMEEMON!
DOOM

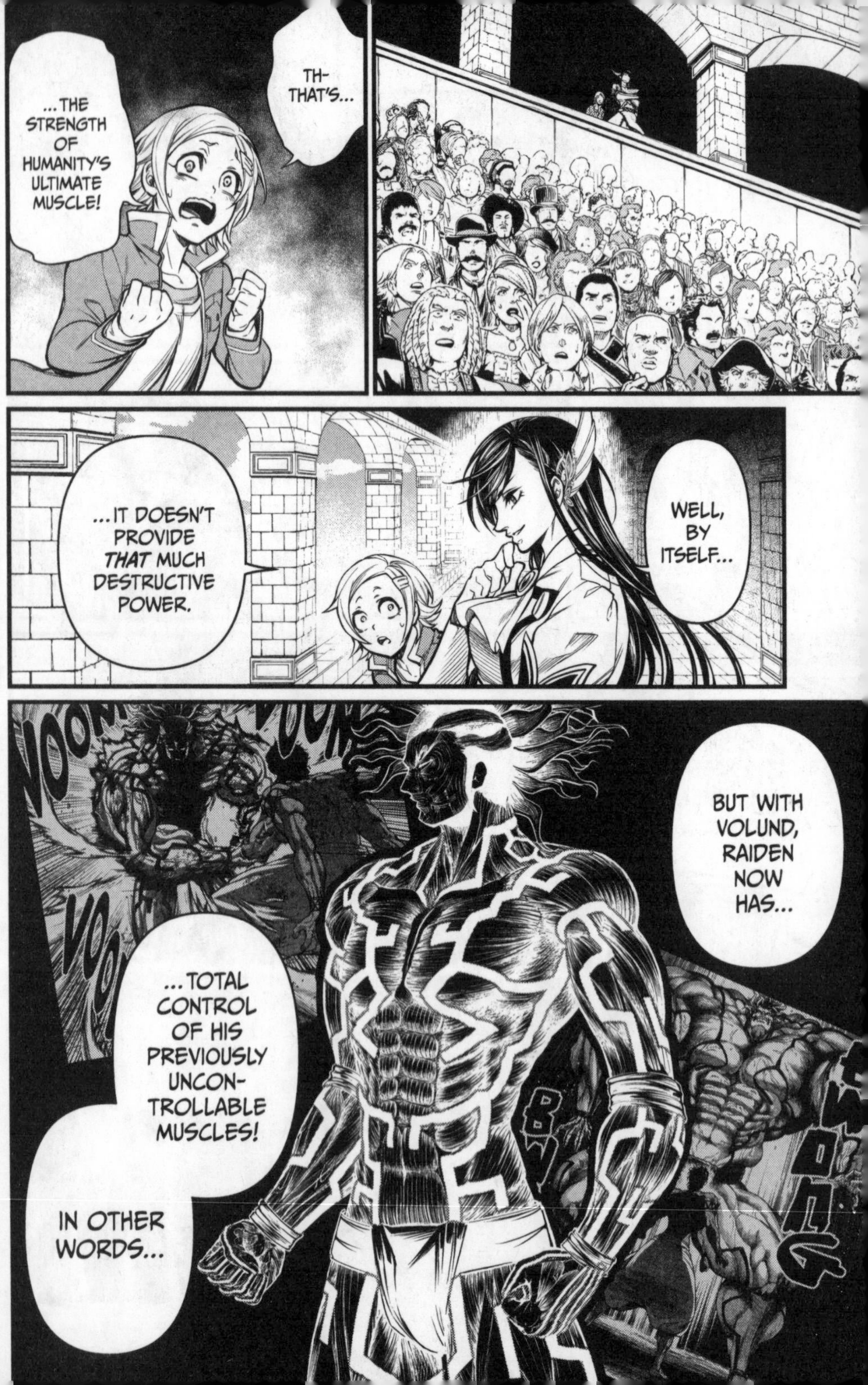
TH- THAT'S...
...THE STRENGTH OF HUMANITY'S ULTIMATE MUSCLE!
WELL, BY ITSELF...
...IT DOESN'T PROVIDE *THAT* MUCH DESTRUCTIVE POWER.
BUT WITH VOLUND, RAIDEN NOW HAS...
...TOTAL CONTROL OF HIS PREVIOUSLY UNCON-TROLLABLE MUSCLES!
IN OTHER WORDS...

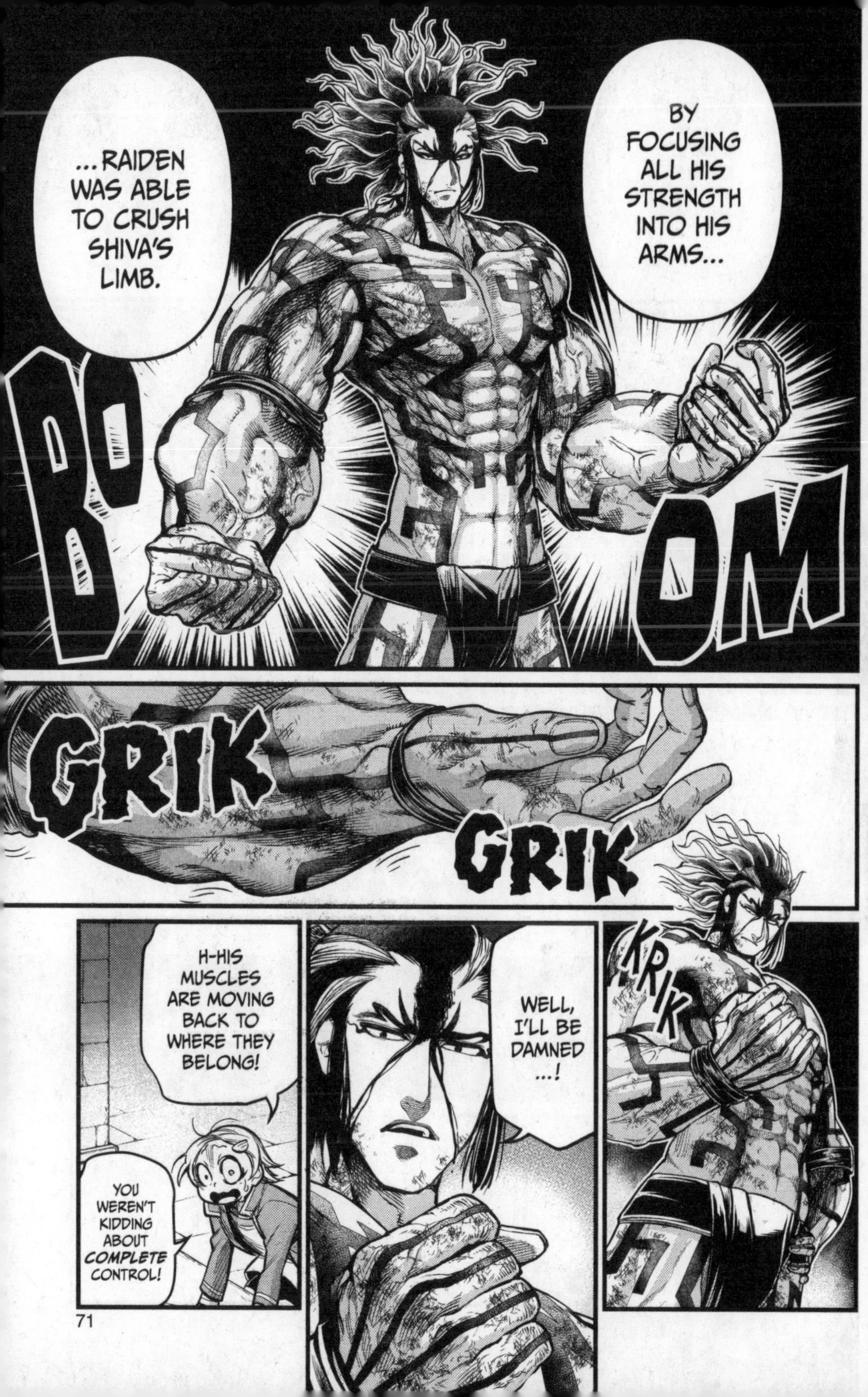
BY FOCUSING ALL HIS STRENGTH INTO HIS ARMS...
...RAIDEN WAS ABLE TO CRUSH SHIVA'S LIMB.
BOOM
GRIK
GRIK
KRIK
KRIK
WELL, I'LL BE DAMNED ...!
H-HIS MUSCLES ARE MOVING BACK TO WHERE THEY BELONG!
YOU WEREN'T KIDDING ABOUT **COMPLETE** CONTROL!

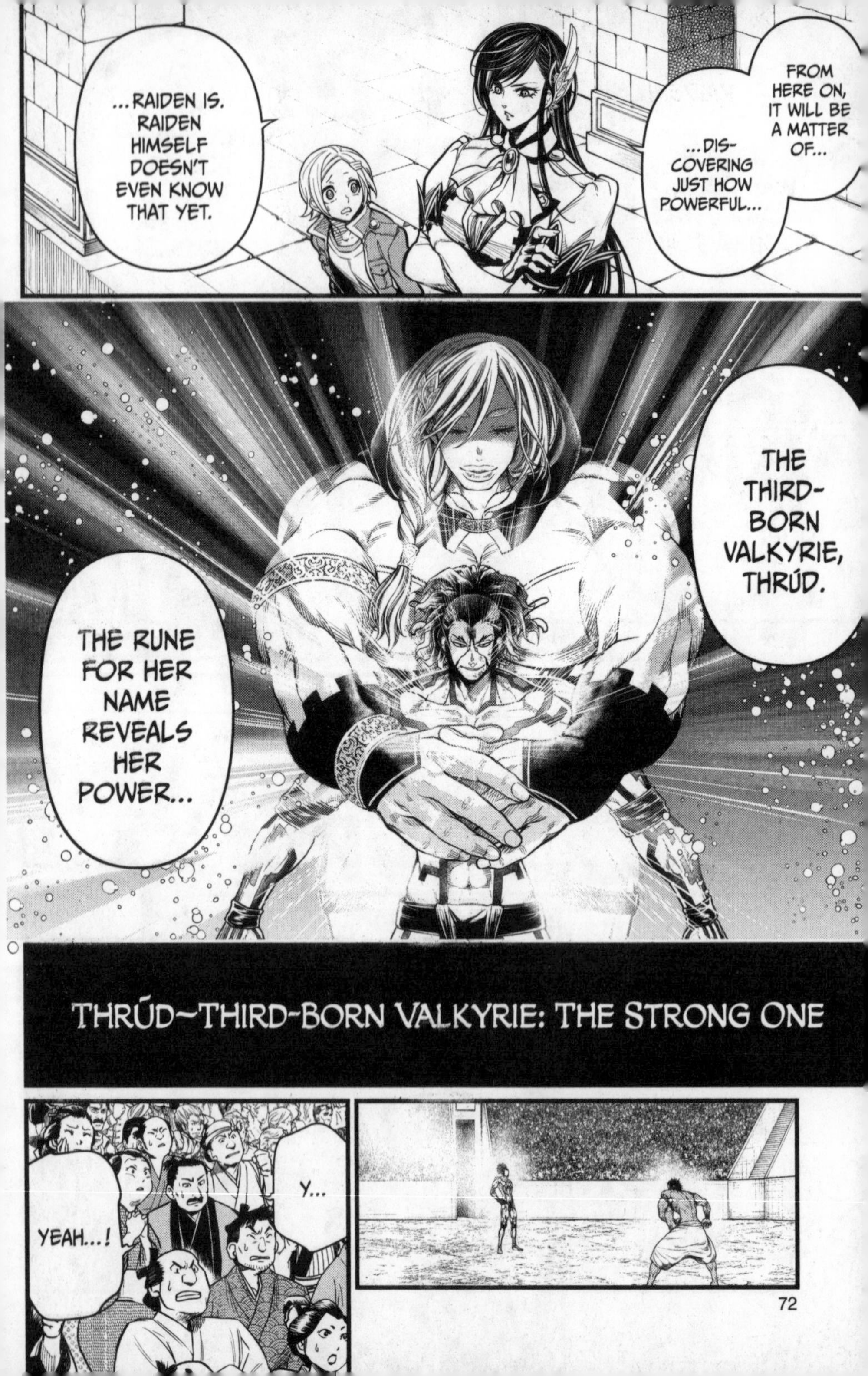
FROM HERE ON, IT WILL BE A MATTER OF...
...DIS-COVERING JUST HOW POWERFUL...
...RAIDEN IS. RAIDEN HIMSELF DOESN'T EVEN KNOW THAT YET.
THE THIRD-BORN VALKYRIE, THRÚD.
THE RUNE FOR HER NAME REVEALS HER POWER...
THRÚD~THIRD-BORN VALKYRIE: THE STRONG ONE
Y...
YEAH...!

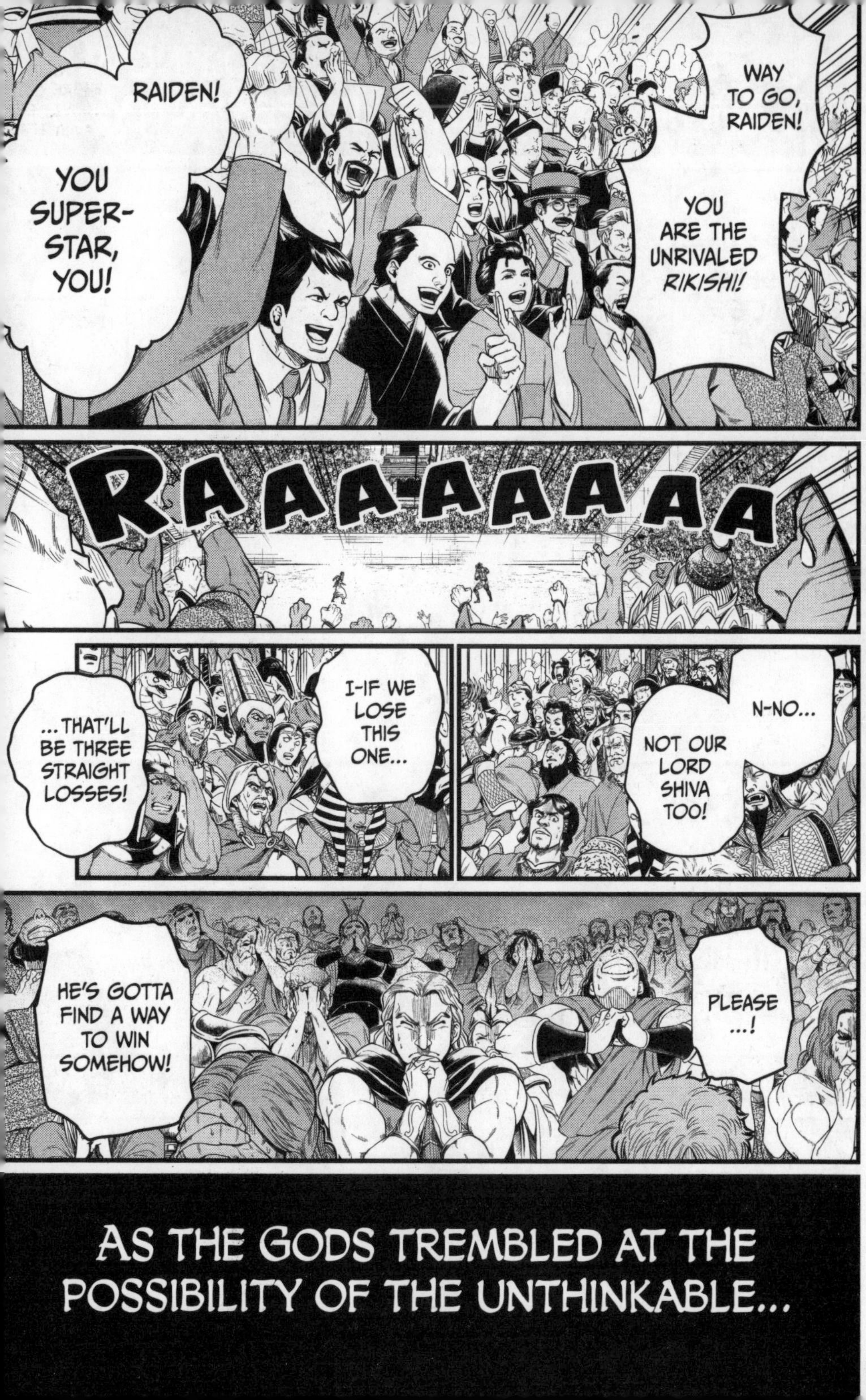
WAY TO GO, RAIDEN!
RAIDEN!
YOU ARE THE UNRIVALED RIKISHI!
YOU SUPER-STAR, YOU!
RAAAAAAA
N-NO...
NOT OUR LORD SHIVA TOO!
I-IF WE LOSE THIS ONE...
...THAT'LL BE THREE STRAIGHT LOSSES!
PLEASE...!
HE'S GOTTA FIND A WAY TO WIN SOMEHOW!
AS THE GODS TREMBLED AT THE POSSIBILITY OF THE UNTHINKABLE...

...THE GODS OF INDIA, WHO KNOW SHIVA, SAW THINGS DIFFERENTLY.

THERE'S NO WAY SHIVA CAN LOSE TO THAT PUNK.

HEH!

HFF

HFF

...1,116 INDIAN GODS DWELL IN HIS FISTS!

OF COURSE NOT!

THE SPIRITS OF ALL...

HFF

HFF

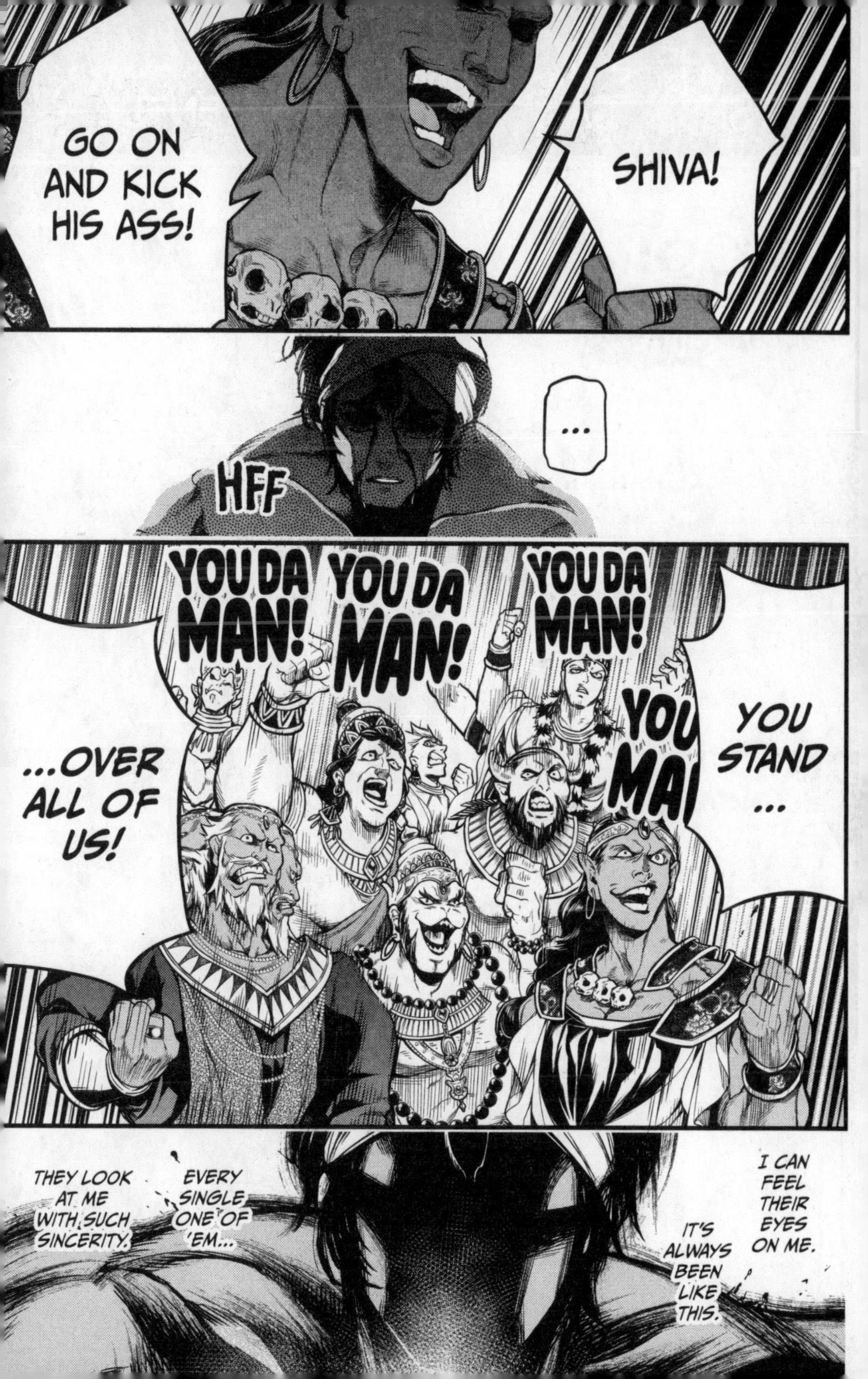
SHIVA!
GO ON AND KICK HIS ASS!
...
HFF
YOU STAND ...
YOU MA
YOU DA MAN!
YOU DA MAN!
YOU DA MAN!
...OVER ALL OF US!
I CAN FEEL THEIR EYES ON ME.
IT'S ALWAYS BEEN LIKE THIS.
EVERY SINGLE ONE OF 'EM...
THEY LOOK AT ME WITH SUCH SINCERITY.

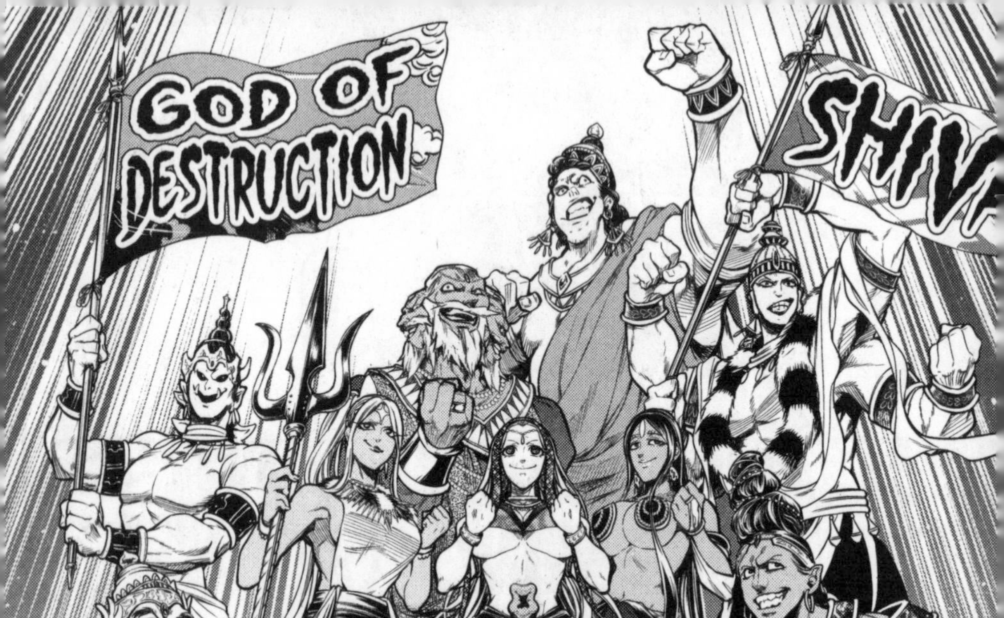
SHIV
GOD OF DESTRUCTION
...HIS FELLOW GODS!!
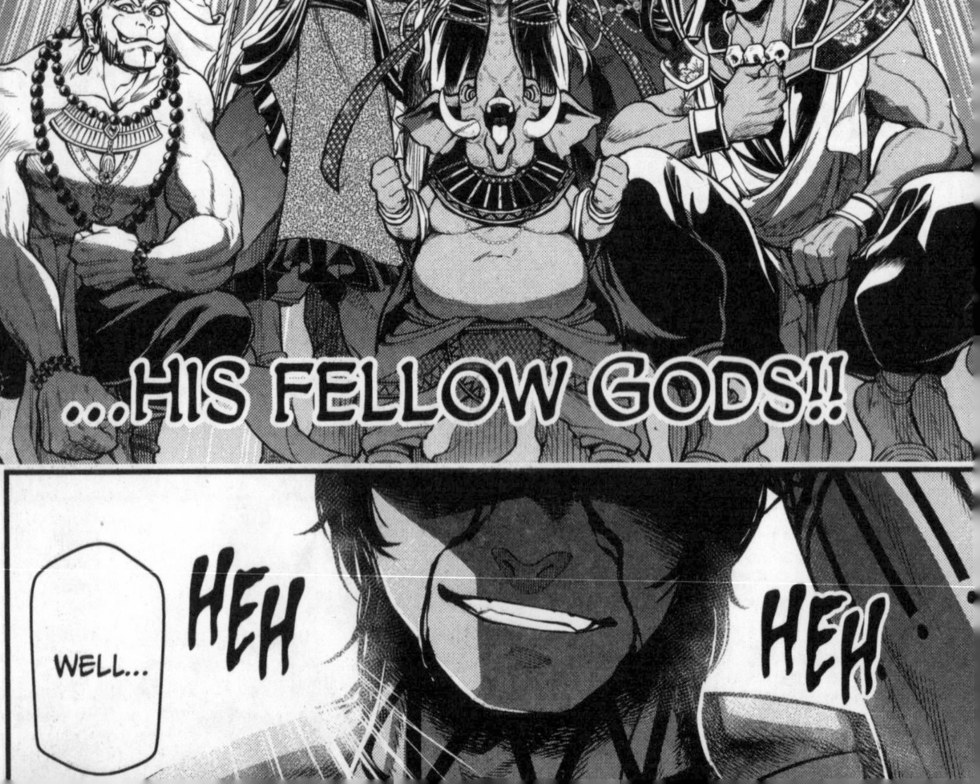
HEH
HEH
WELL...

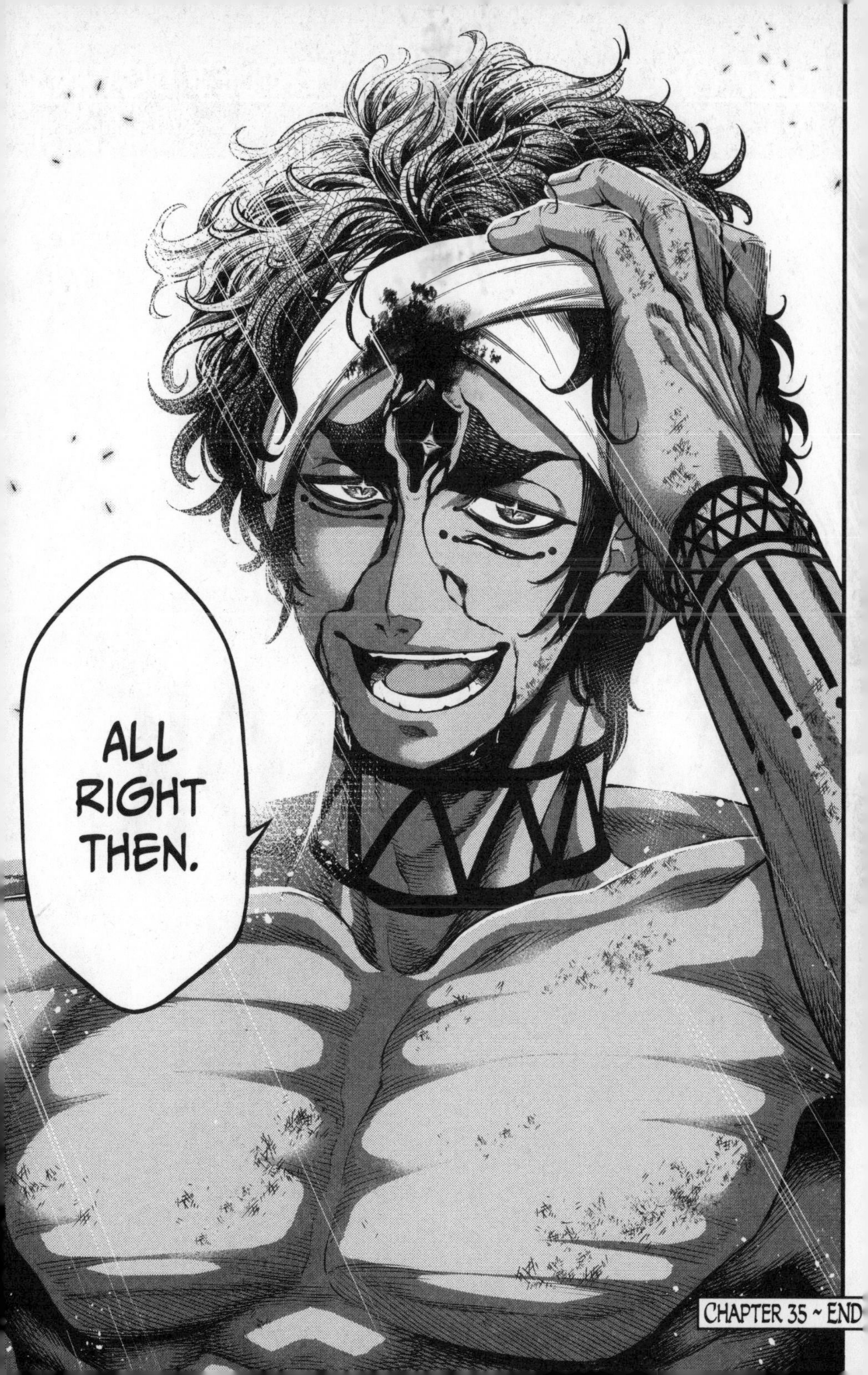
ALL RIGHT THEN.
CHAPTER 35 ~ END

RECORD OF
RAGNAROK

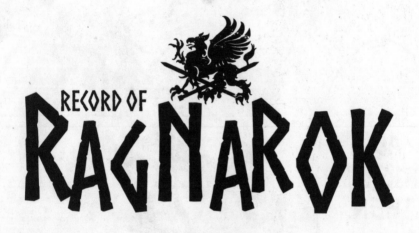

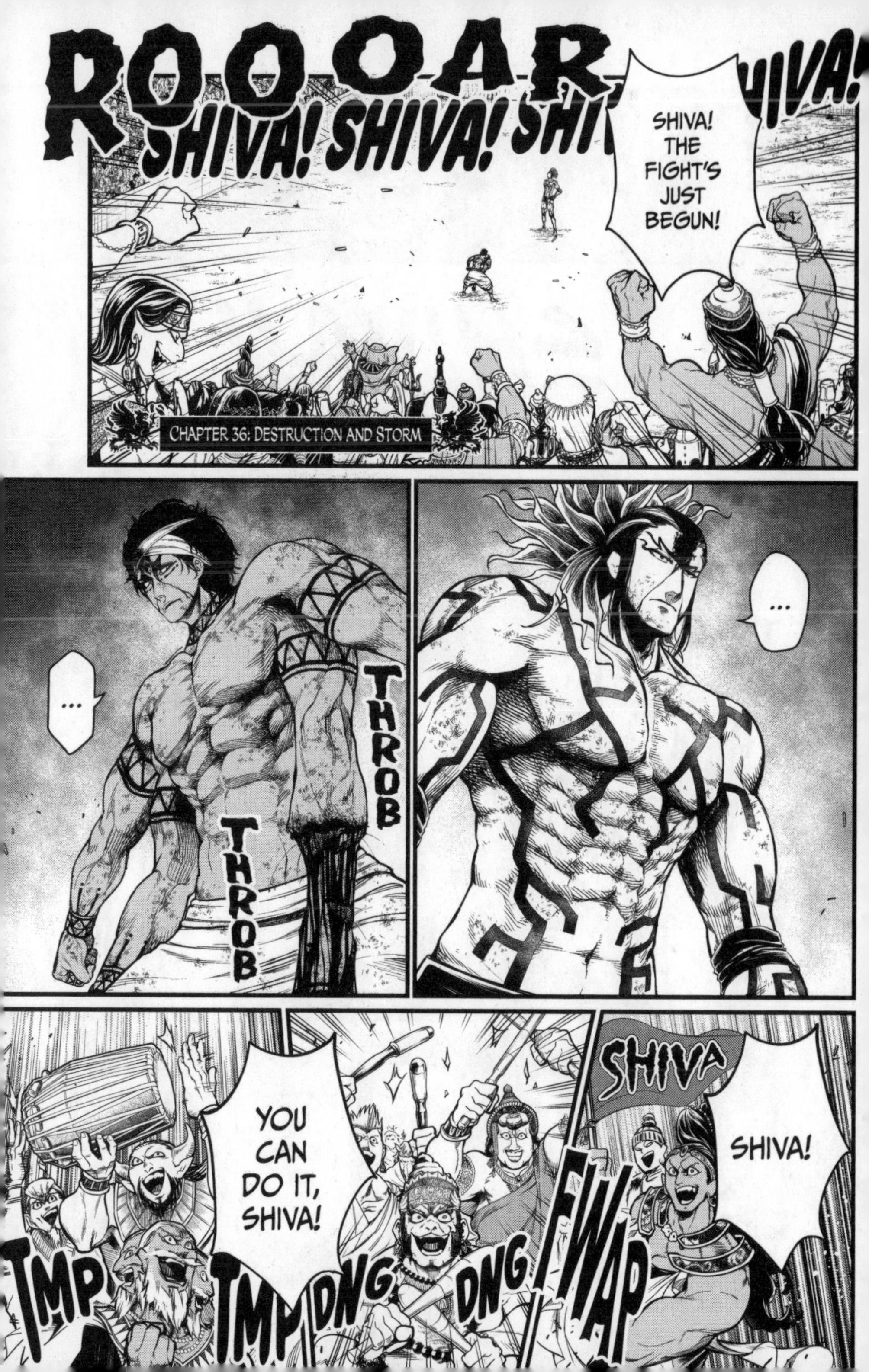
ROOOAR
SHIVA! SHIVA! SHI
HIVA!
SHIVA! THE FIGHT'S JUST BEGUN!
CHAPTER 36: DESTRUCTION AND STORM
...
...
THROB
THROB
SHIVA!
SHIVA
FWAP
DNG
DNG
YOU CAN DO IT, SHIVA!
TMP
TMP

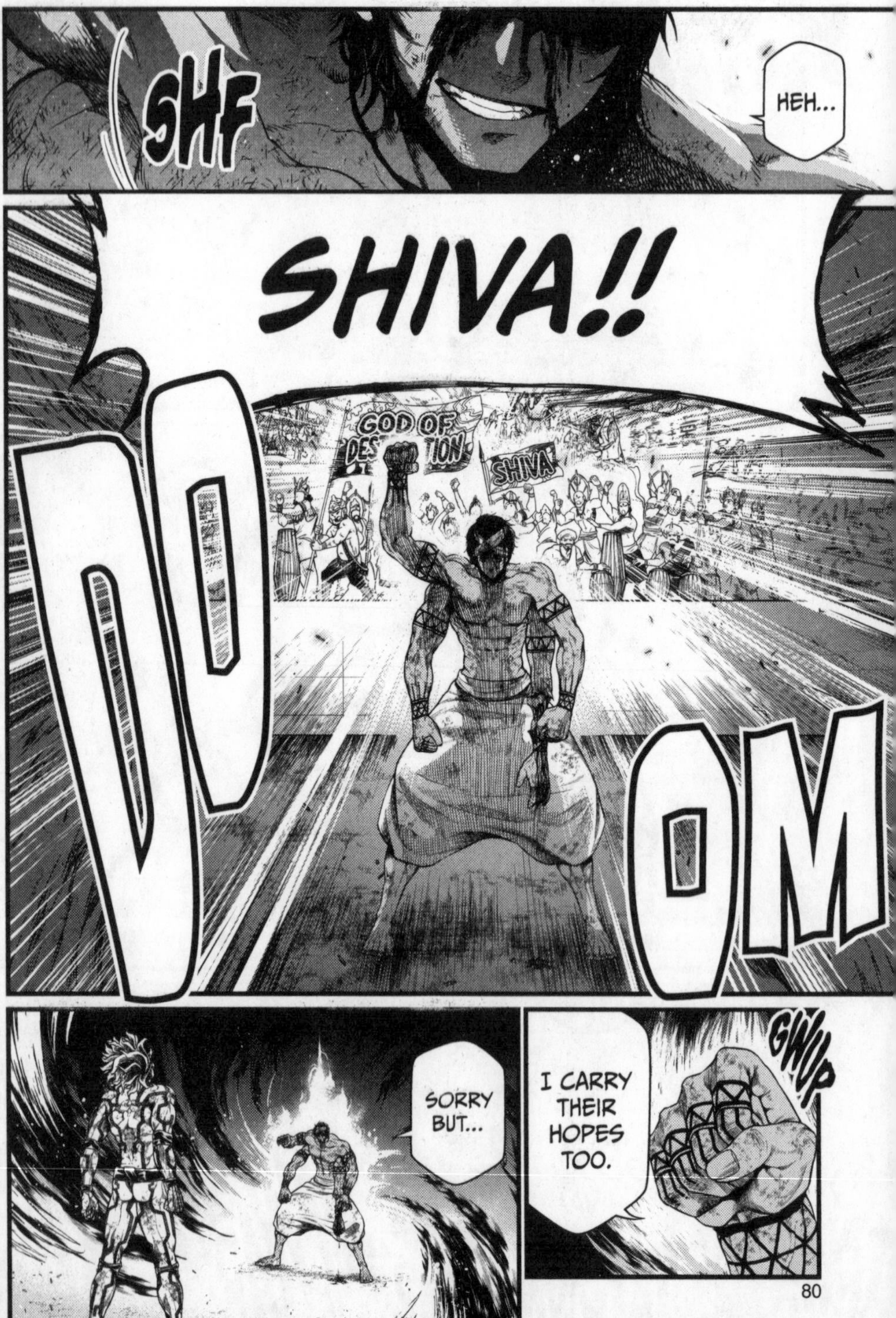
HEH...
SHF
SHIVA!!
GOD OF DES TION
SHIVA
DOOM
GWUP
I CARRY THEIR HOPES TOO.
SORRY BUT...

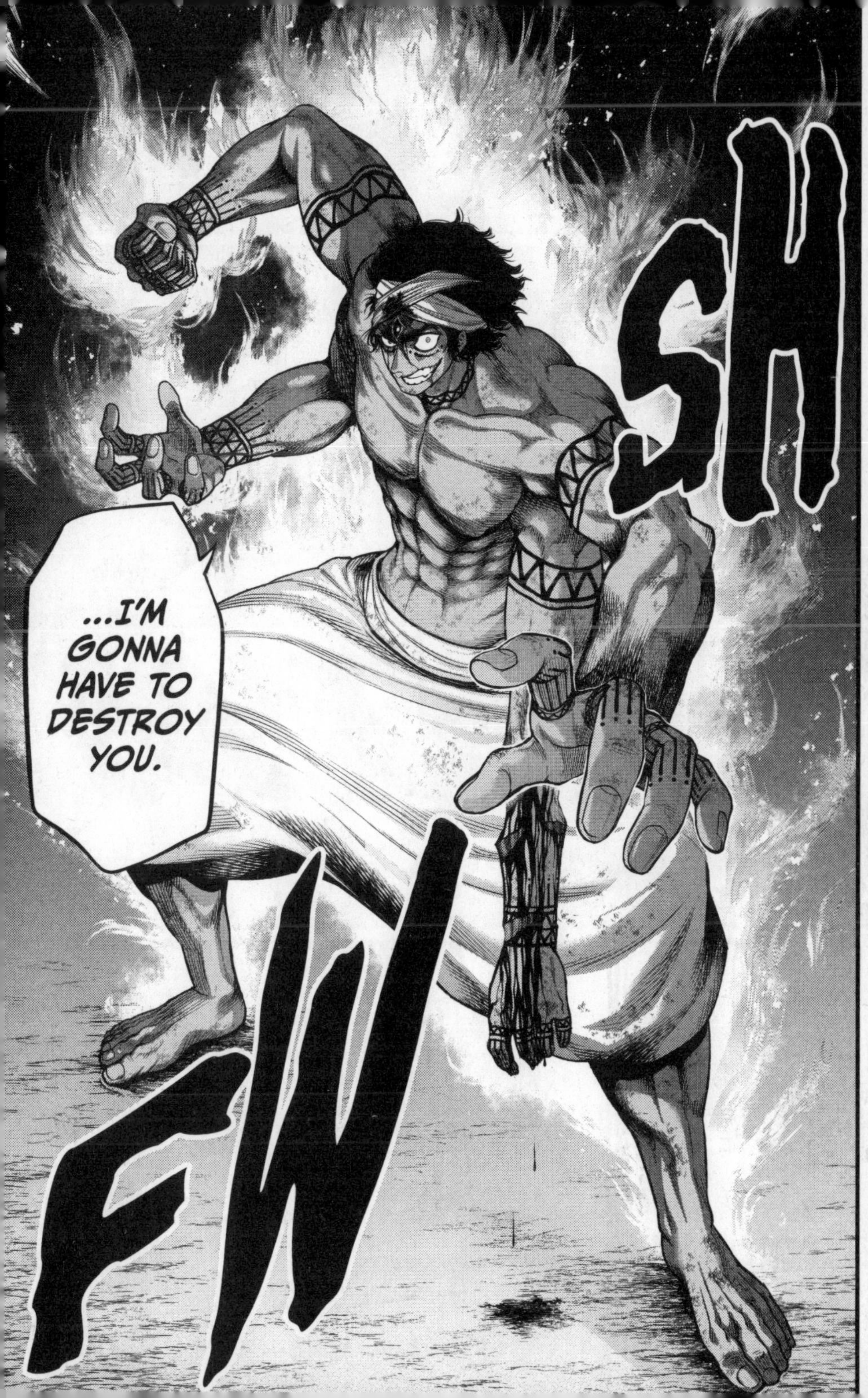
SH
...I'M GONNA HAVE TO DESTROY YOU.
FW

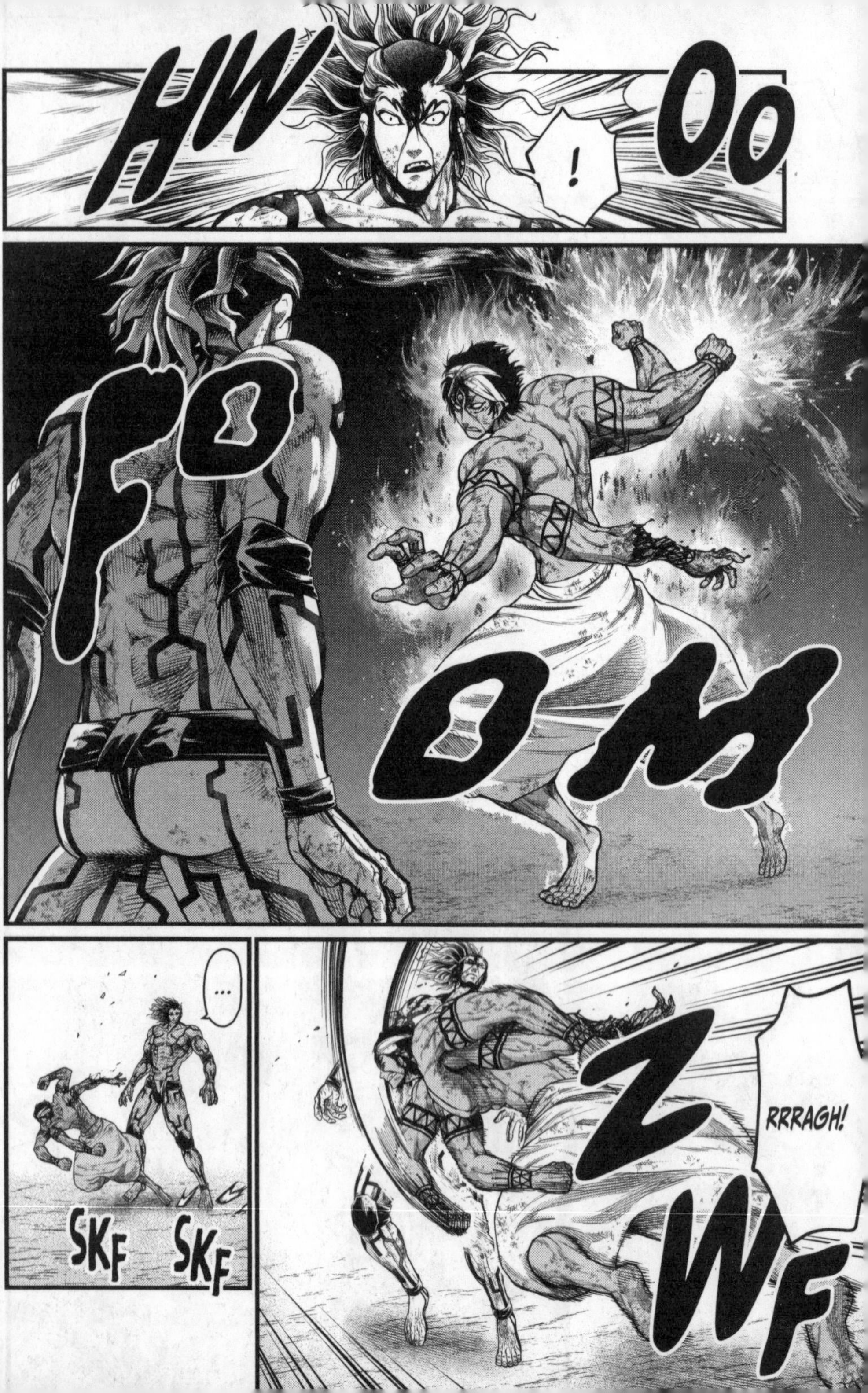
HWOO
!
FOOM
RRRAGH!
ZWF
...
SKF
SKF

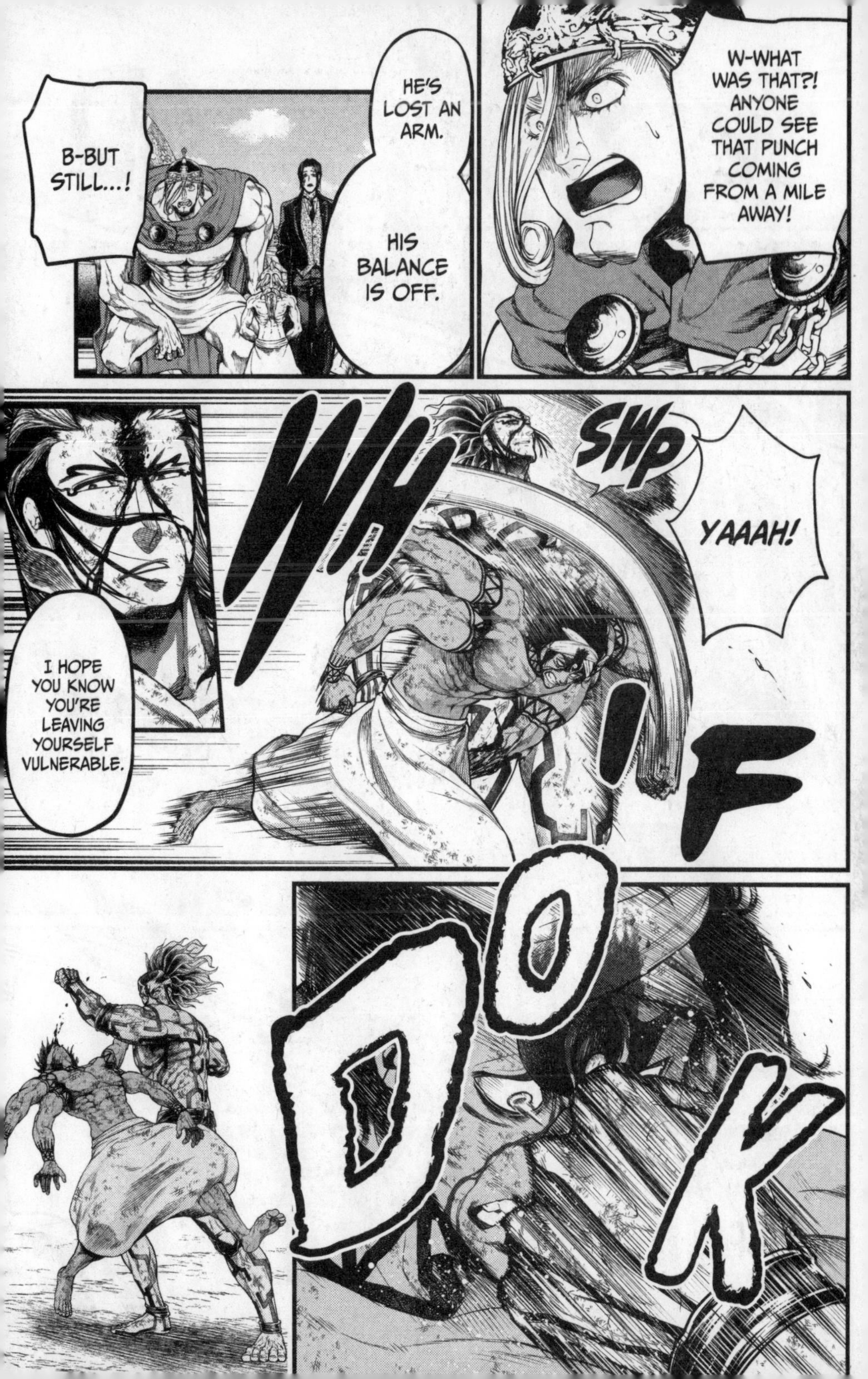
W-WHAT WAS THAT?! ANYONE COULD SEE THAT PUNCH COMING FROM A MILE AWAY!
HE'S LOST AN ARM.
HIS BALANCE IS OFF.
B-BUT STILL...!
SWP
YAAAH!
WHIFF
I HOPE YOU KNOW YOU'RE LEAVING YOURSELF VULNERABLE.
DOK

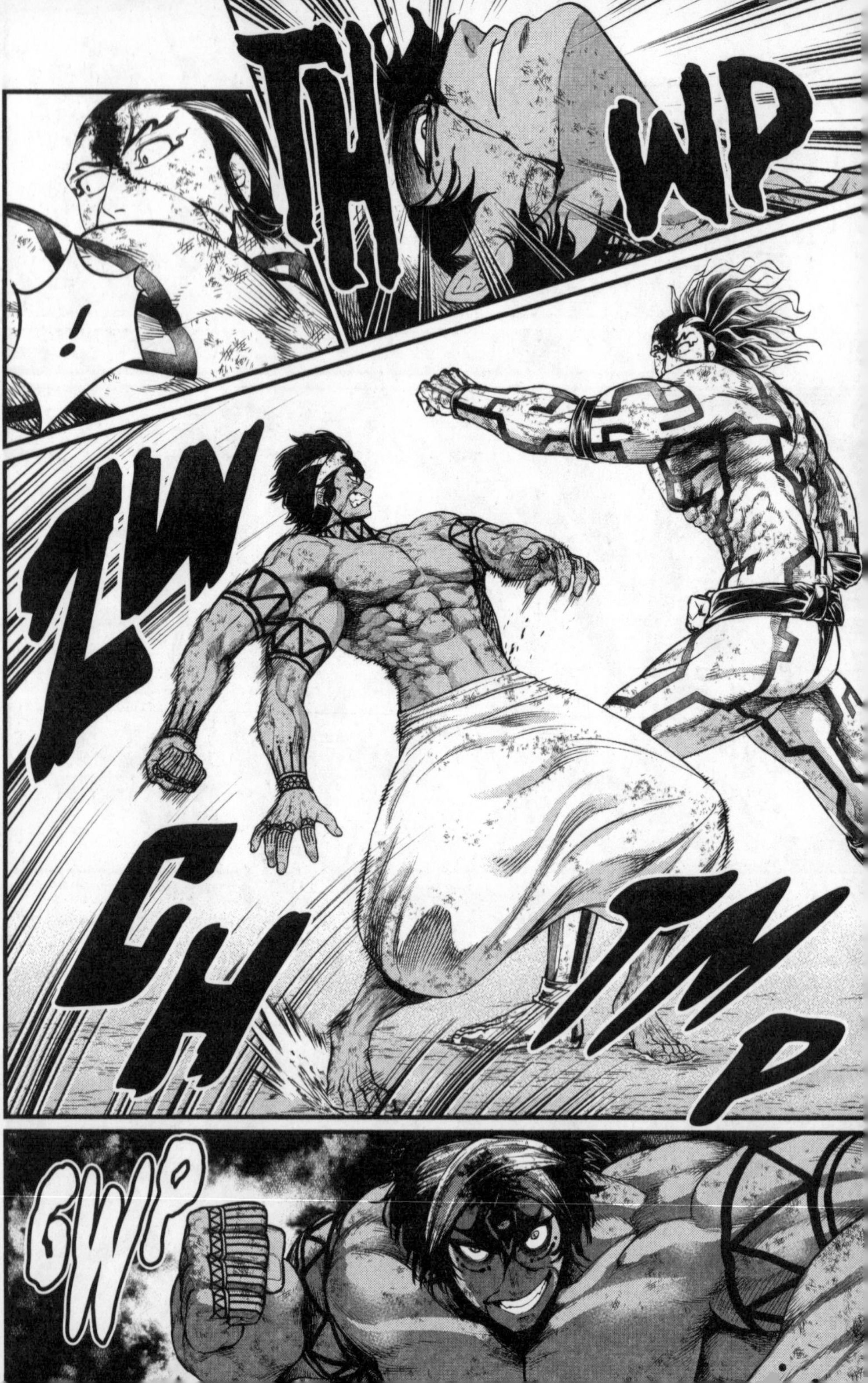
THWP
!
ZW
CHMP
GWP

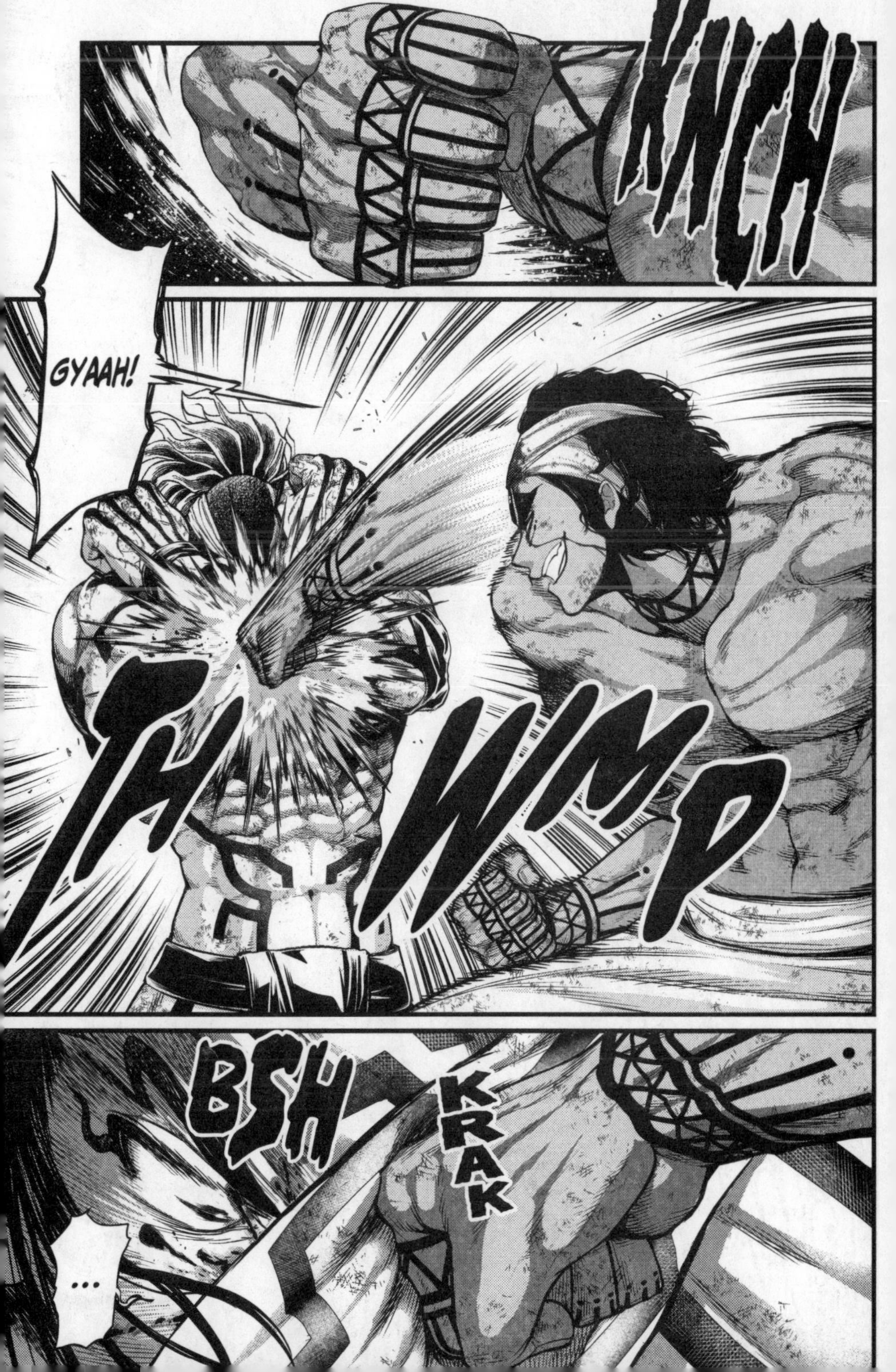
KNCH
GYAAH!
THWMP
KRAK
BSH
...

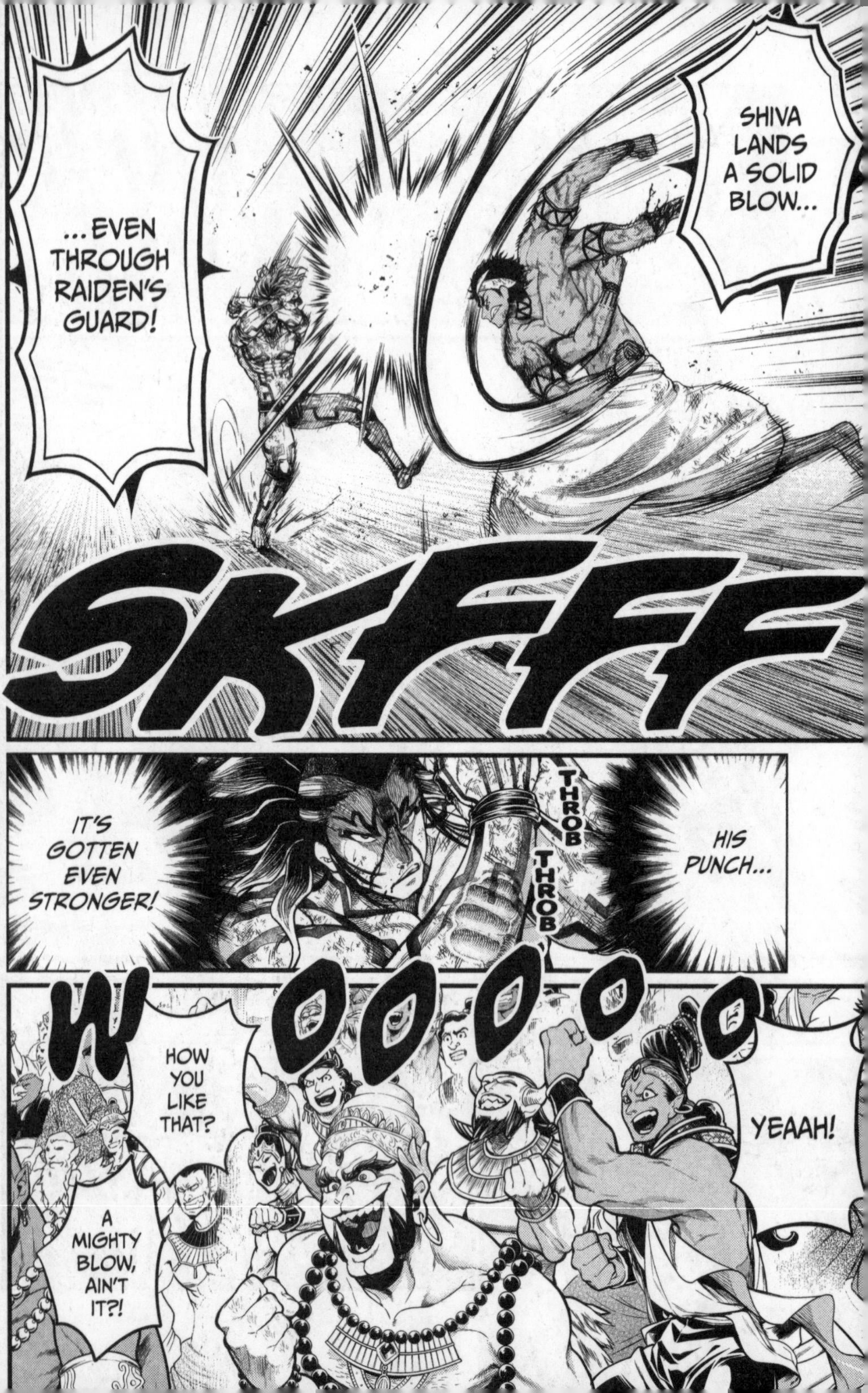
SHIVA LANDS A SOLID BLOW...
...EVEN THROUGH RAIDEN'S GUARD!
SKFFF
HIS PUNCH...
THROB THROB
IT'S GOTTEN EVEN STRONGER!
WOOOOO
YEAAH!
HOW YOU LIKE THAT?
A MIGHTY BLOW, AIN'T IT?!

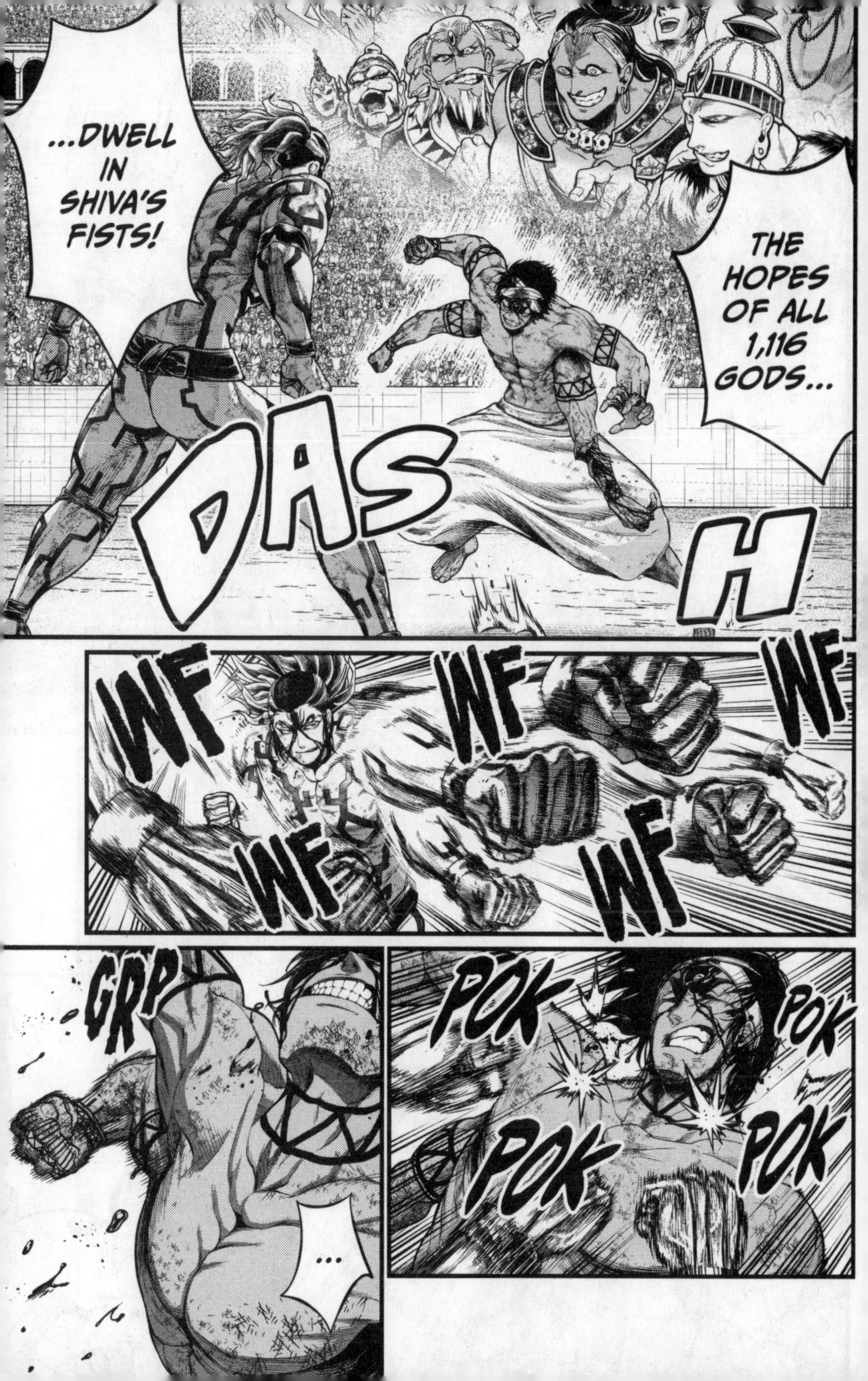
THE HOPES OF ALL 1,116 GODS...
...DWELL IN SHIVA'S FISTS!
DASH
WF
WF
WF
WF
WF
POK
POK
POK
POK
GRP
...

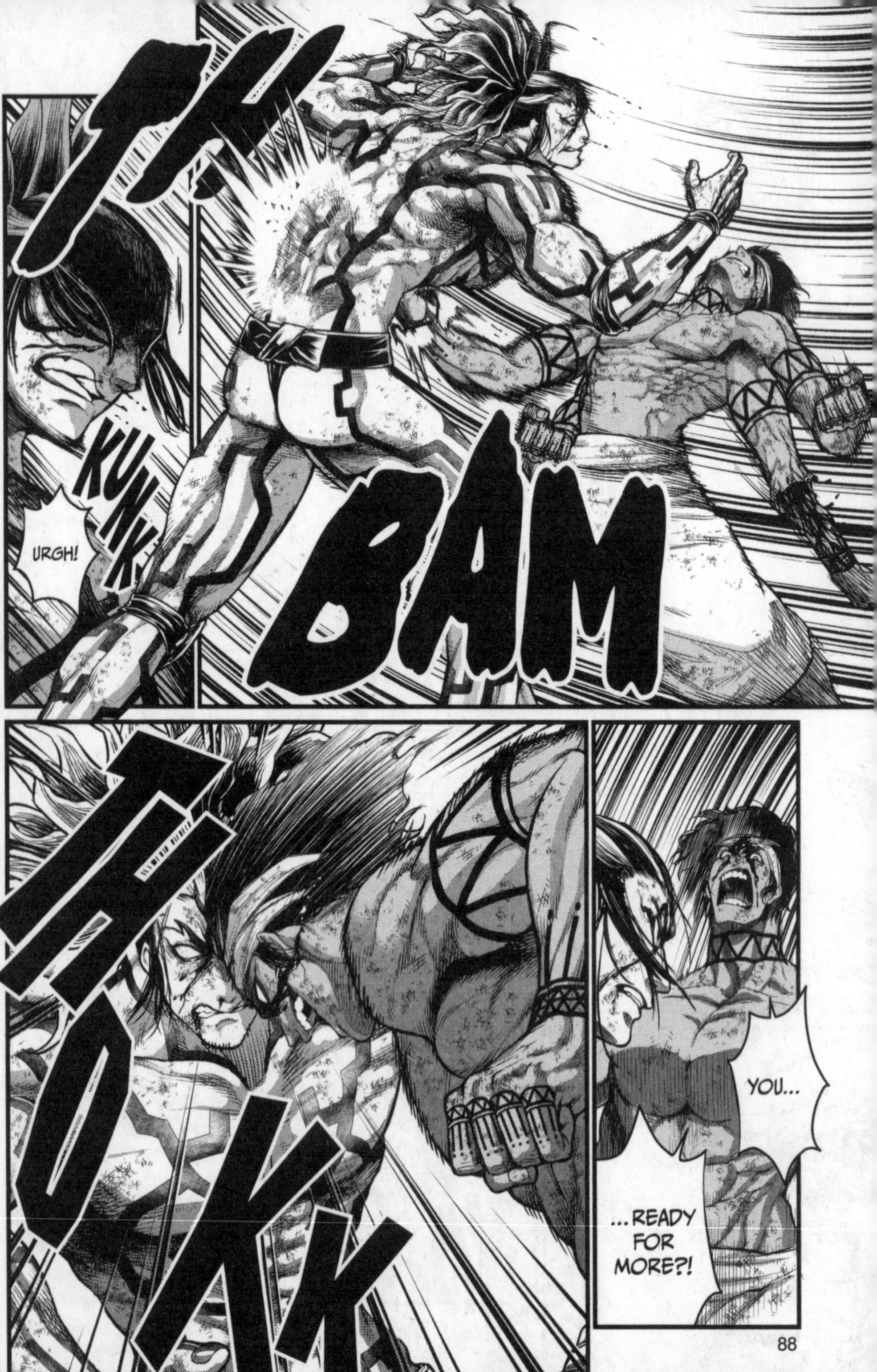
BAM
KUNK
URGH!
YOU...
...READY FOR MORE?!

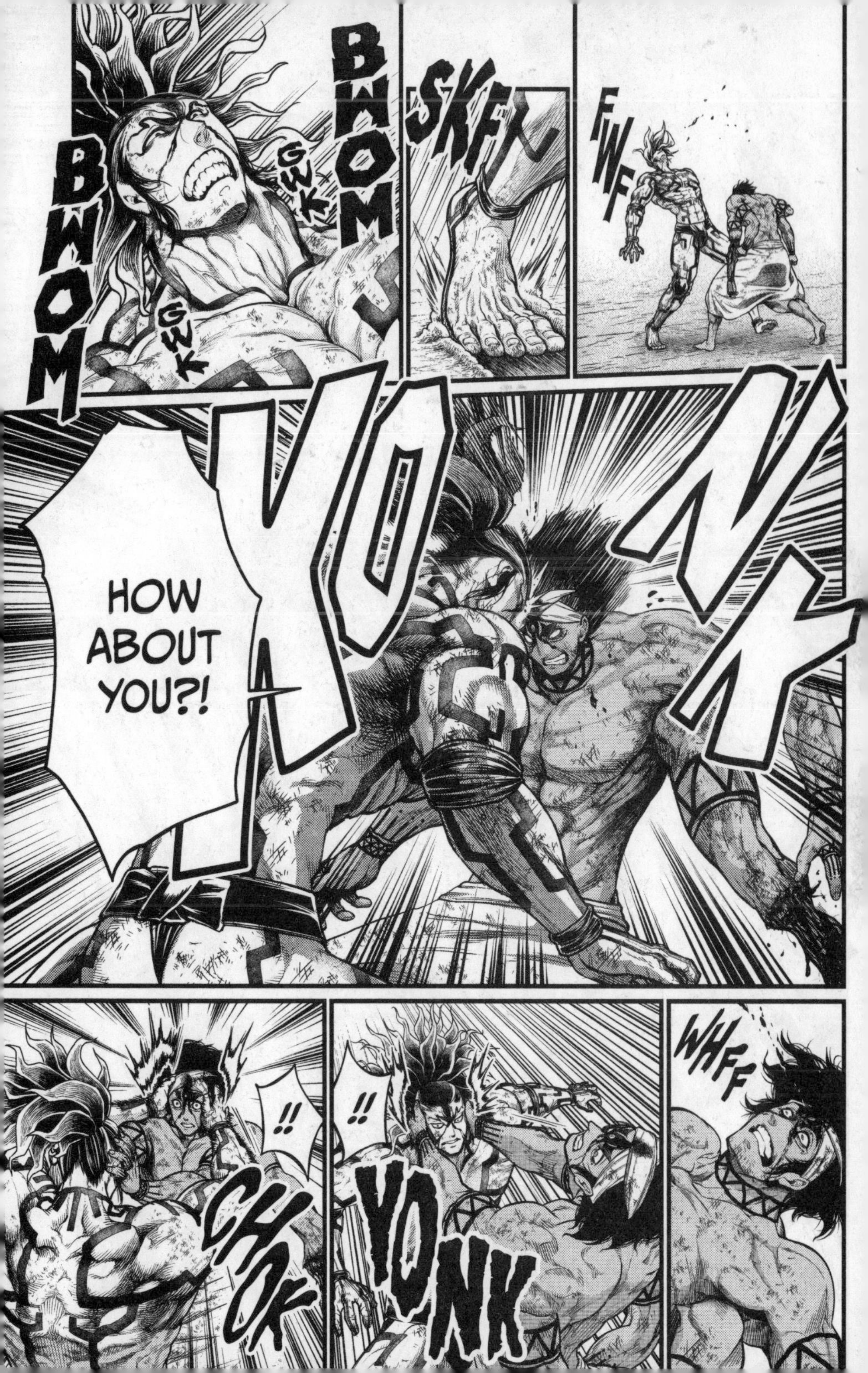
FWF
SKFF
BWHOM
GWK
BWHOM
GWK
YONK
HOW ABOUT YOU?!
WHFF
!!
YONK
!!
CHOK

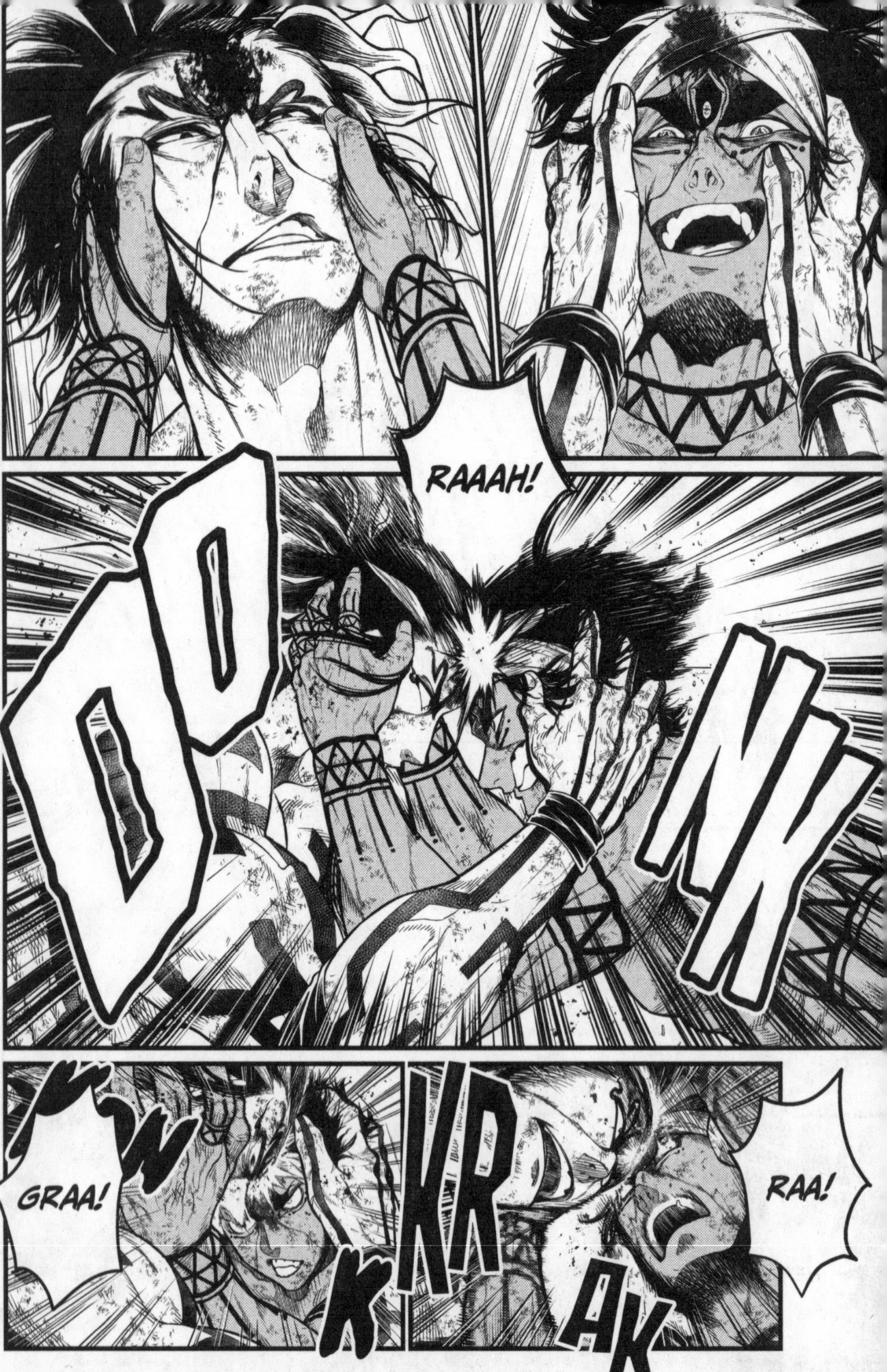
RAAAH!
RAA!
GRAA!

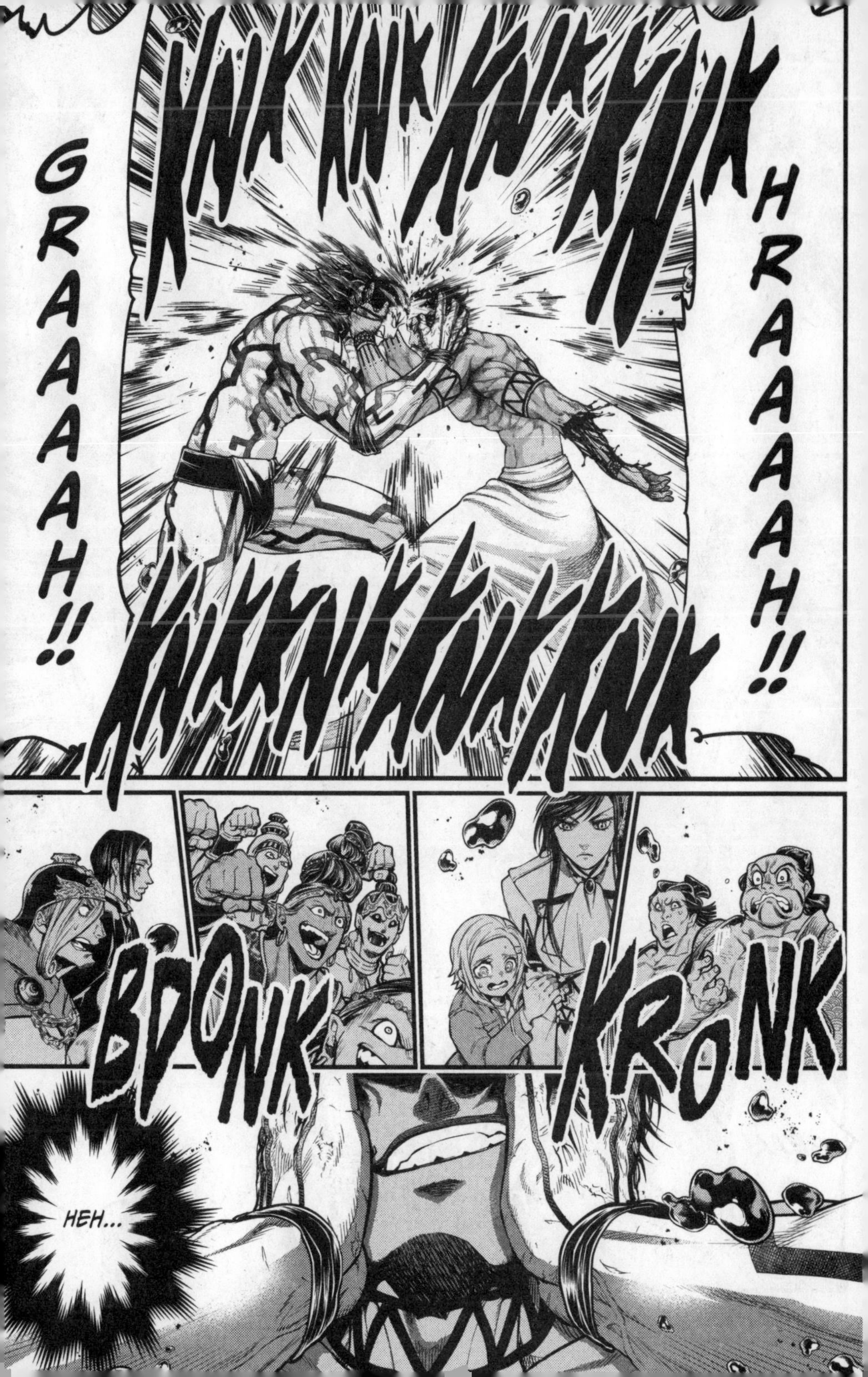
HRAAAAAH!!
GRAAAAAH!!
KRONK
BDONK
HEH...

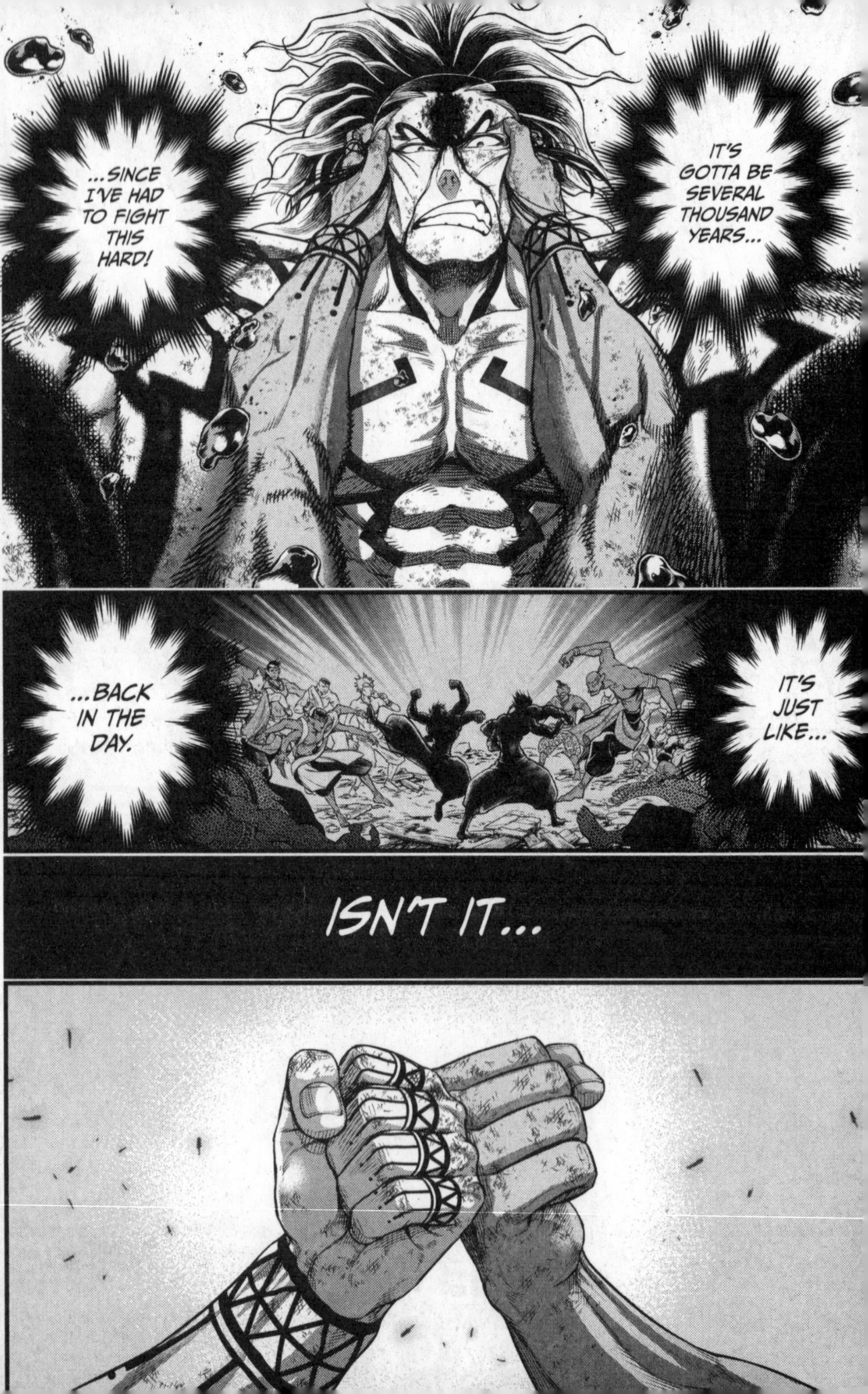
IT'S GOTTA BE SEVERAL THOUSAND YEARS...
...SINCE I'VE HAD TO FIGHT THIS HARD!
IT'S JUST LIKE...
...BACK IN THE DAY.
ISN'T IT...

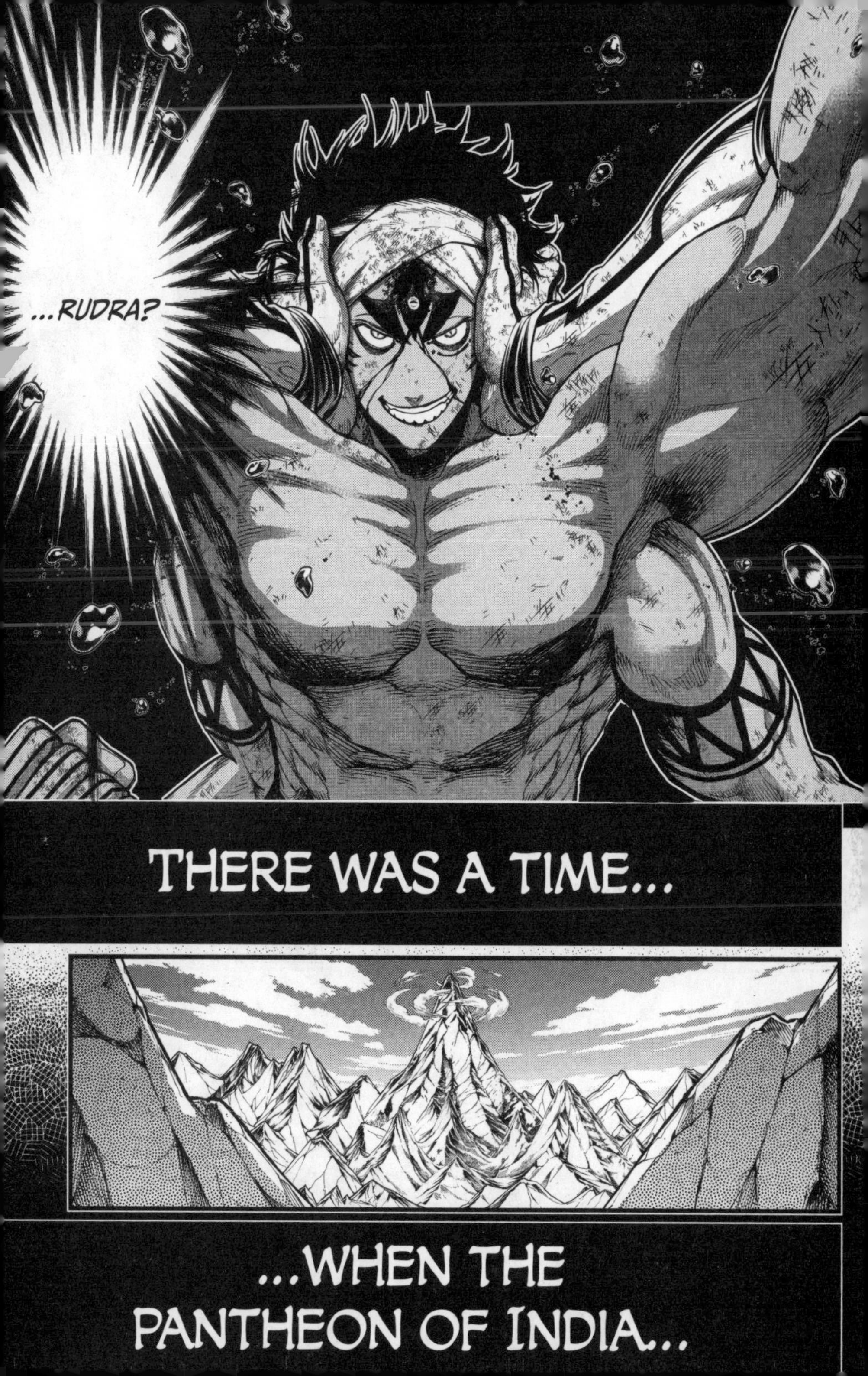
...RUDRA?
THERE WAS A TIME...
...WHEN THE PANTHEON OF INDIA...

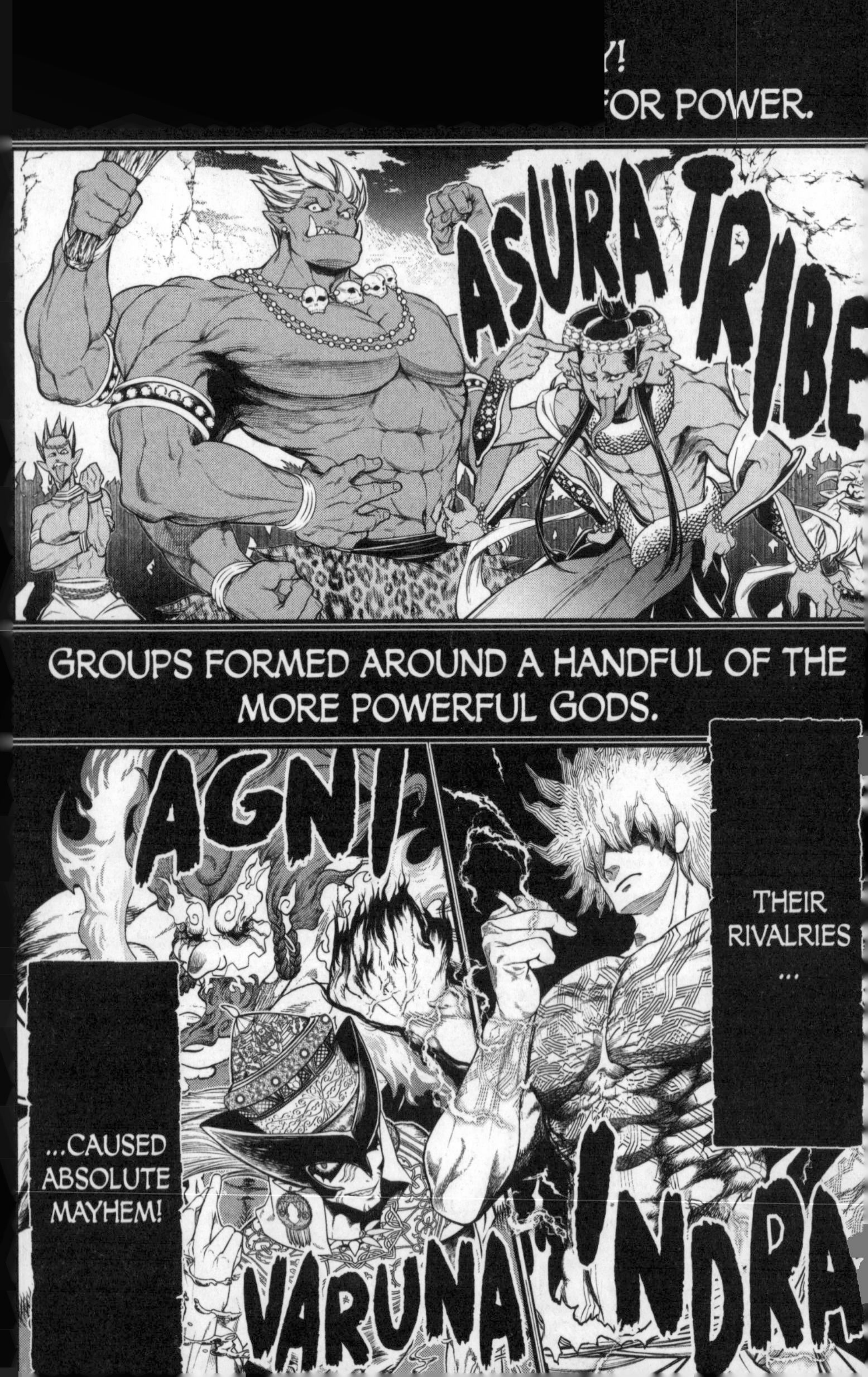
[redacted]
FOR POWER.
ASURA TRIBE
GROUPS FORMED AROUND A HANDFUL OF THE MORE POWERFUL GODS.
AGNI
THEIR RIVALRIES ...
...CAUSED ABSOLUTE MAYHEM!
INDRA
VARUNA

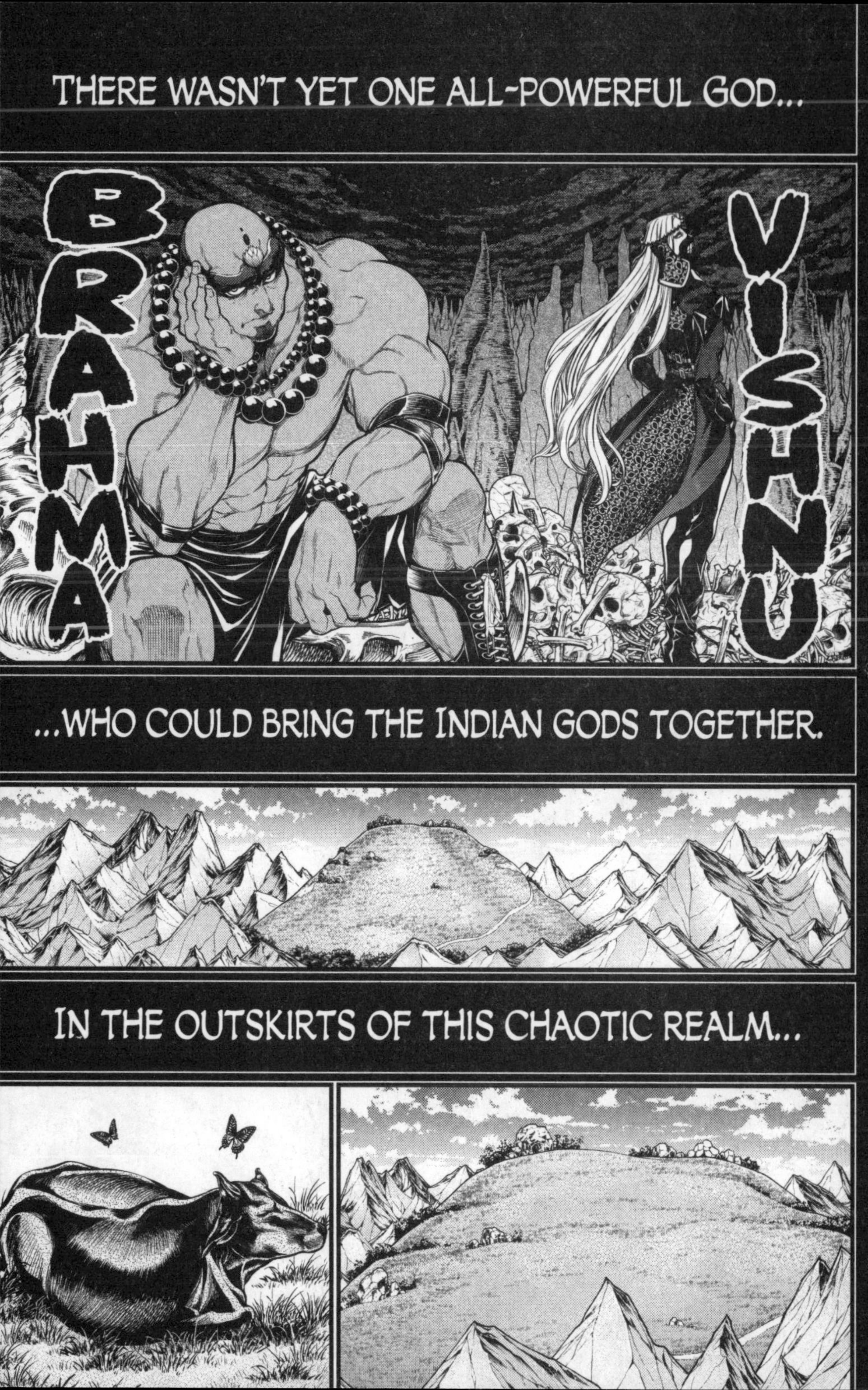
THERE WASN'T YET ONE ALL-POWERFUL GOD...
VISHNU
BRAHMA
...WHO COULD BRING THE INDIAN GODS TOGETHER.
IN THE OUTSKIRTS OF THIS CHAOTIC REALM...

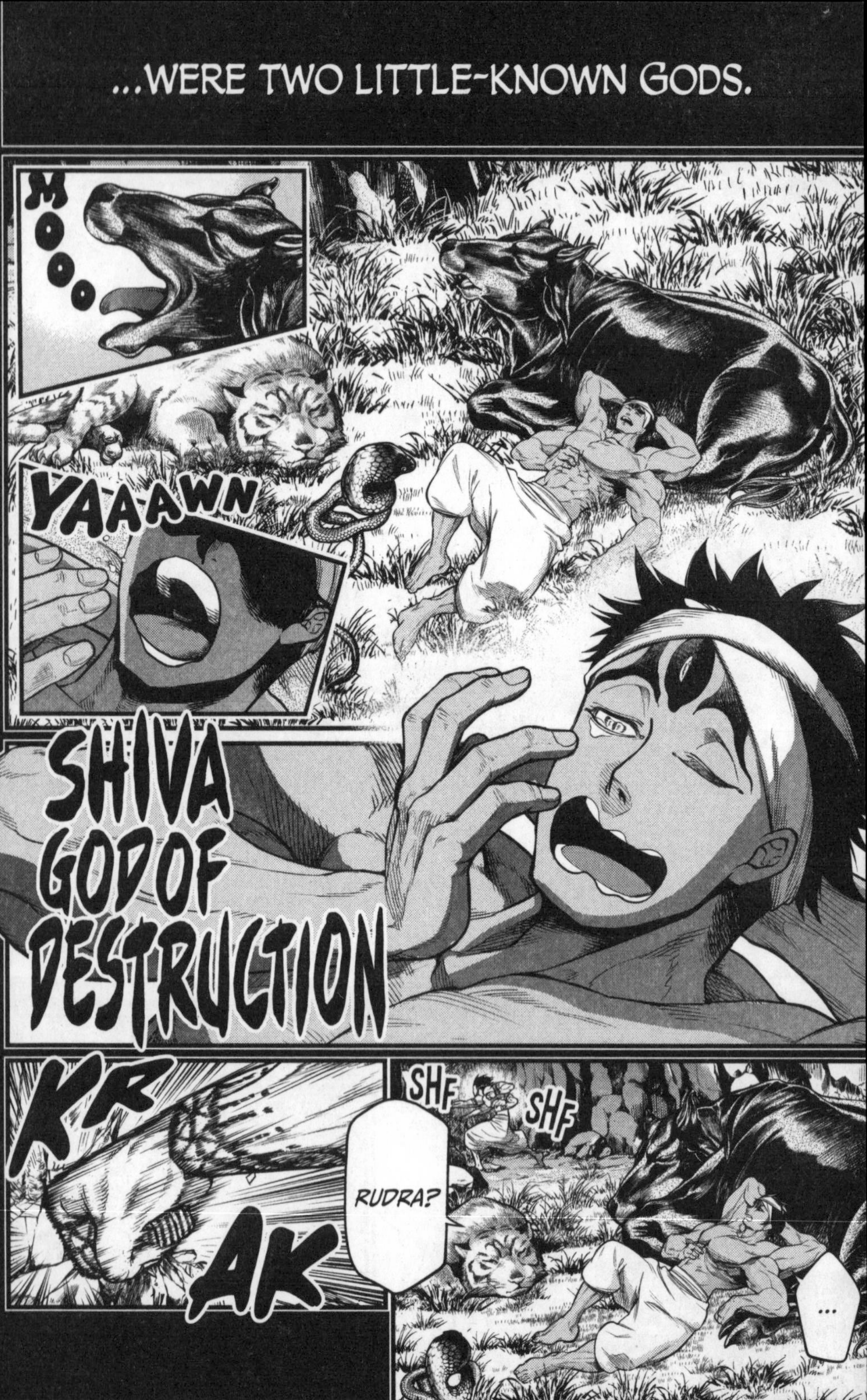
...WERE TWO LITTLE-KNOWN GODS.
MOOOO
YAAAWN
SHIVA GOD OF DESTRUCTION
SHF SHF
RUDRA?
...
KRAK

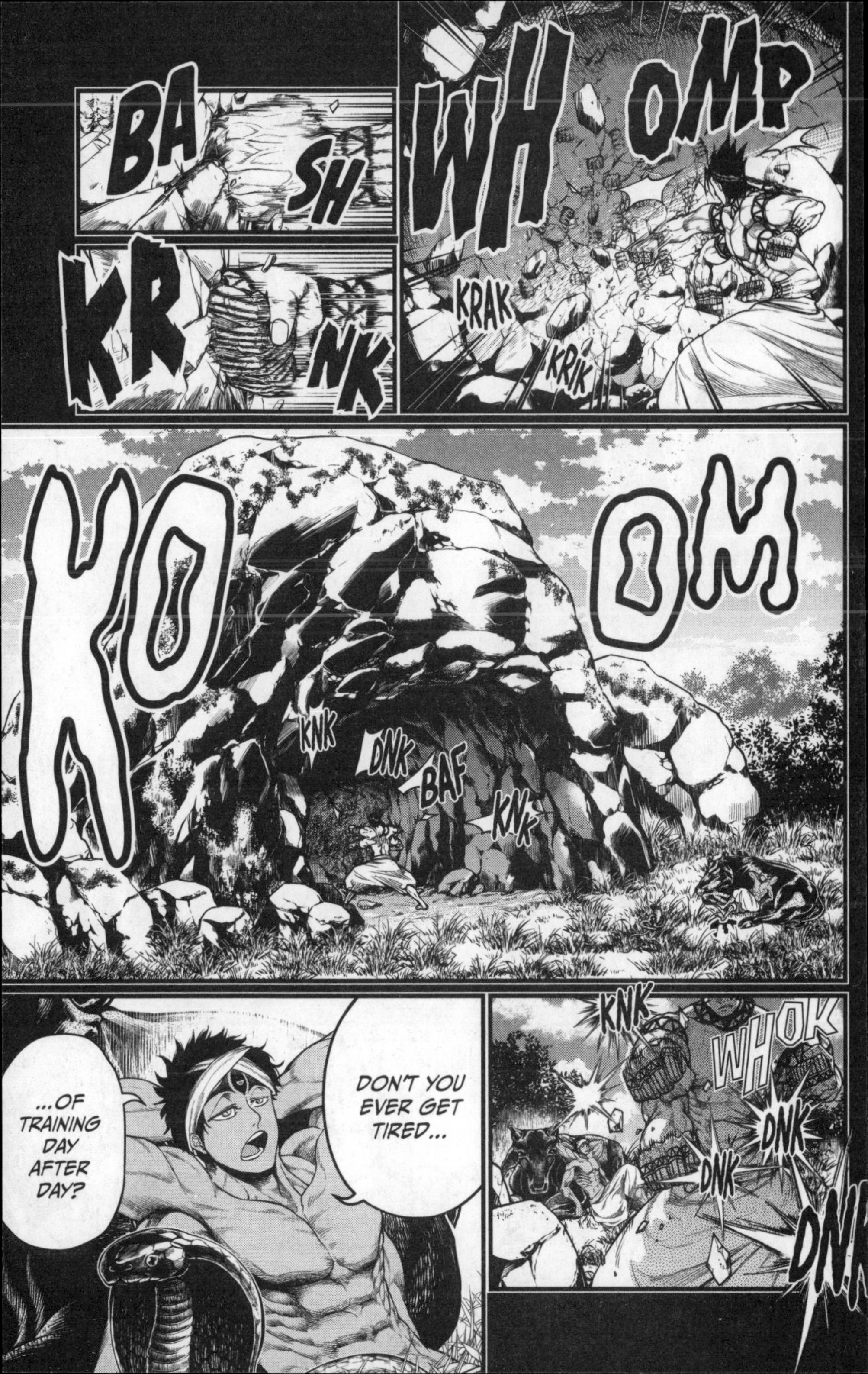
WHOMP
KRAK
KRIK
BASH
KRNK
KOOM
KNK
DNK
BAF
KNK
KNK
WHOK
DNK
DNK
DN
DON'T YOU EVER GET TIRED...
...OF TRAINING DAY AFTER DAY?

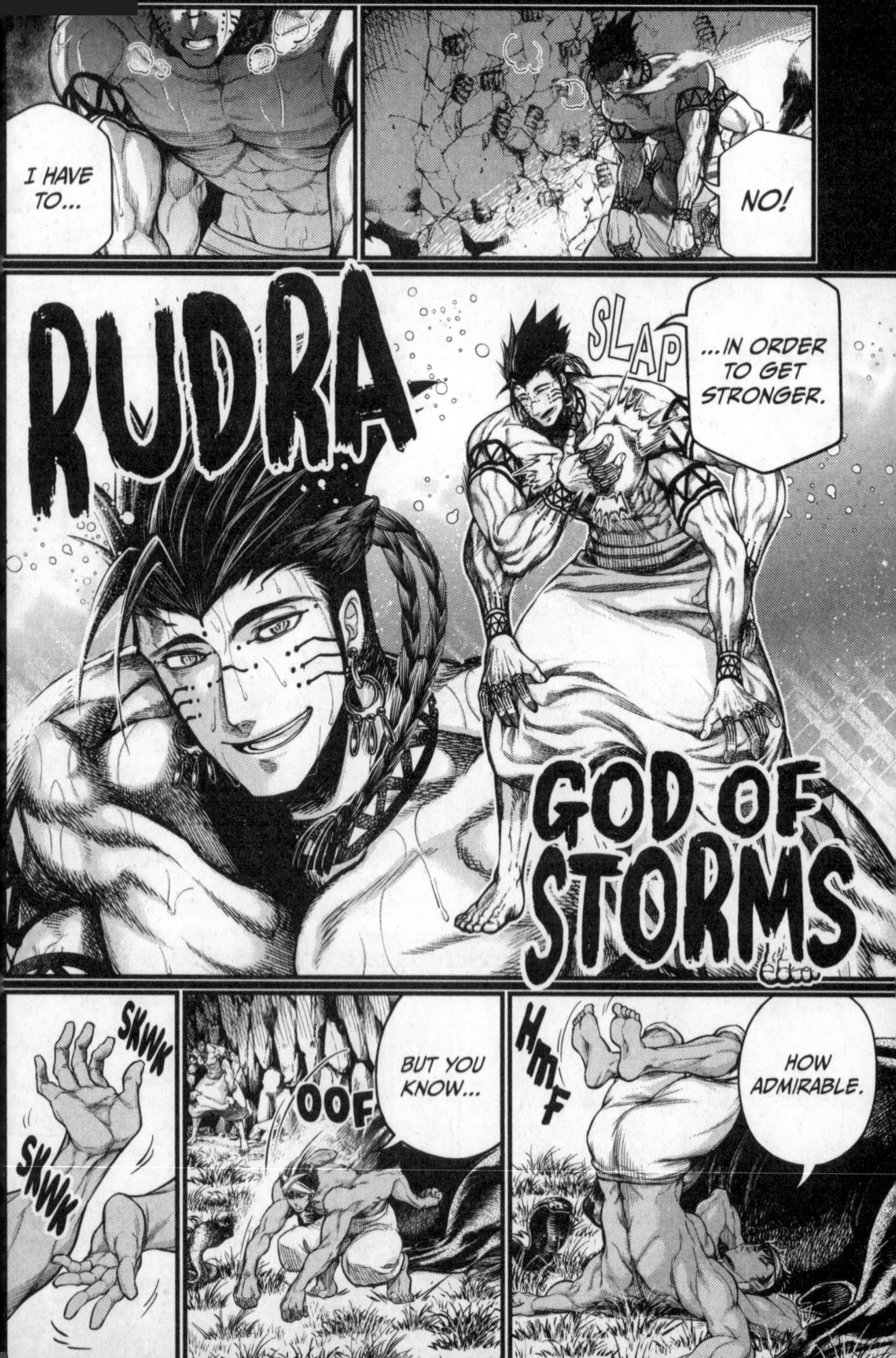
NO!
I HAVE TO...
SLAP
...IN ORDER TO GET STRONGER.
RUDRA
GOD OF STORMS
HOW ADMIRABLE.
HMF
BUT YOU KNOW...
OOF
SKWK
SKWK

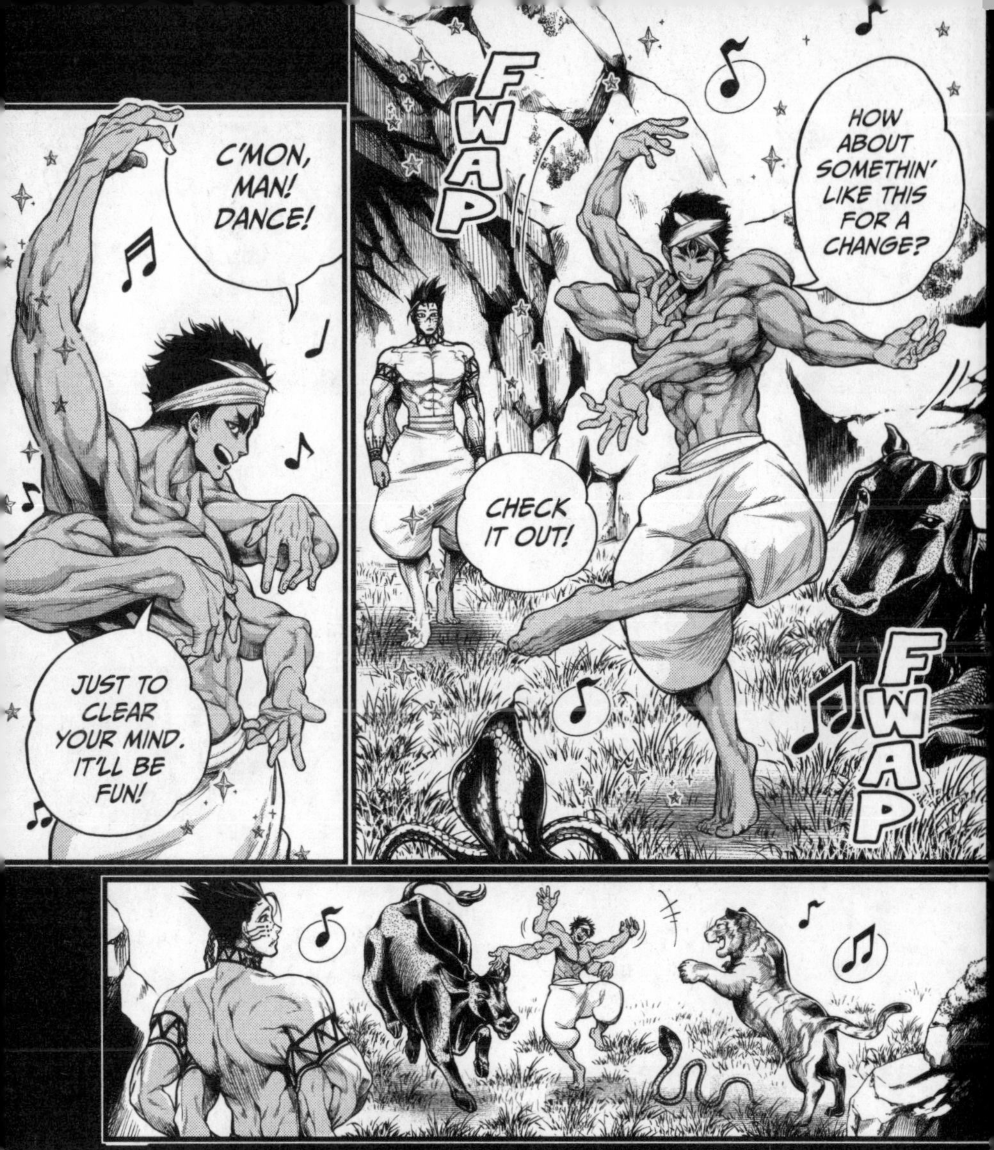

FWAP
HOW ABOUT SOMETHIN' LIKE THIS FOR A CHANGE?
CHECK IT OUT!
FWAP
C'MON, MAN! DANCE!
JUST TO CLEAR YOUR MIND. IT'LL BE FUN!
GIMME A BREAK...

THESE TWO GODS HAD COMPLETELY OPPOSITE PERSONALITIES. HOWEVER...

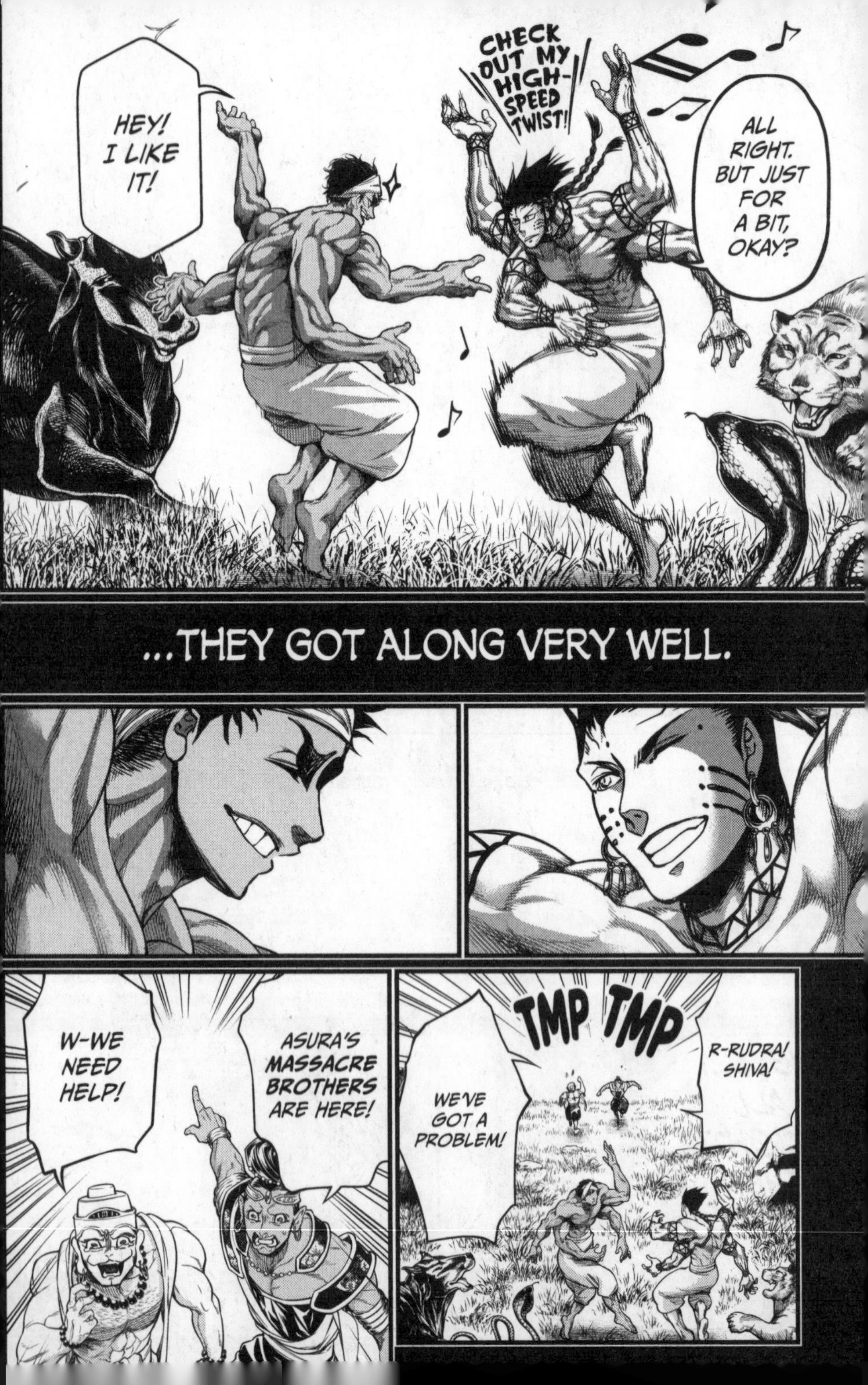
ALL RIGHT. BUT JUST FOR A BIT, OKAY?
CHECK OUT MY HIGH-SPEED TWIST!
HEY! I LIKE IT!
...THEY GOT ALONG VERY WELL.
TMP TMP
R-RUDRA! SHIVA!
WE'VE GOT A PROBLEM!
ASURA'S MASSACRE BROTHERS ARE HERE!
W-WE NEED HELP!

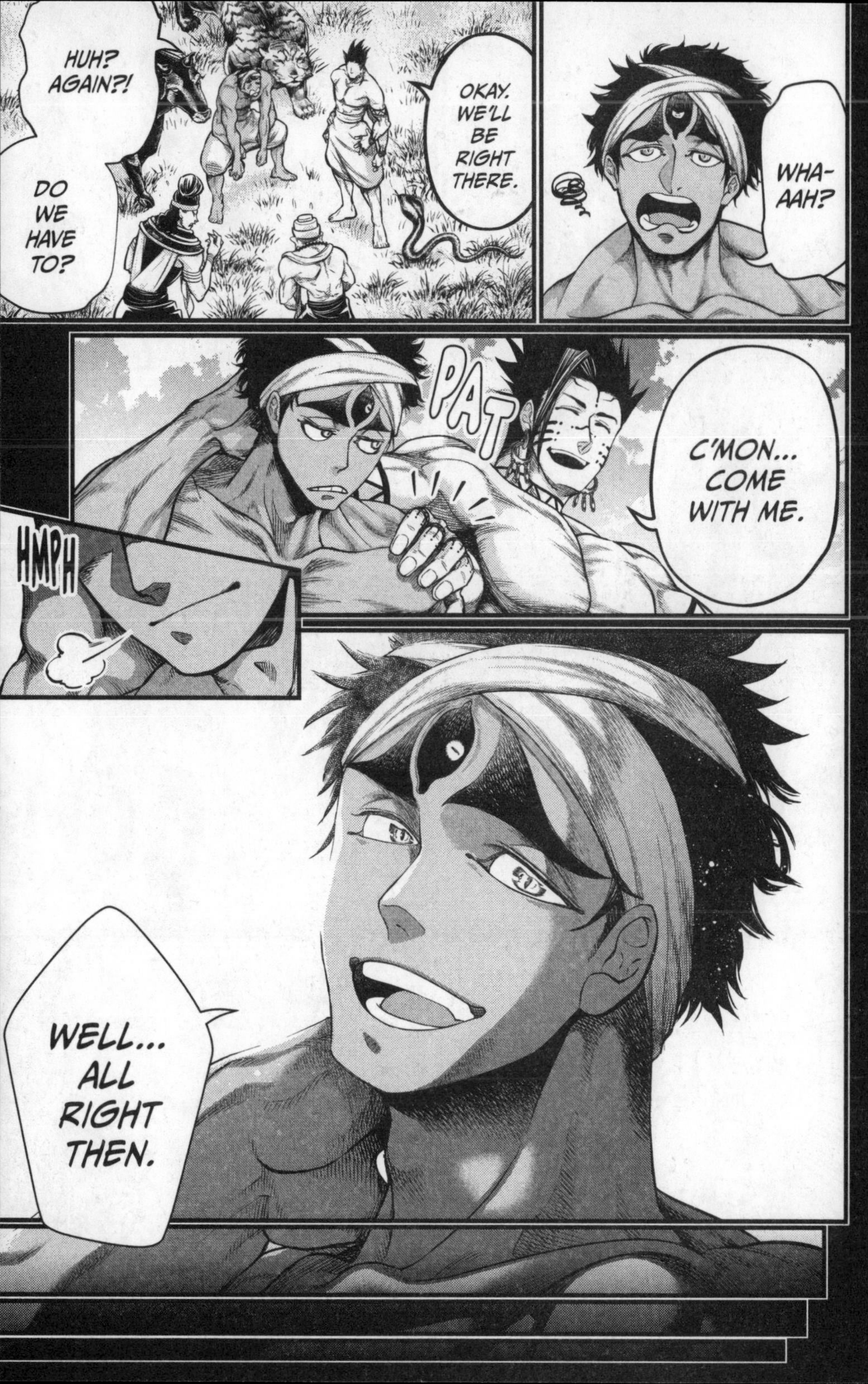
WHA-AAH?
OKAY. WE'LL BE RIGHT THERE.
HUH? AGAIN?!
DO WE HAVE TO?
C'MON... COME WITH ME.
PAT
HMPH
WELL... ALL RIGHT THEN.

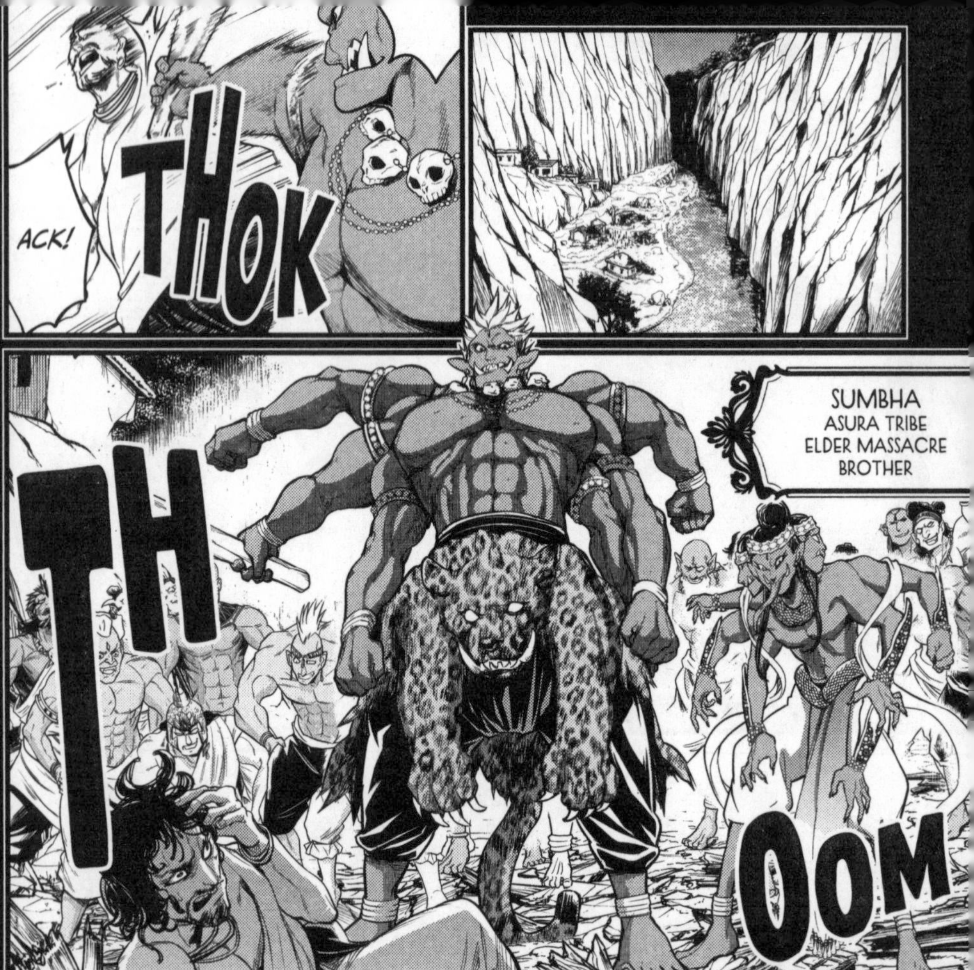
THOK
ACK!
SUMBHA
ASURA TRIBE
ELDER MASSACRE
BROTHER
TH
OOM
AIEE!
WHERE'S THE LOCAL GOD THAT RULES THIS VILLAGE?!

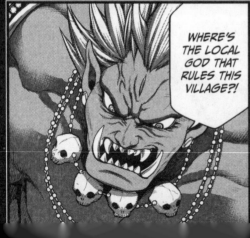

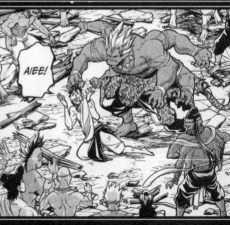

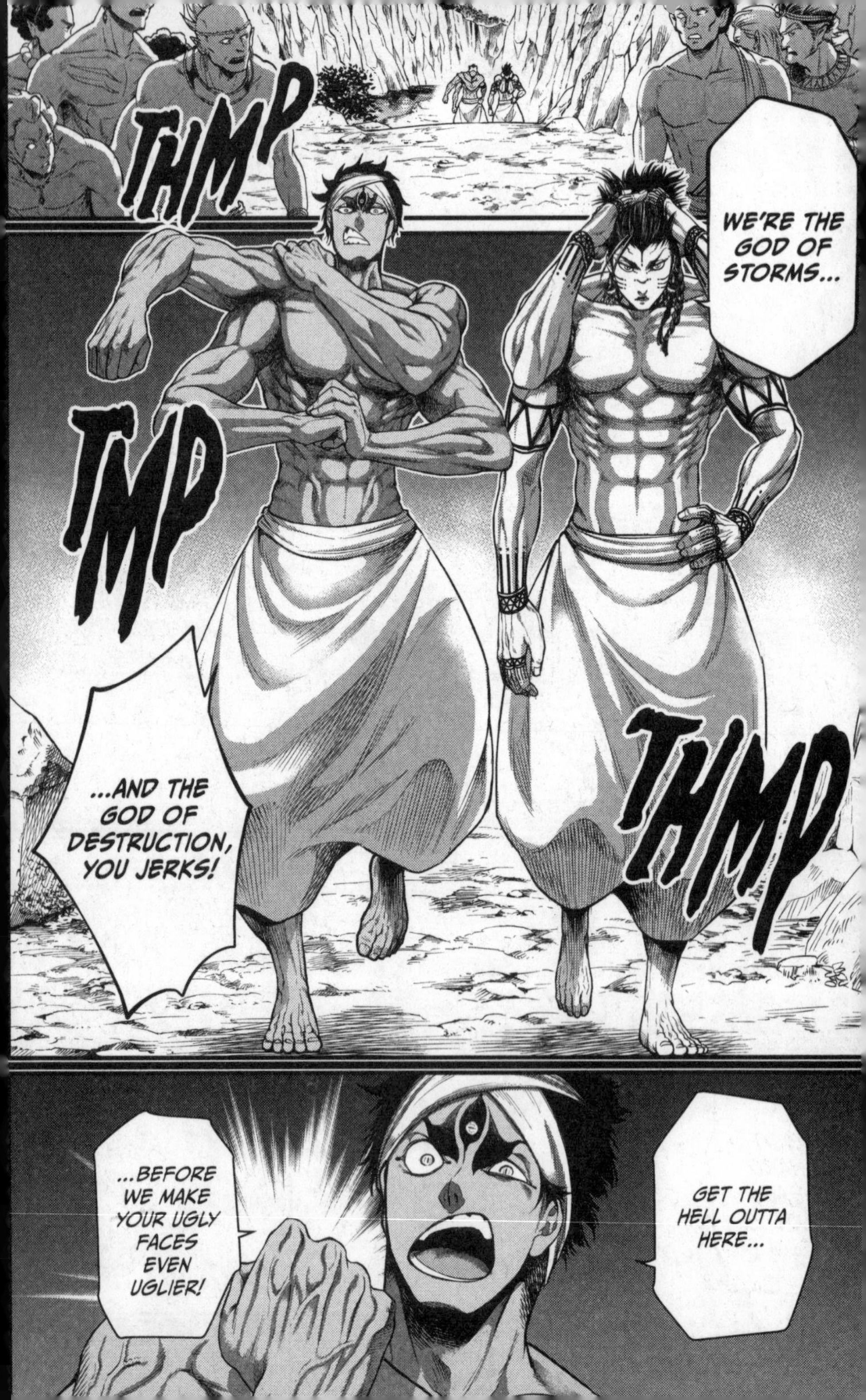
THMP
WE'RE THE GOD OF STORMS...
TMP
THMP
...AND THE GOD OF DESTRUCTION, YOU JERKS!
GET THE HELL OUTTA HERE...
...BEFORE WE MAKE YOUR UGLY FACES EVEN UGLIER!

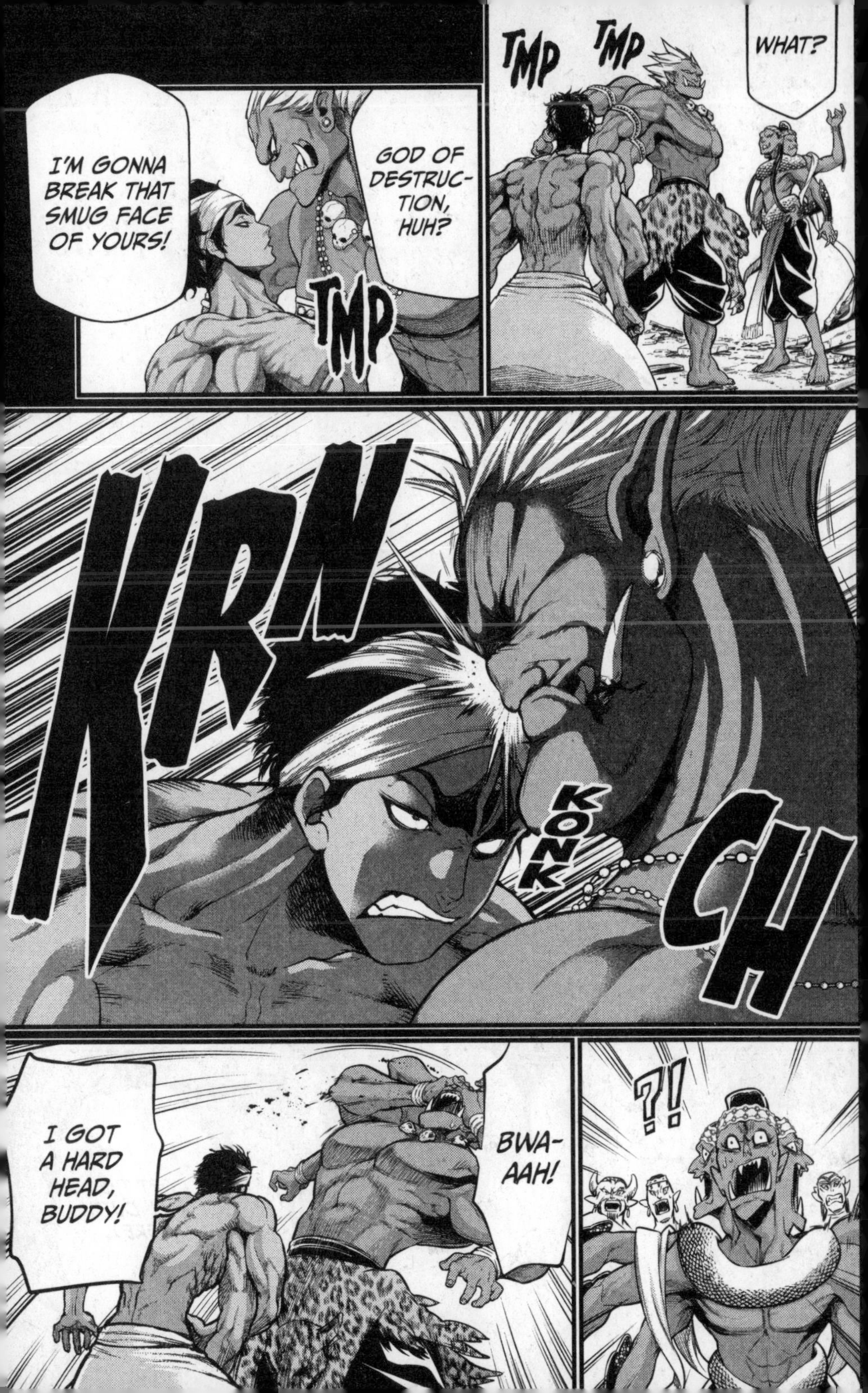
WHAT?
TMP
TMP
GOD OF DESTRUC-TION, HUH?
I'M GONNA BREAK THAT SMUG FACE OF YOURS!
TMP
KRN
KONK
CH
?!
BWA-AAH!
I GOT A HARD HEAD, BUDDY!

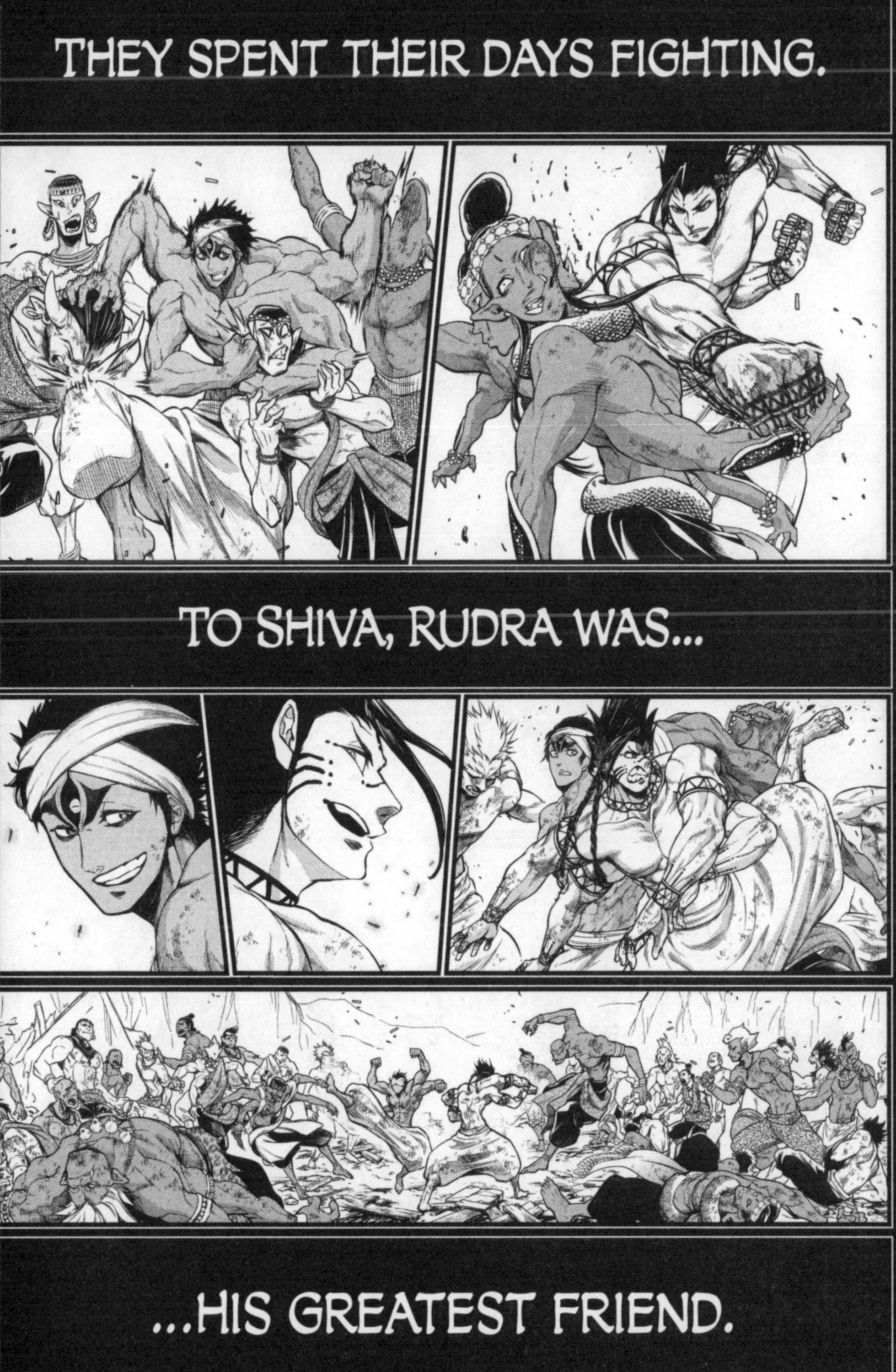
THEY SPENT THEIR DAYS FIGHTING.
TO SHIVA, RUDRA WAS...
...HIS GREATEST FRIEND.

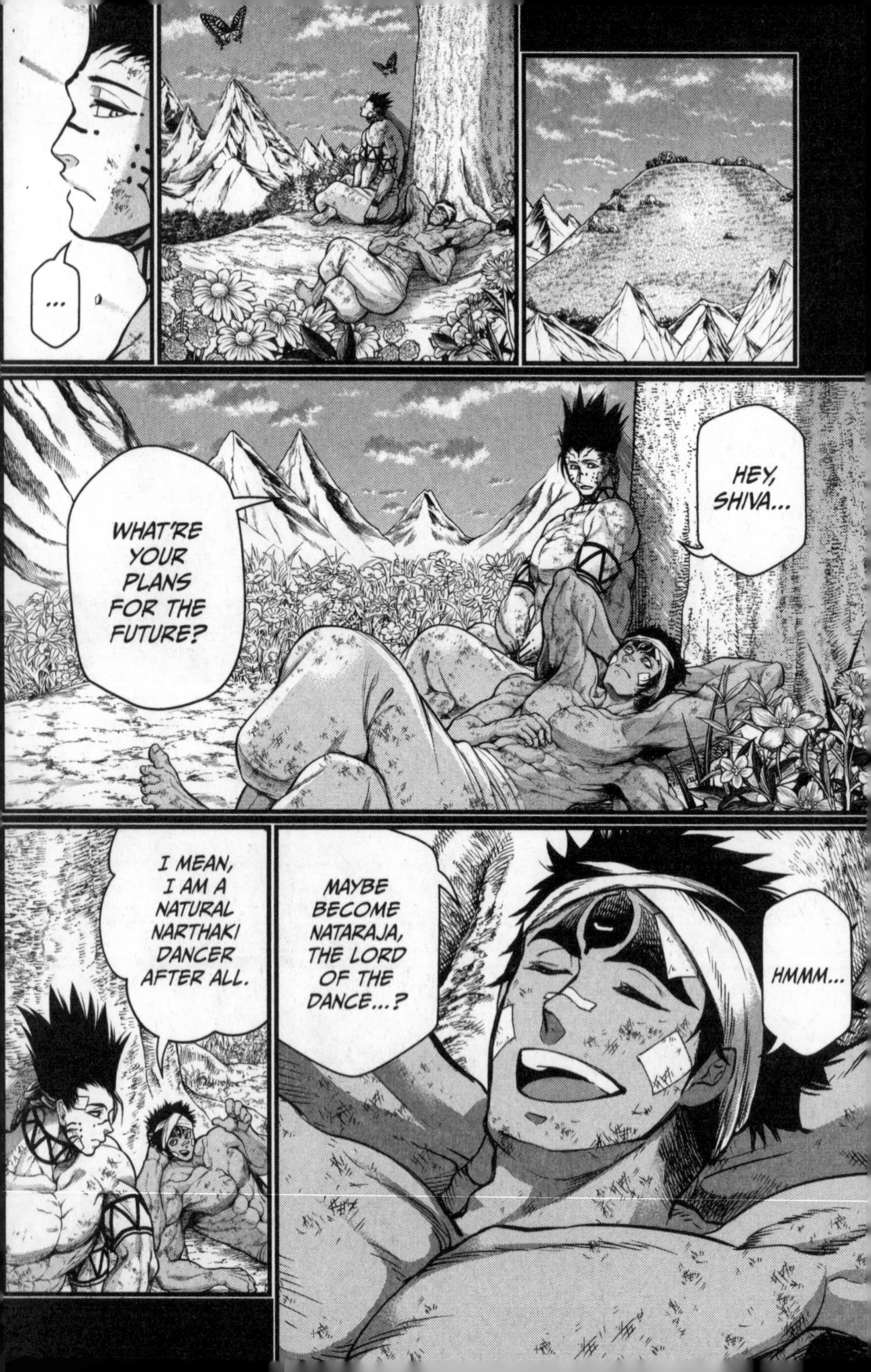
...
HEY, SHIVA...
WHAT'RE YOUR PLANS FOR THE FUTURE?
HMMM...
MAYBE BECOME NATARAJA, THE LORD OF THE DANCE...?
I MEAN, I AM A NATURAL NARTHAKI DANCER AFTER ALL.

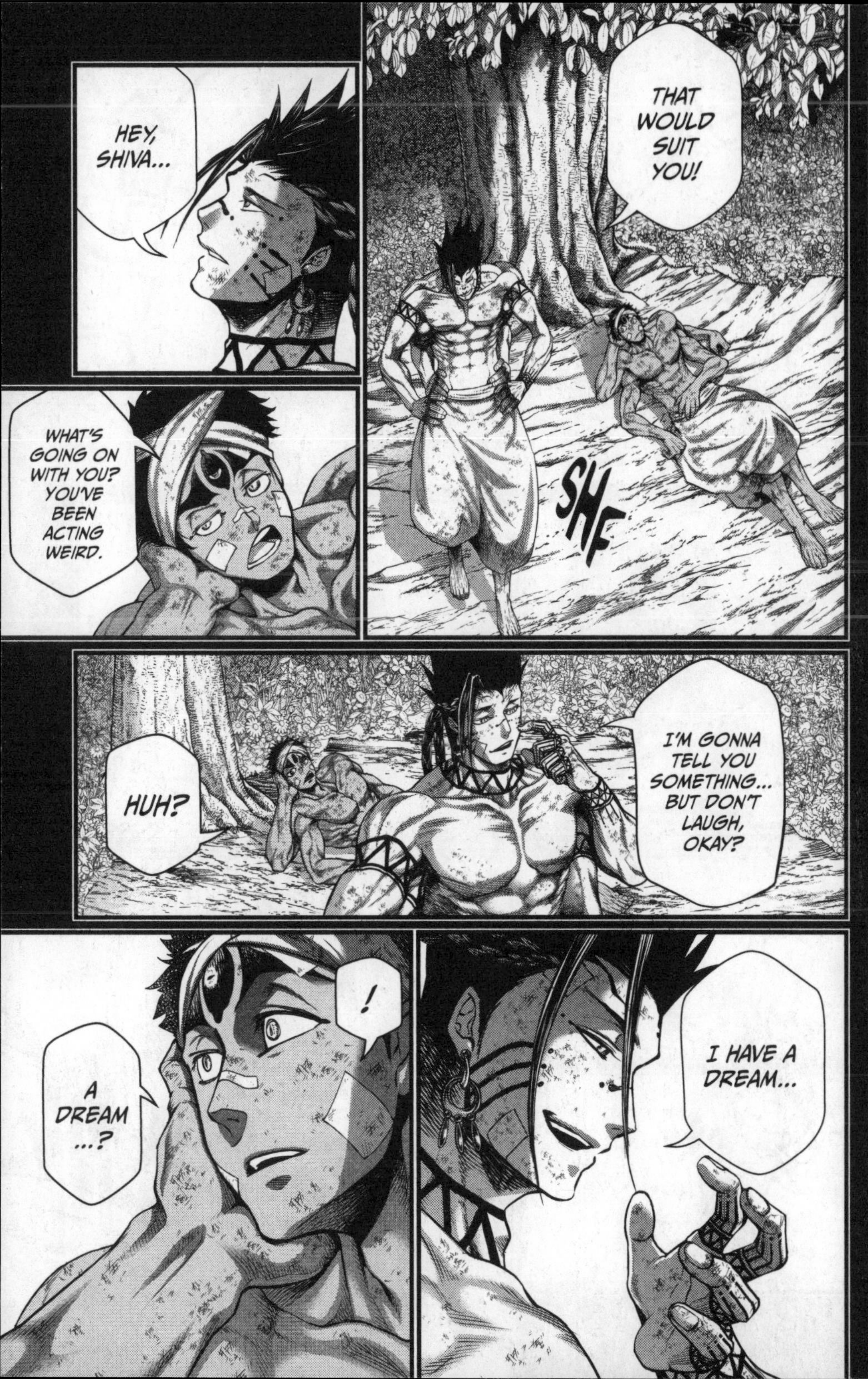
THAT WOULD SUIT YOU!
SHF
HEY, SHIVA...
WHAT'S GOING ON WITH YOU? YOU'VE BEEN ACTING WEIRD.
I'M GONNA TELL YOU SOMETHING... BUT DON'T LAUGH, OKAY?
HUH?
I HAVE A DREAM...
!
A DREAM ...?

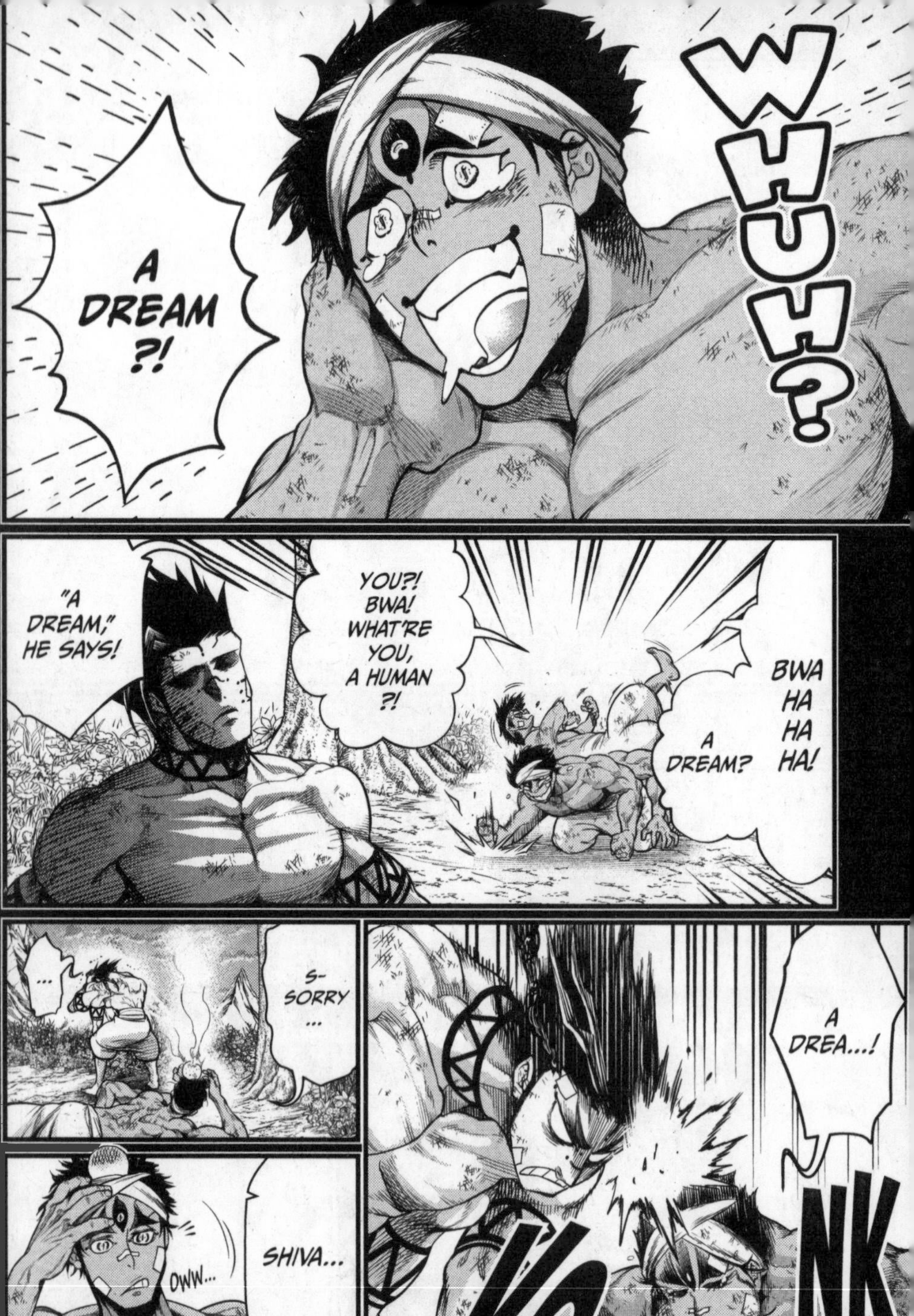
WHUH?
A DREAM ?!
BWA HA HA HA!
A DREAM?
YOU?! BWA! WHAT'RE YOU, A HUMAN ?!
"A DREAM," HE SAYS!
A DREA...!
KONK
S-SORRY ...
...
SHIVA...
OWW...

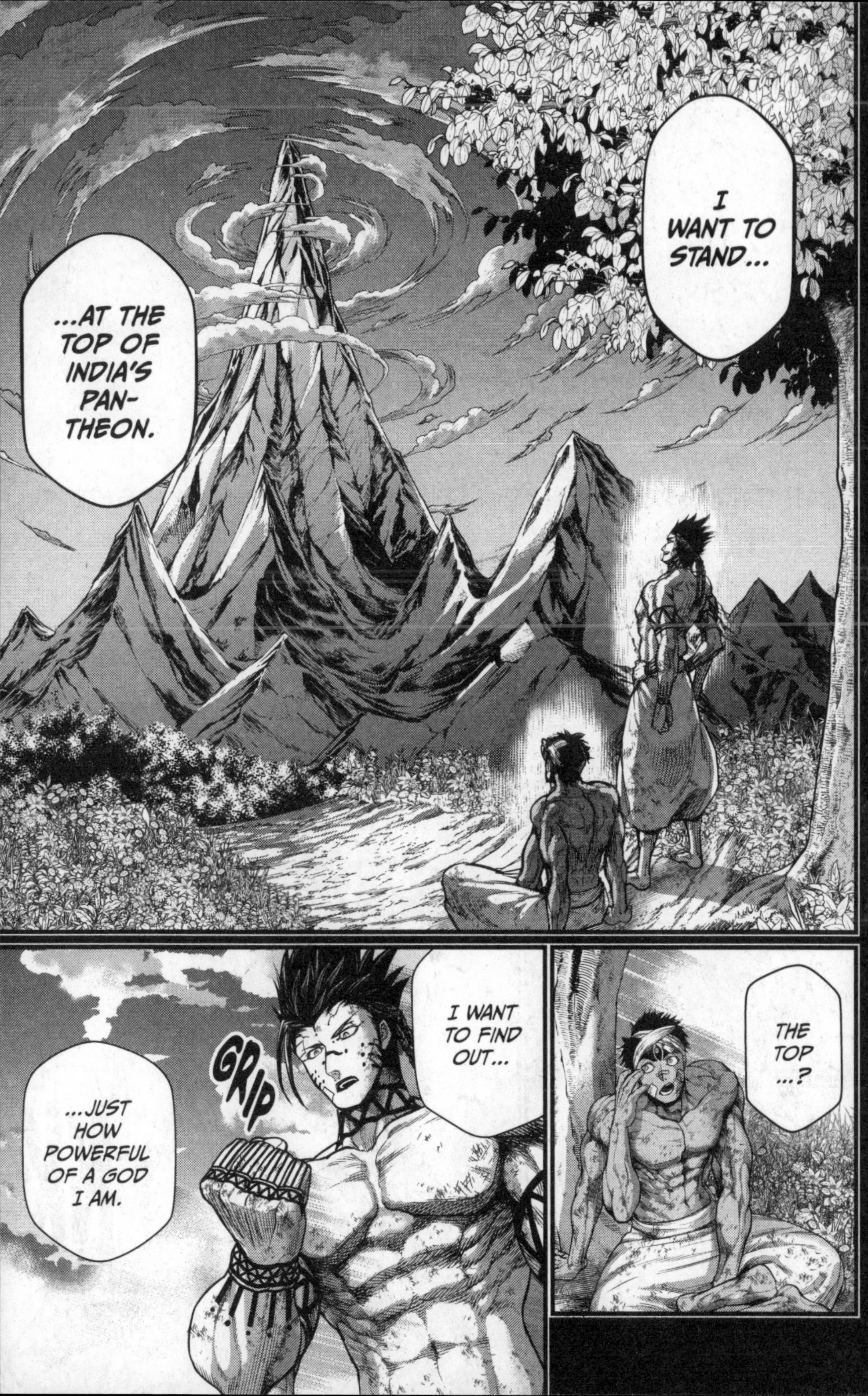
I WANT TO STAND...
...AT THE TOP OF INDIA'S PAN-THEON.
THE TOP ...?
I WANT TO FIND OUT...
GRIP
...JUST HOW POWERFUL OF A GOD I AM.

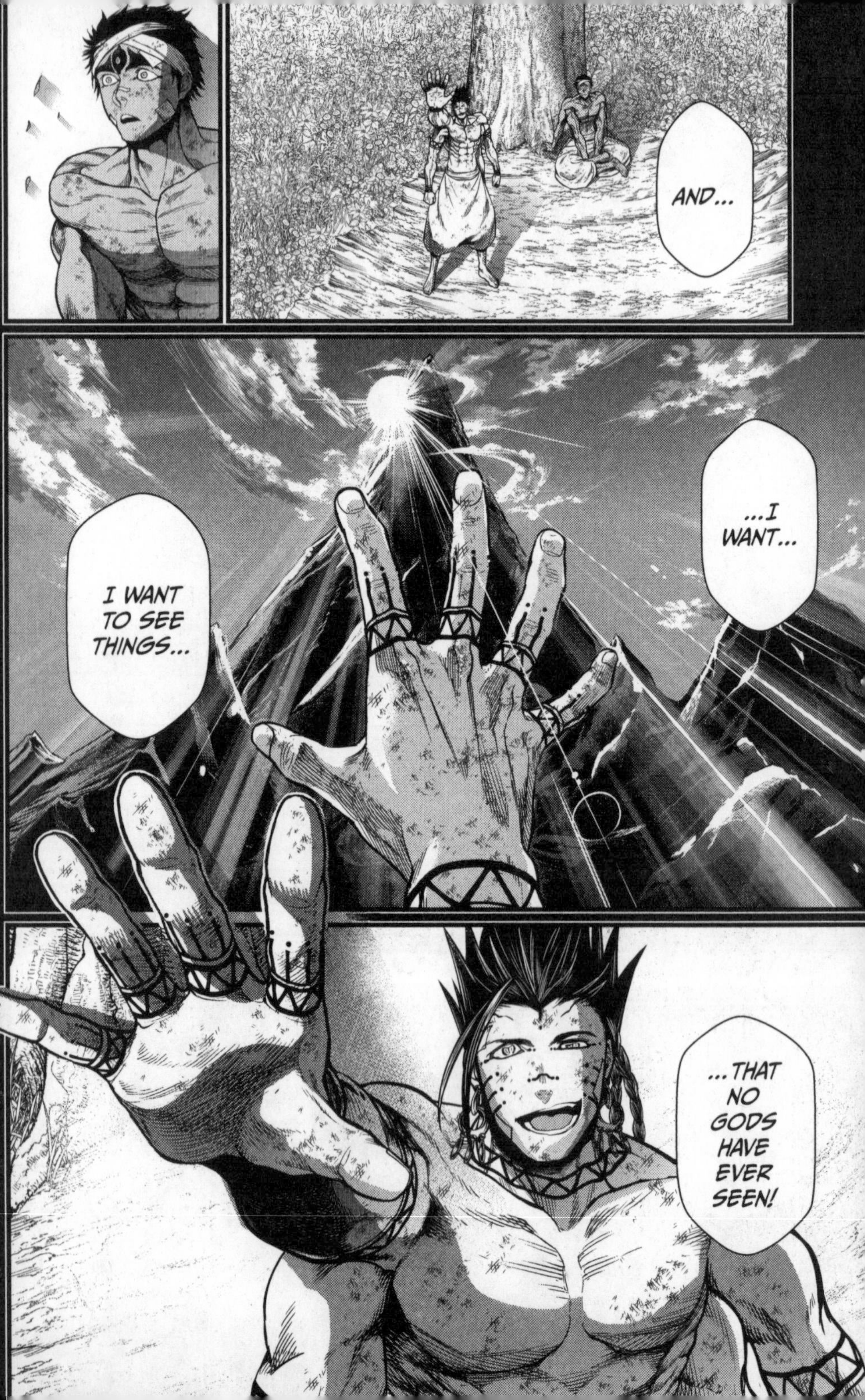
AND...
...I WANT...
I WANT TO SEE THINGS...
...THAT NO GODS HAVE EVER SEEN!

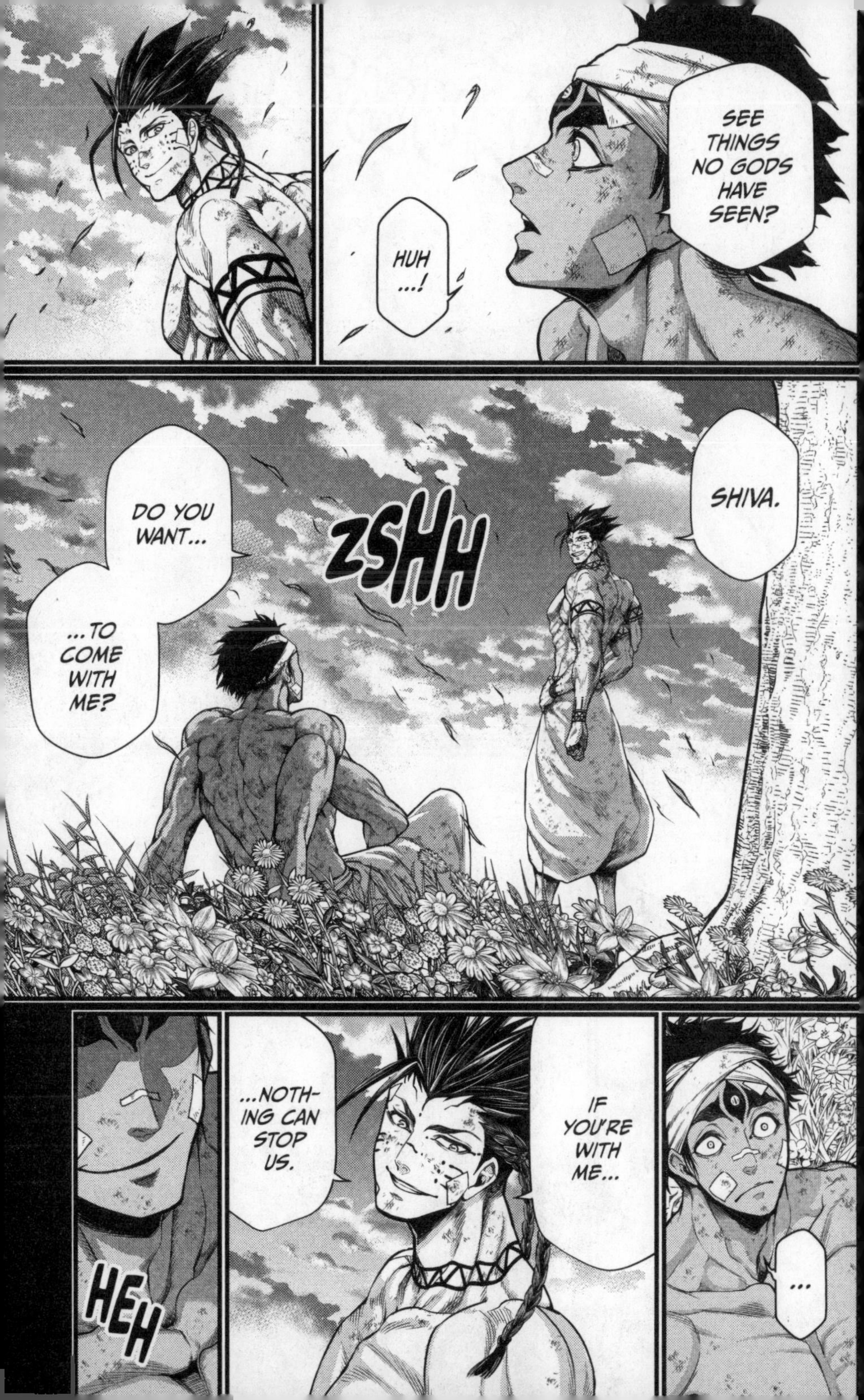
SEE THINGS NO GODS HAVE SEEN?
HUH ...!
SHIVA.
ZSHH
DO YOU WANT...
...TO COME WITH ME?
...
IF YOU'RE WITH ME...
...NOTHING CAN STOP US.
HEH

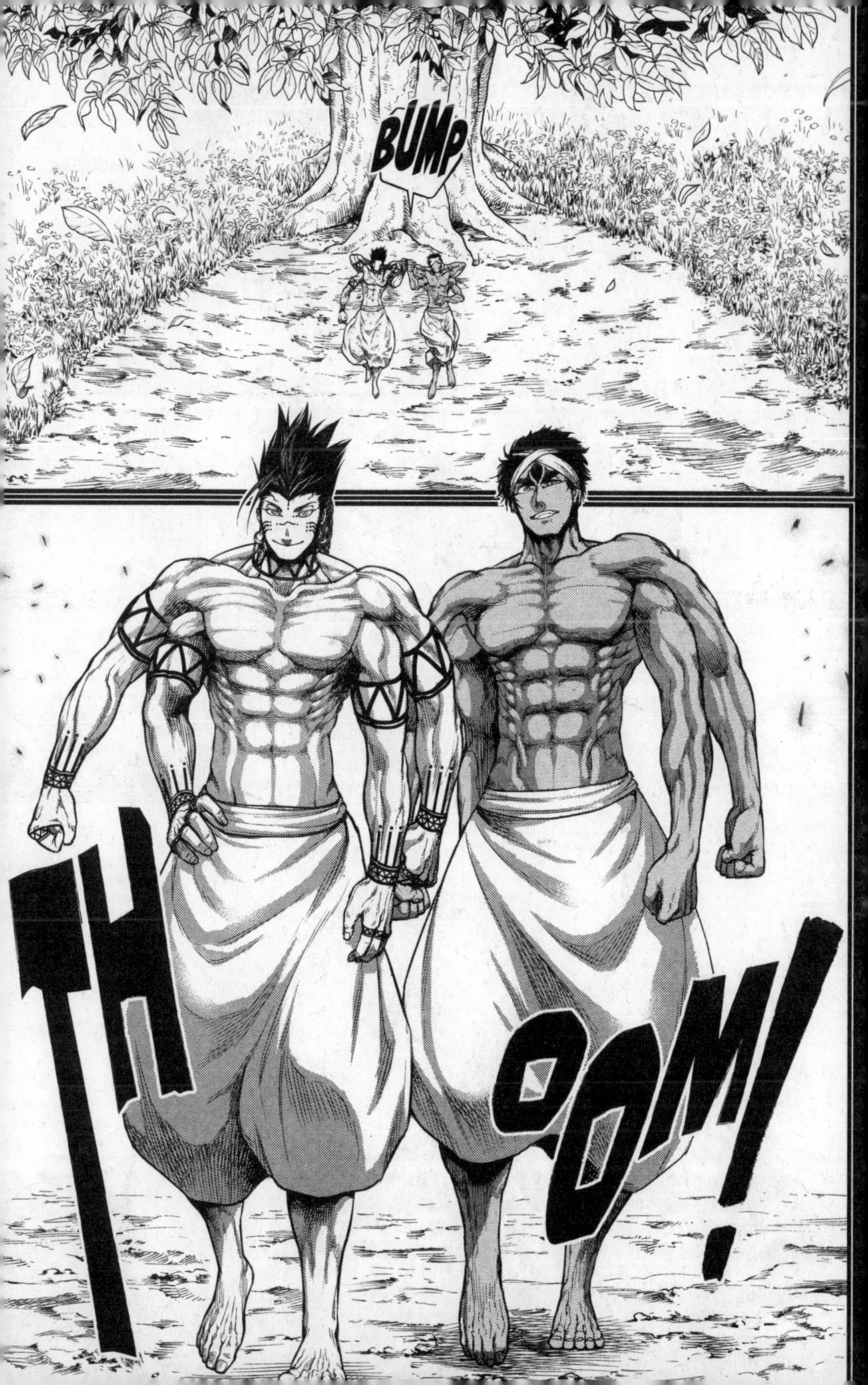
BUMP
THOOM!

AT THE TIME, NO ONE COULD IMAGINE
HOW THEIR DREAM WOULD CONCLUDE.

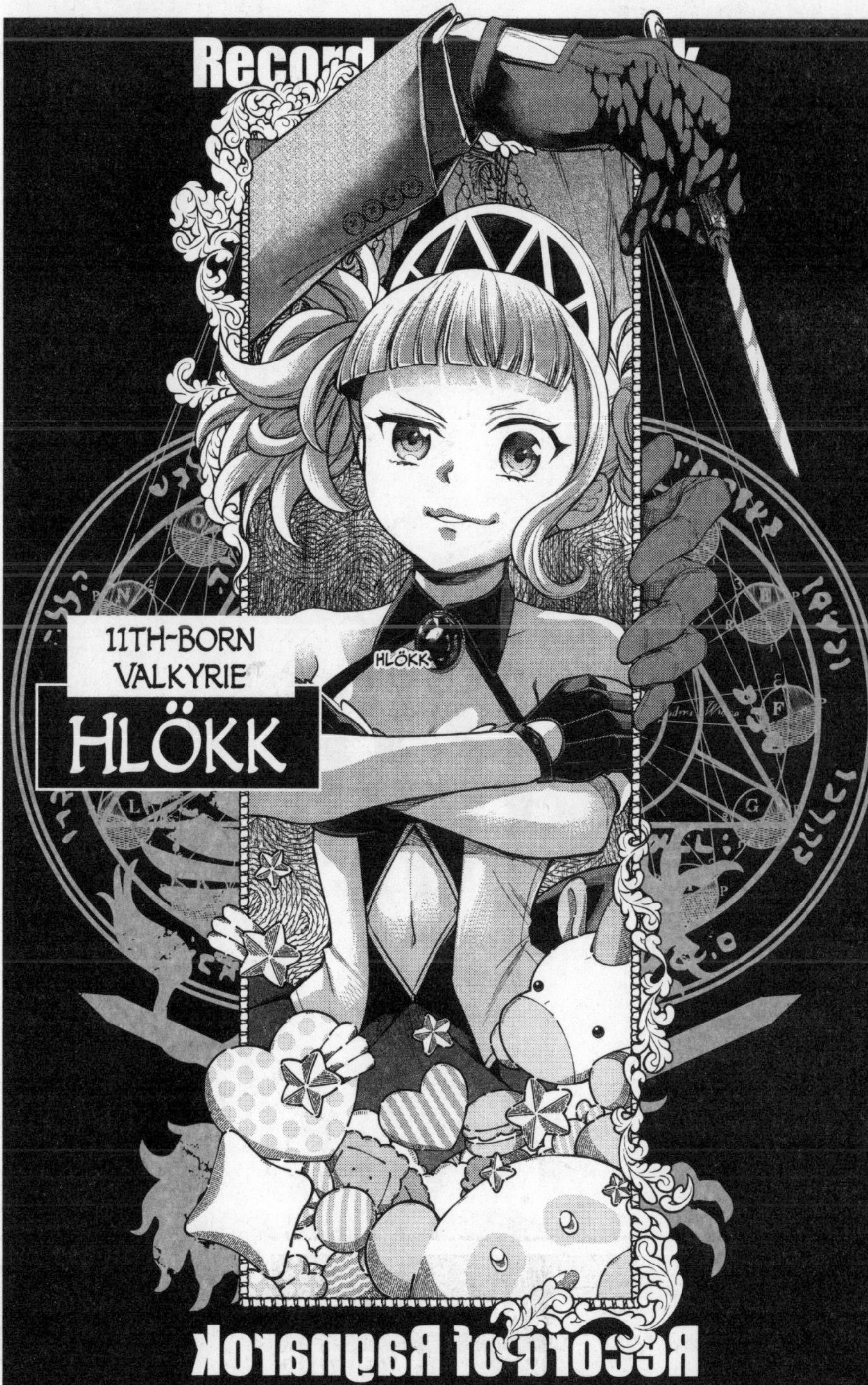
Record of Ragnarok
11TH-BORN VALKYRIE
HLÖKK
HLÖKK
Record of Ragnarok

RECORD OF RAGNAROK

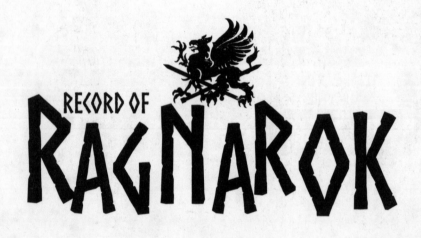

THERE ARE TWO FOOLS ATTEMPTING STAND ATOP THE PANTHEON OF INDIA...

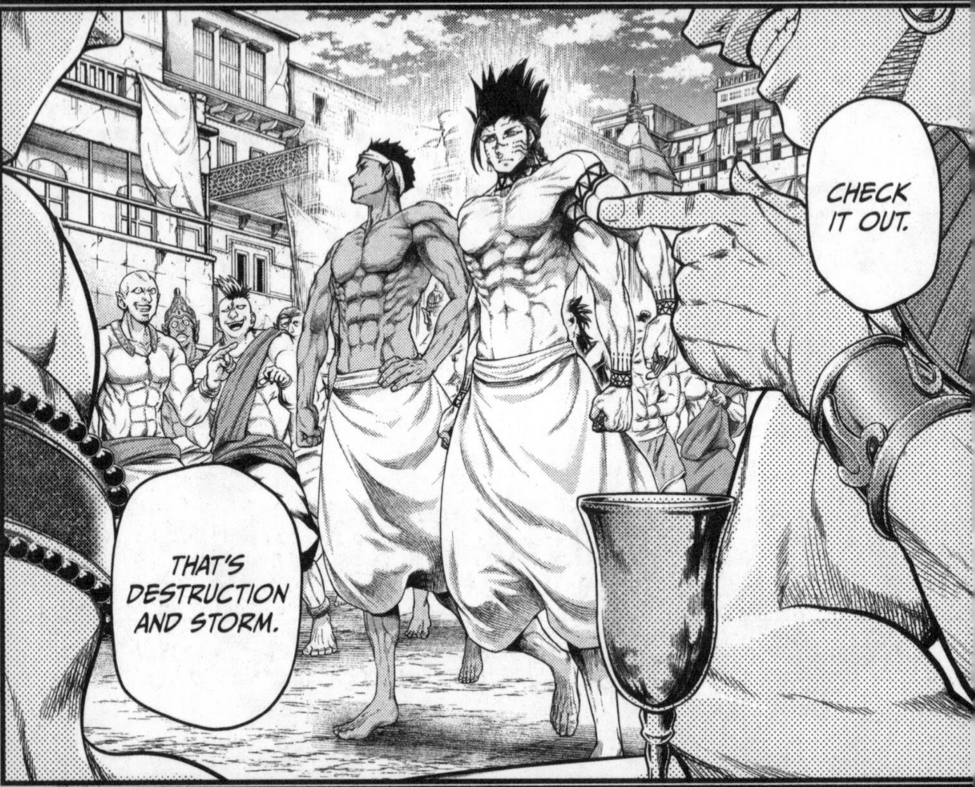
CHECK IT OUT.
THAT'S DESTRUCTION AND STORM.

AT FIRST, THEY WERE LAUGHED AT.

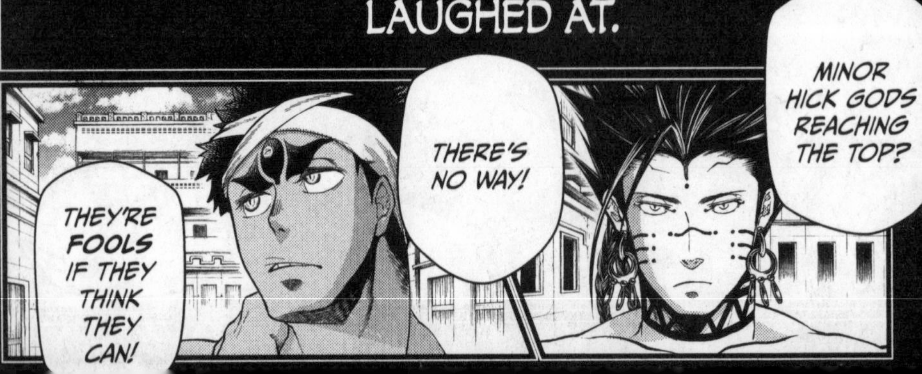
MINOR HICK GODS REACHING THE TOP?
THERE'S NO WAY!
THEY'RE FOOLS IF THEY THINK THEY CAN!

HOWEVER...

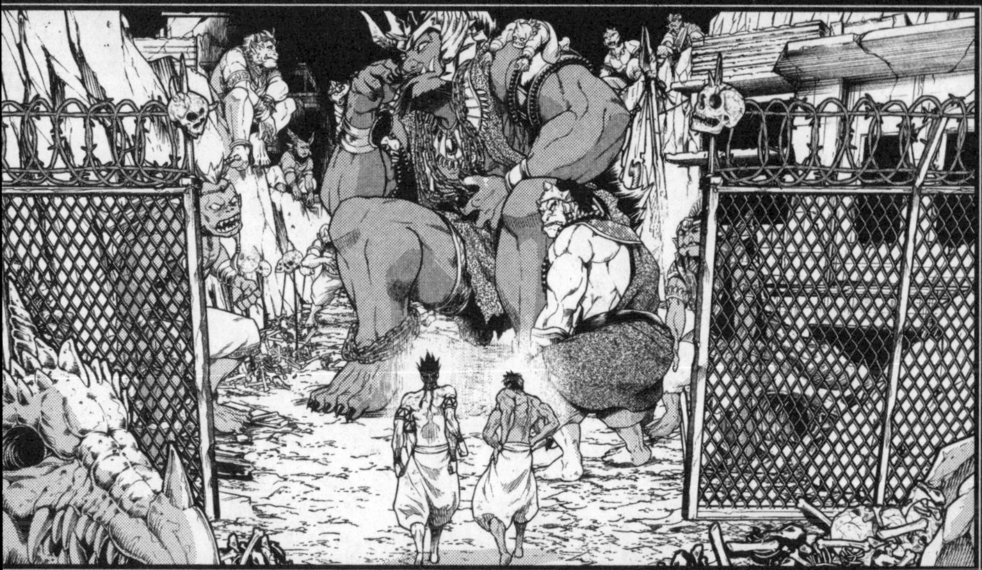

HOWEVER...

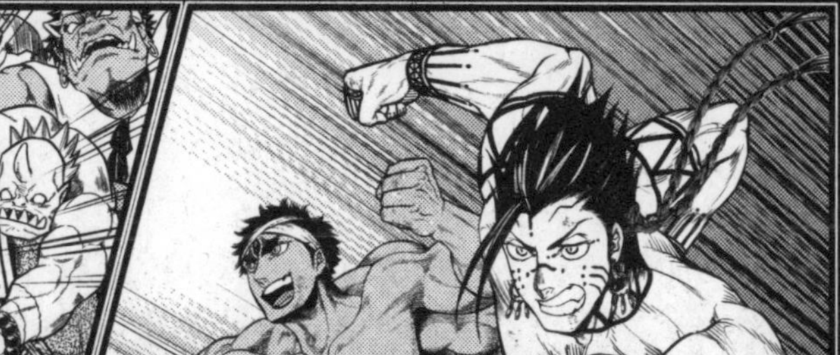

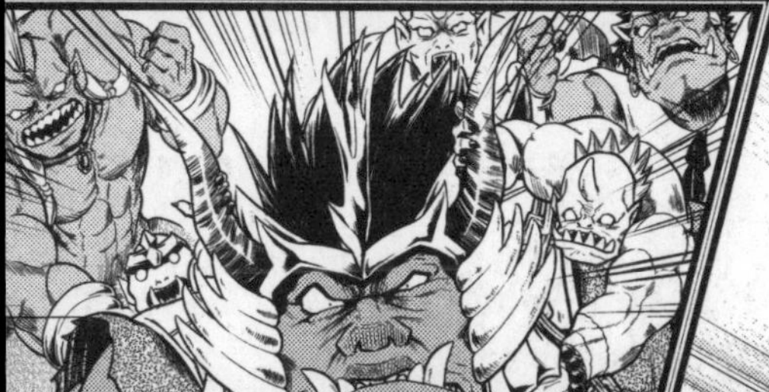

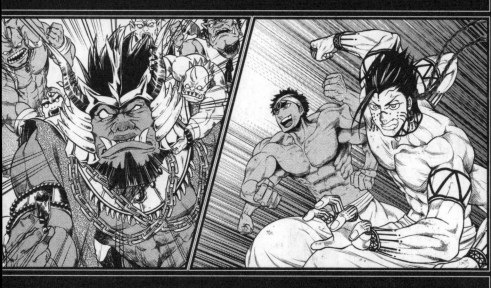

HOWEVER!

AS THEY CONTINUED MOVING FORWARD...

JUST THE TWO OF 'EM... I CAN'T BELIEVE IT!

YEAH... SHIVA AND RUDRA!

THOSE ARE THE GUYS WHO WIPED OUT THE ASURA TRIBE!

...RIDICULE TURNED TO RESPECT.

CONTEMPT TURNED TO HOPE.

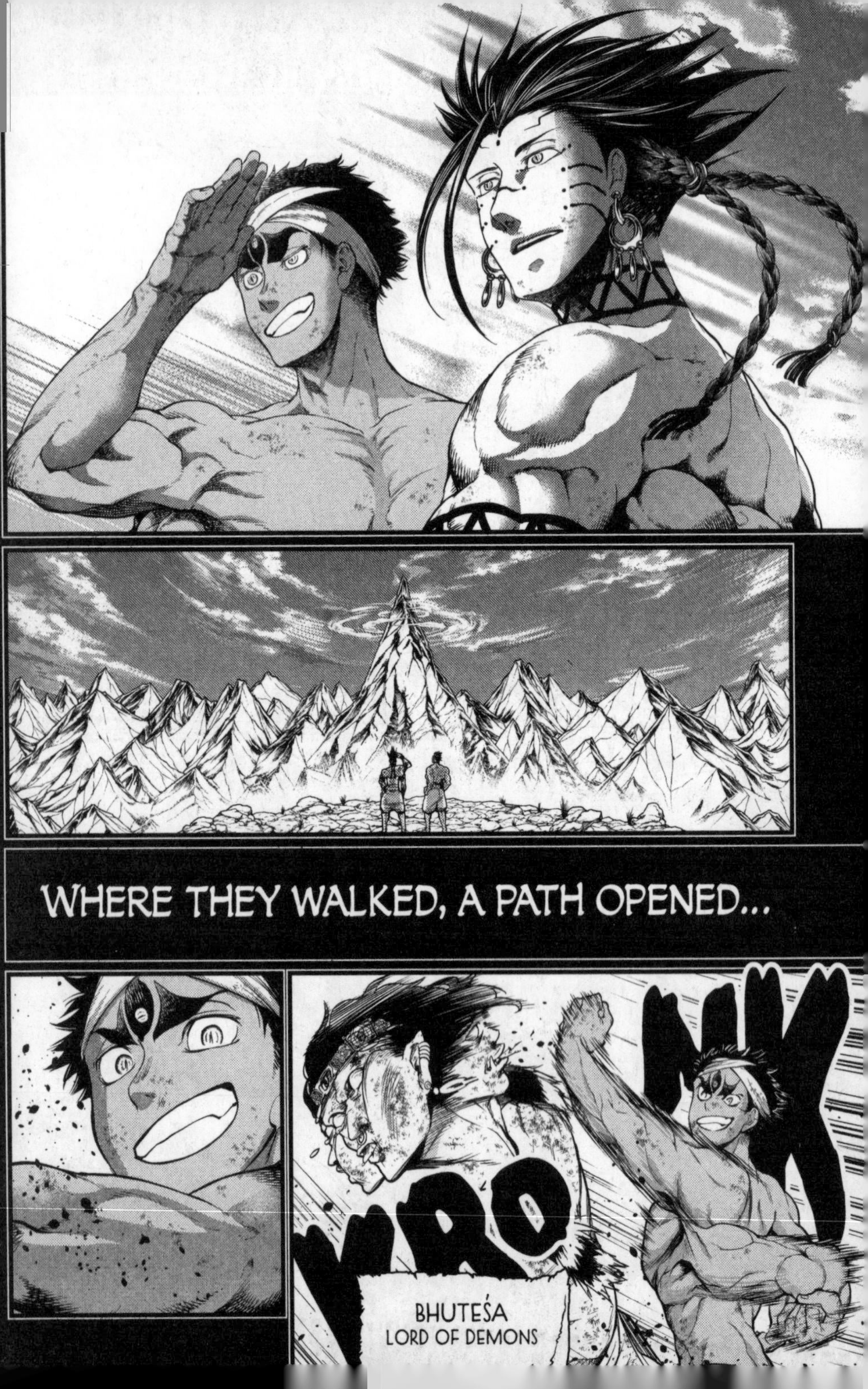
WHERE THEY WALKED, A PATH OPENED...
KRONK
BHUTEŚA
LORD OF DEMONS

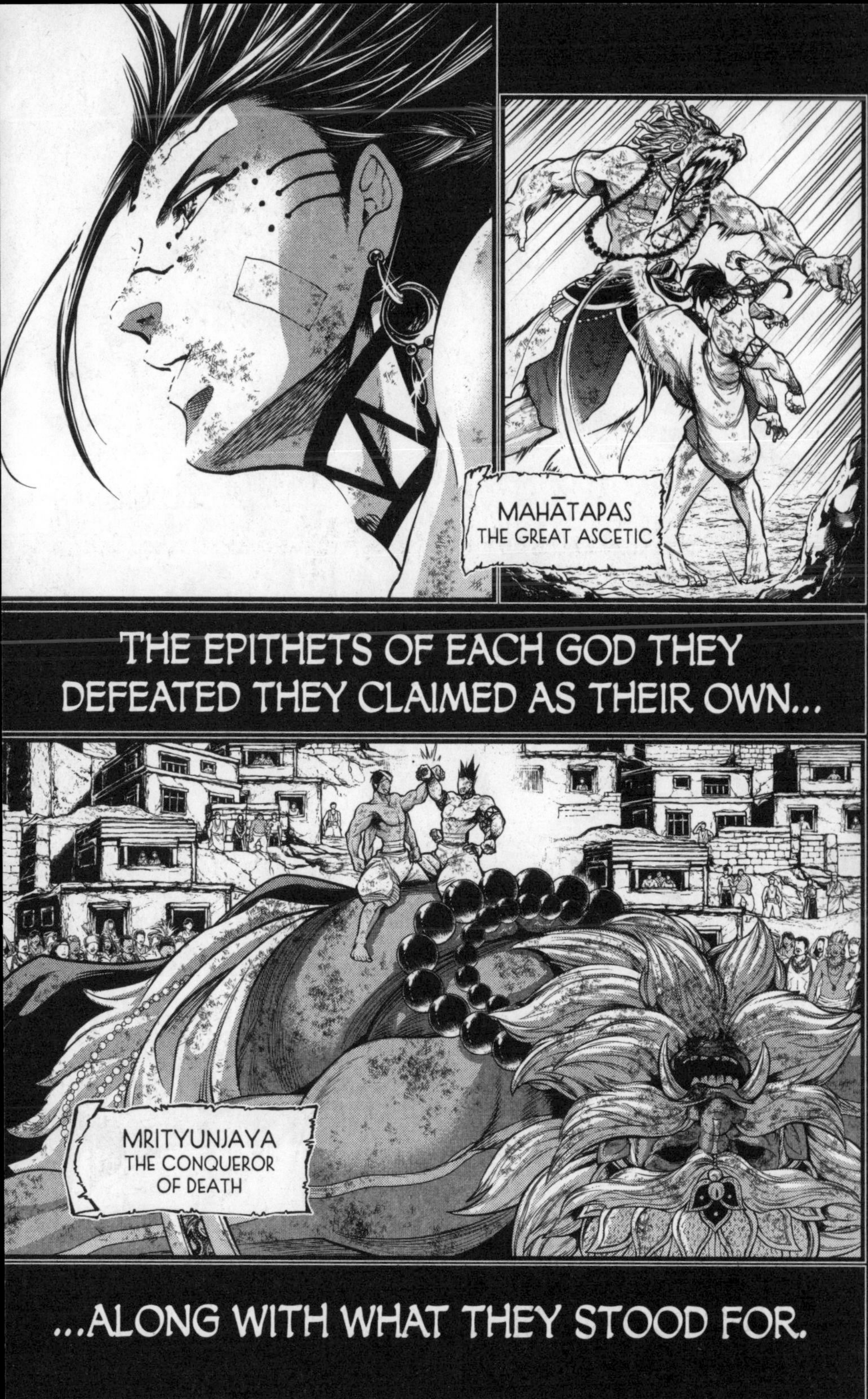
MAHĀTAPAS
THE GREAT ASCETIC
THE EPITHETS OF EACH GOD THEY DEFEATED THEY CLAIMED AS THEIR OWN...
MRITYUNJAYA
THE CONQUEROR OF DEATH
...ALONG WITH WHAT THEY STOOD FOR.

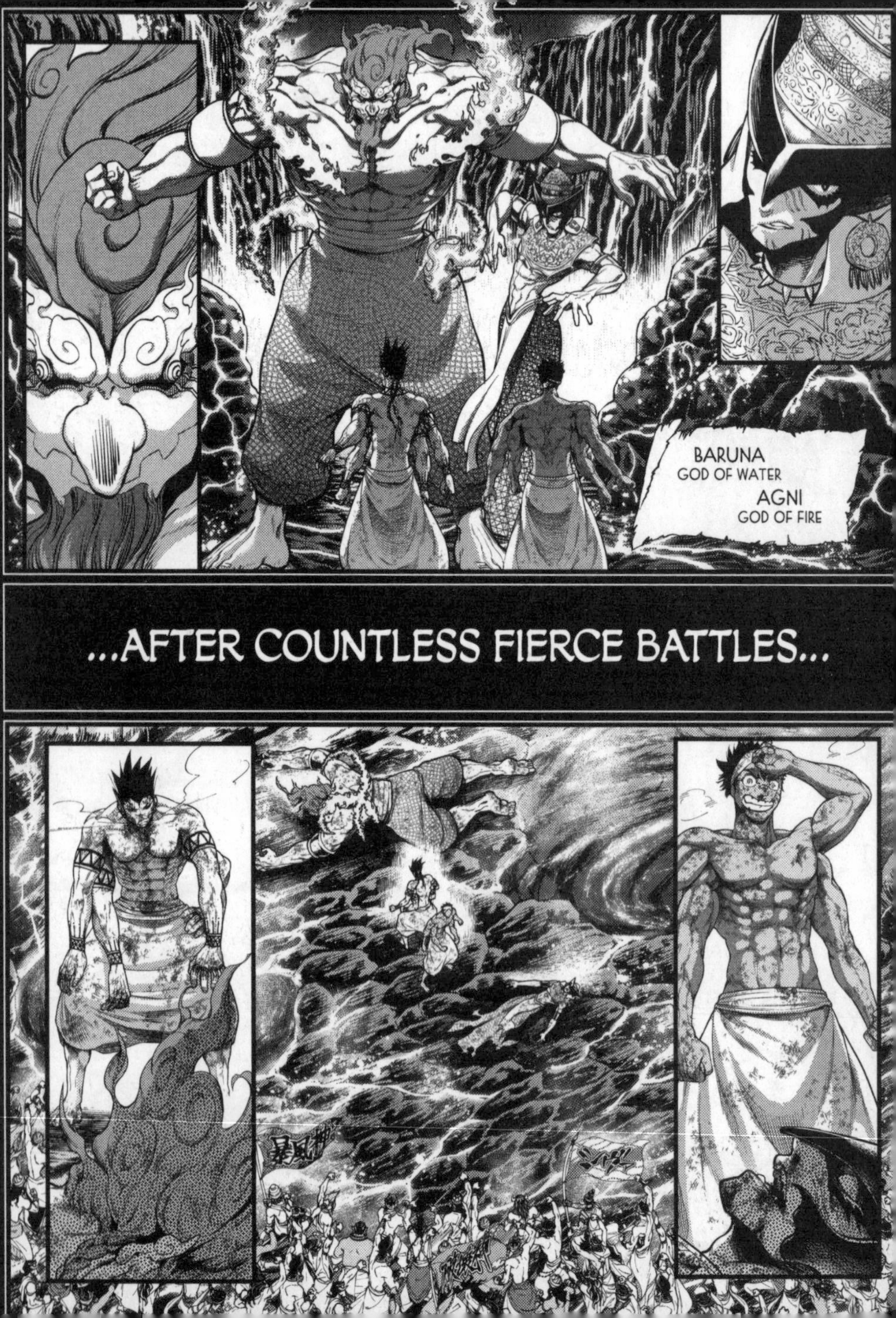
BARUNA
GOD OF WATER
AGNI
GOD OF FIRE
...AFTER COUNTLESS FIERCE BATTLES...

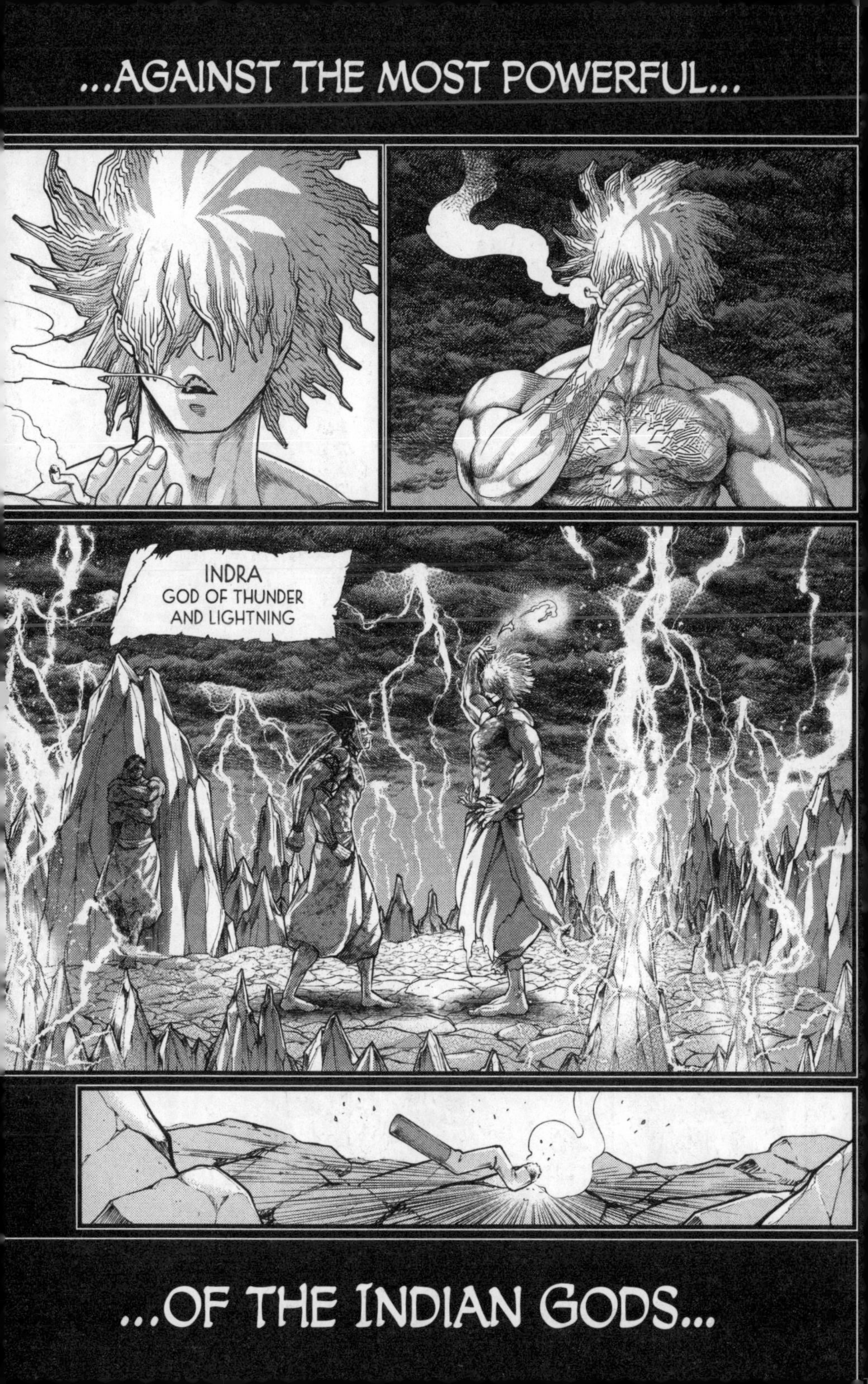
...AGAINST THE MOST POWERFUL...
INDRA
GOD OF THUNDER
AND LIGHTNING
...OF THE INDIAN GODS...

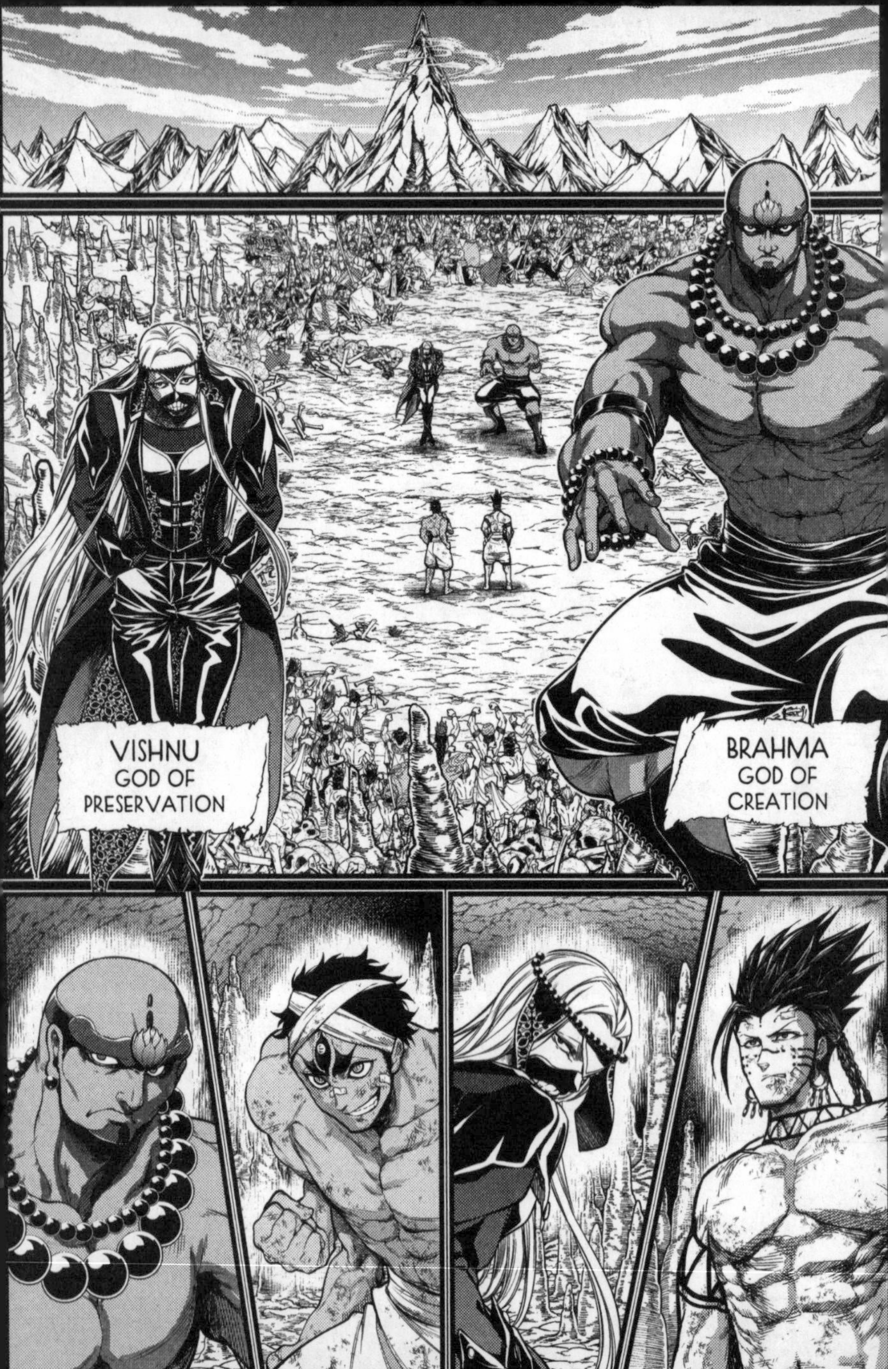
BRAHMA
GOD OF
CREATION
VISHNU
GOD OF
PRESERVATION

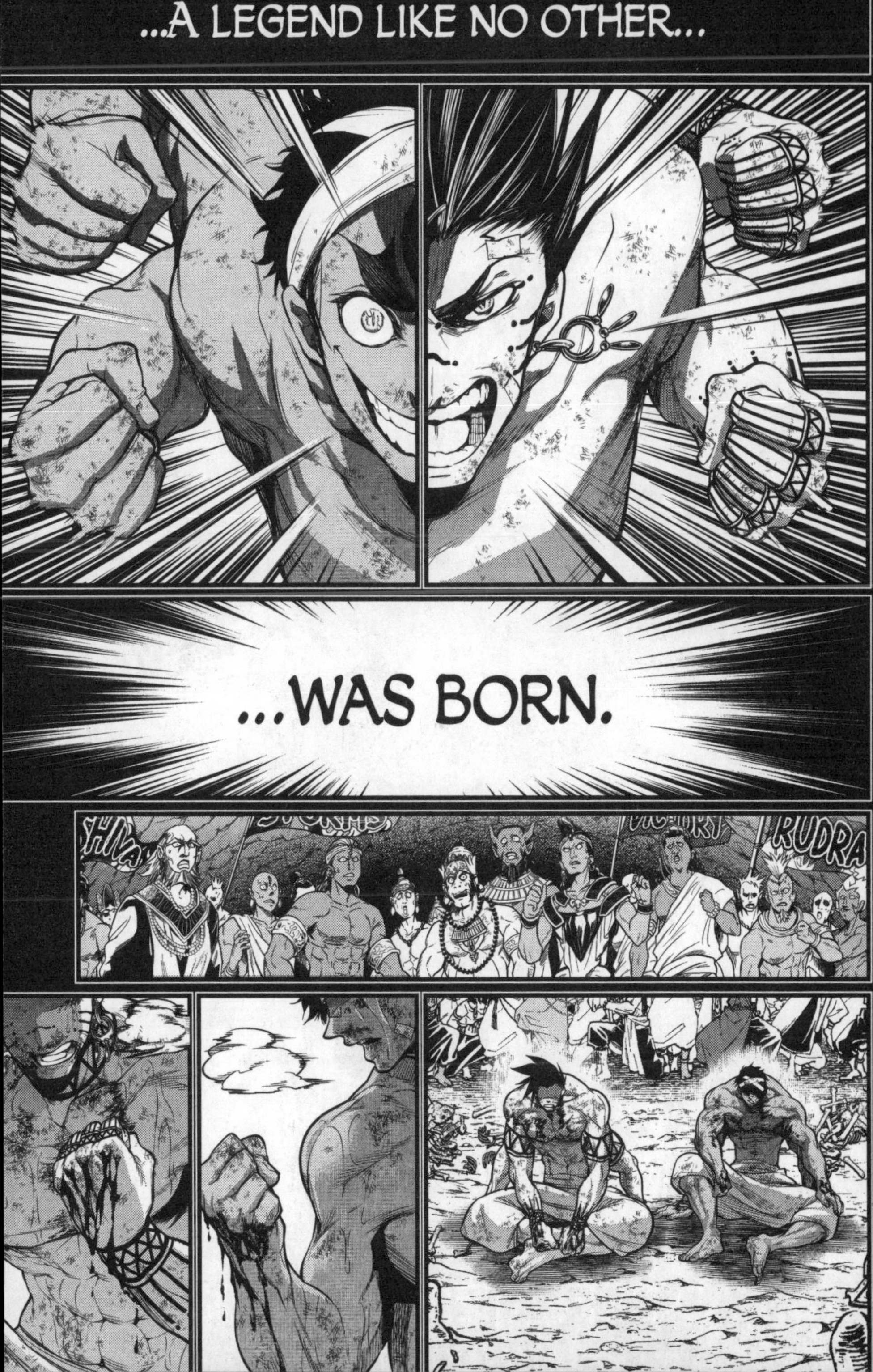
...A LEGEND LIKE NO OTHER...
...WAS BORN.
RUDRA

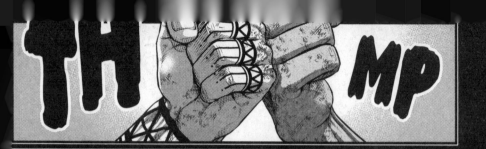

SHIVA AND RUDRA...

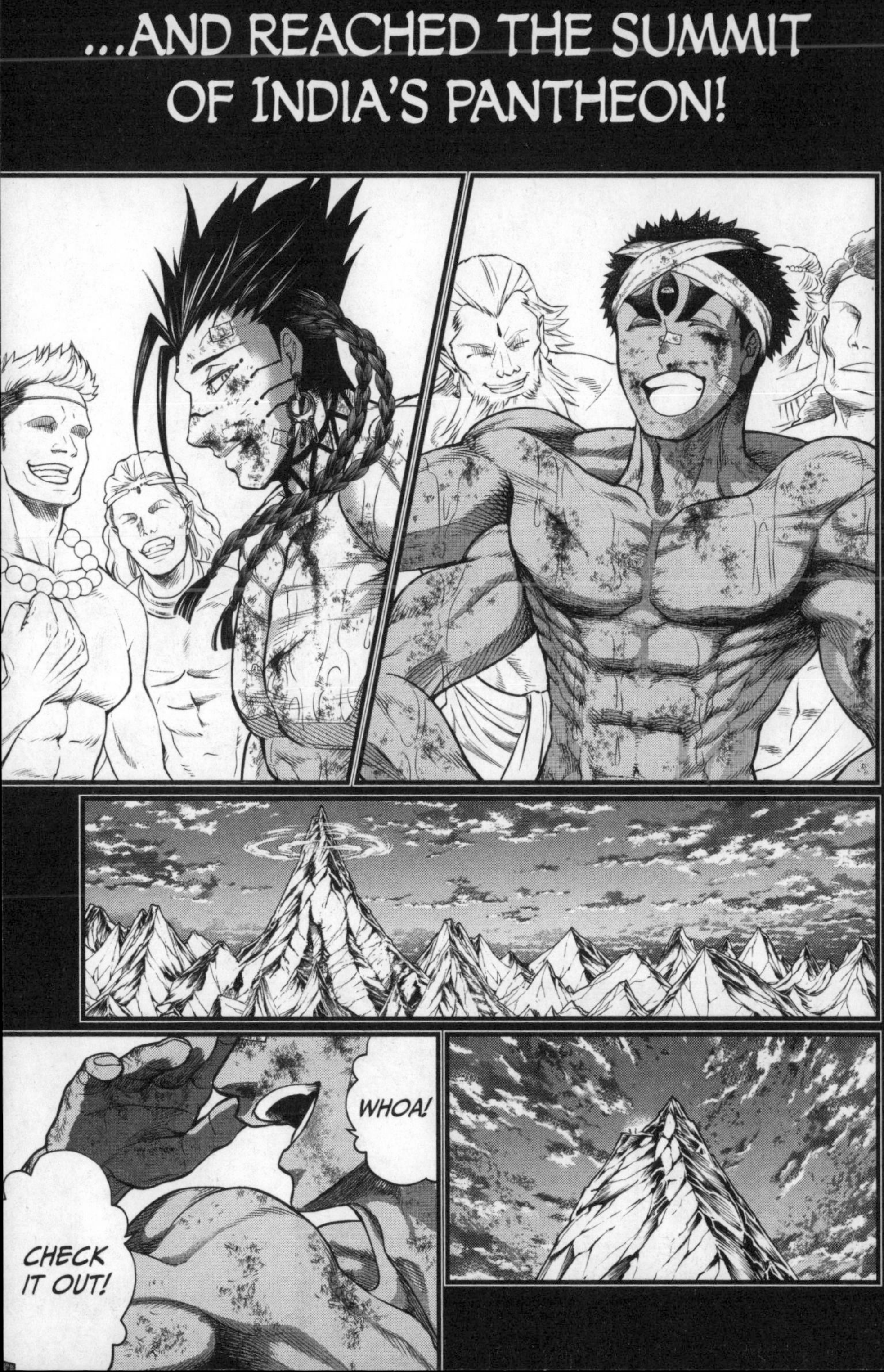
...AND REACHED THE SUMMIT OF INDIA'S PANTHEON!
WHOA!
CHECK IT OUT!

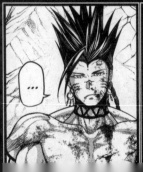

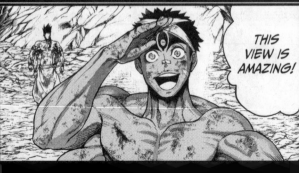

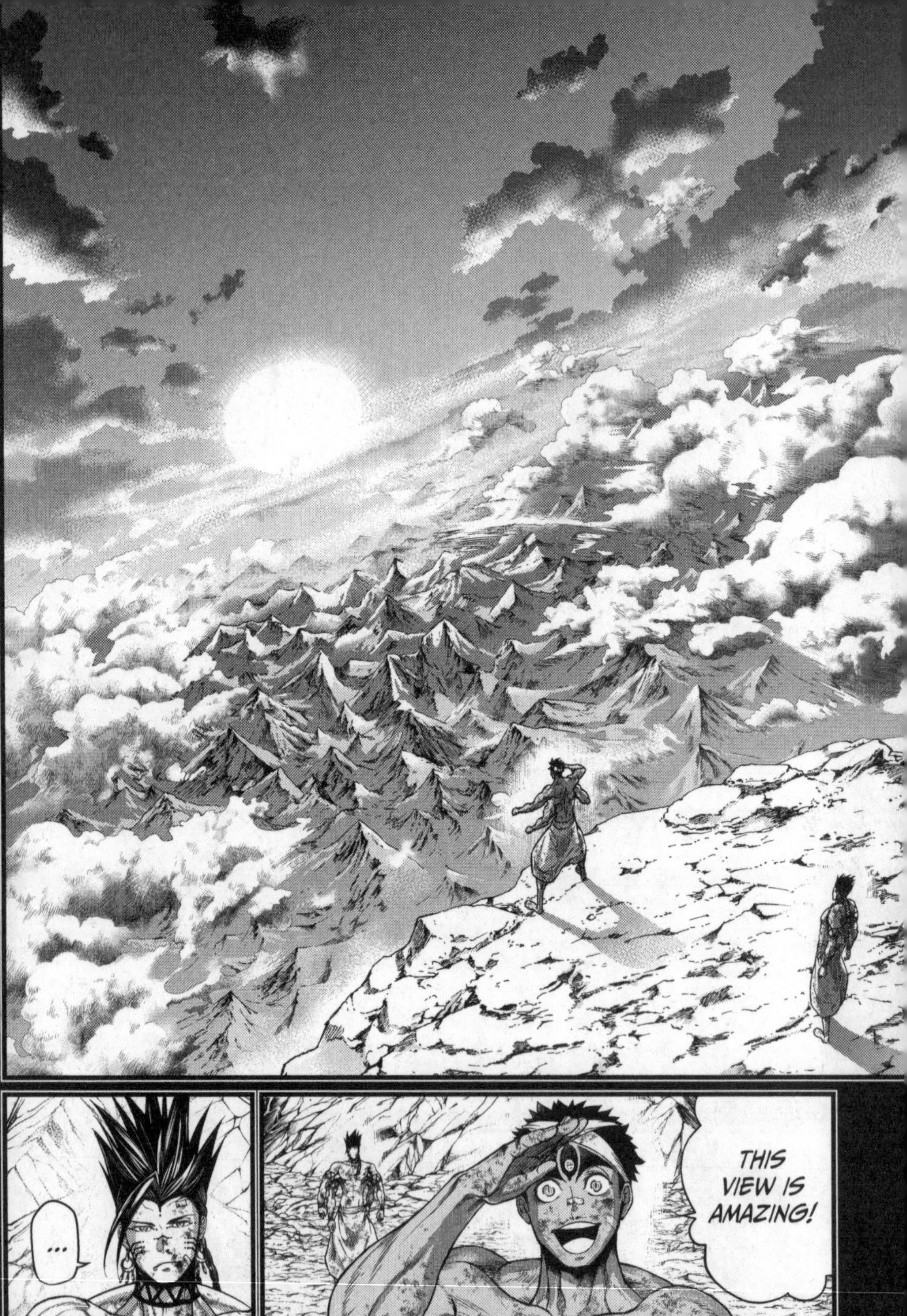
THIS VIEW IS AMAZING!
...

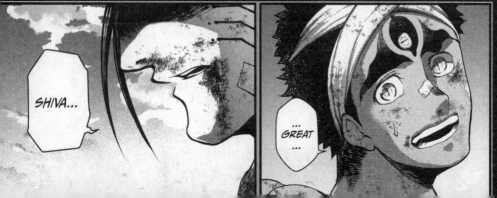

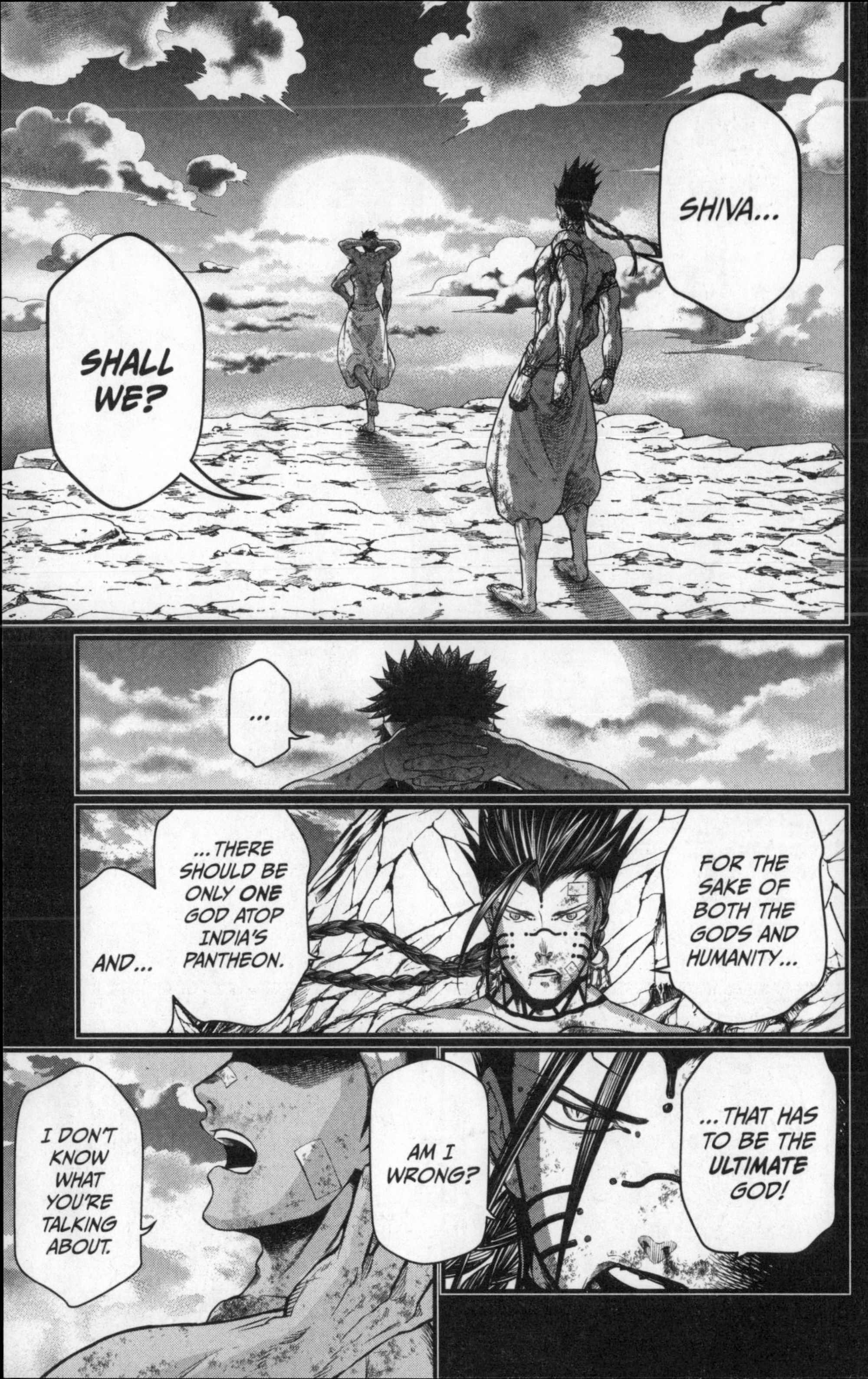
SHIVA...
SHALL WE?
...
FOR THE SAKE OF BOTH THE GODS AND HUMANITY...
...THERE SHOULD BE ONLY ONE GOD ATOP INDIA'S PANTHEON.
AND...
...THAT HAS TO BE THE ULTIMATE GOD!
AM I WRONG?
I DON'T KNOW WHAT YOU'RE TALKING ABOUT.

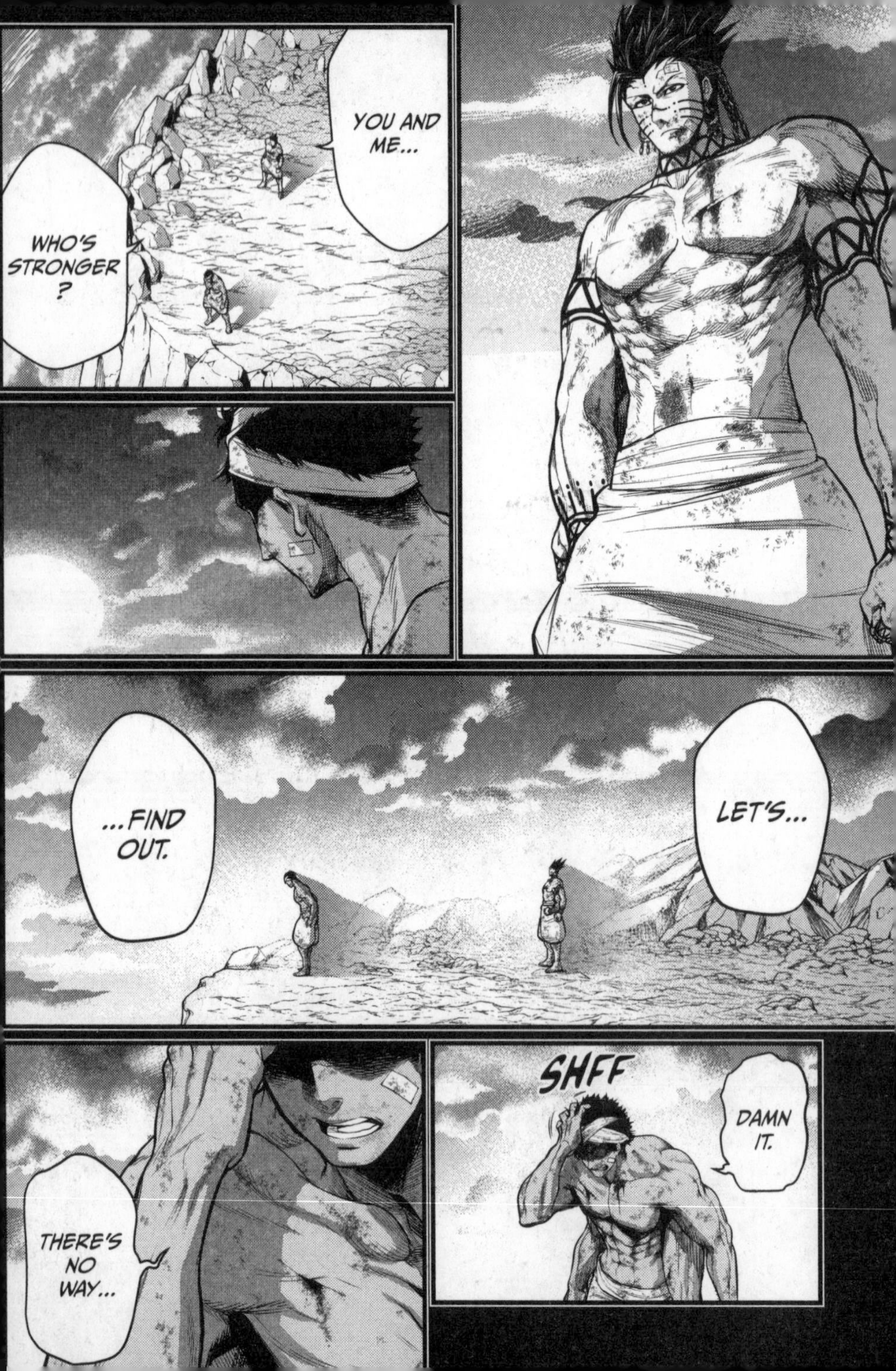
YOU AND ME...
WHO'S STRONGER?
LET'S...
...FIND OUT.
DAMN IT.
SHFF
THERE'S NO WAY...

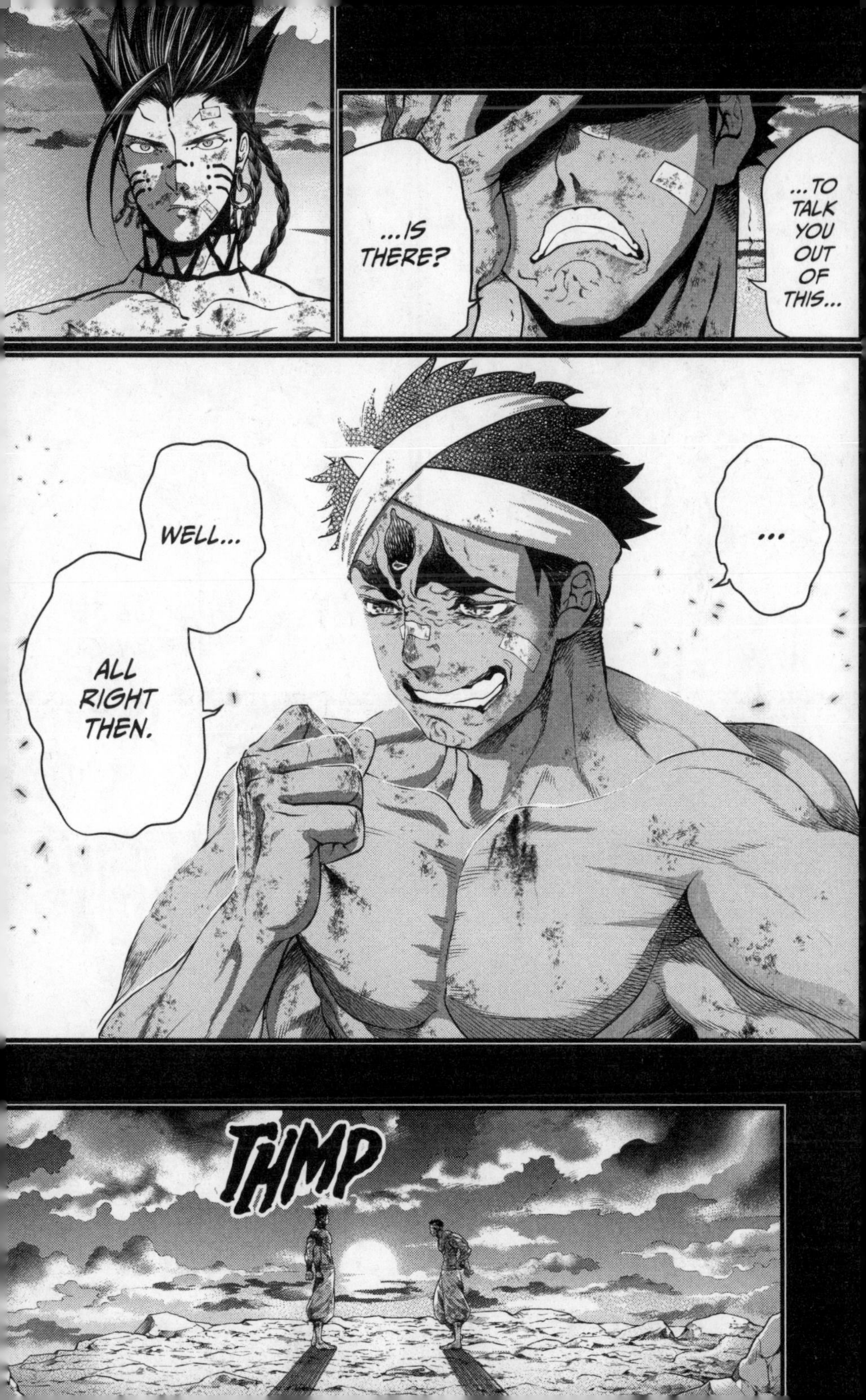
...TO TALK YOU OUT OF THIS...
...IS THERE?
...
WELL...
ALL RIGHT THEN.
THMP

WITH ALL MY HEART.

LET'S ENJOY THIS DANCE.

TH MP

HEH

GRIN

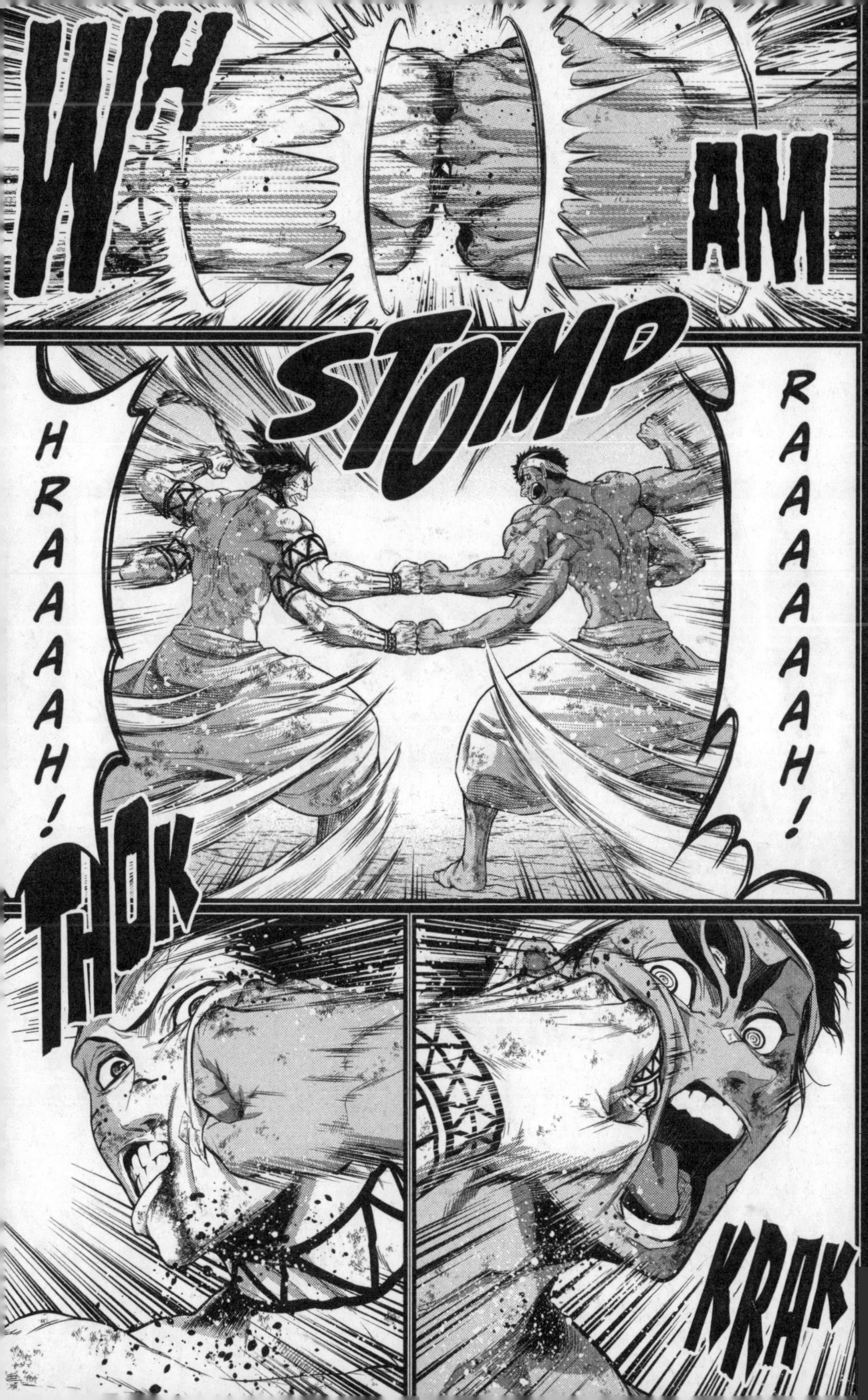
WH
AM
STOMP
RAAAAAAH!
HRAAAAH!
KRAK
THOK

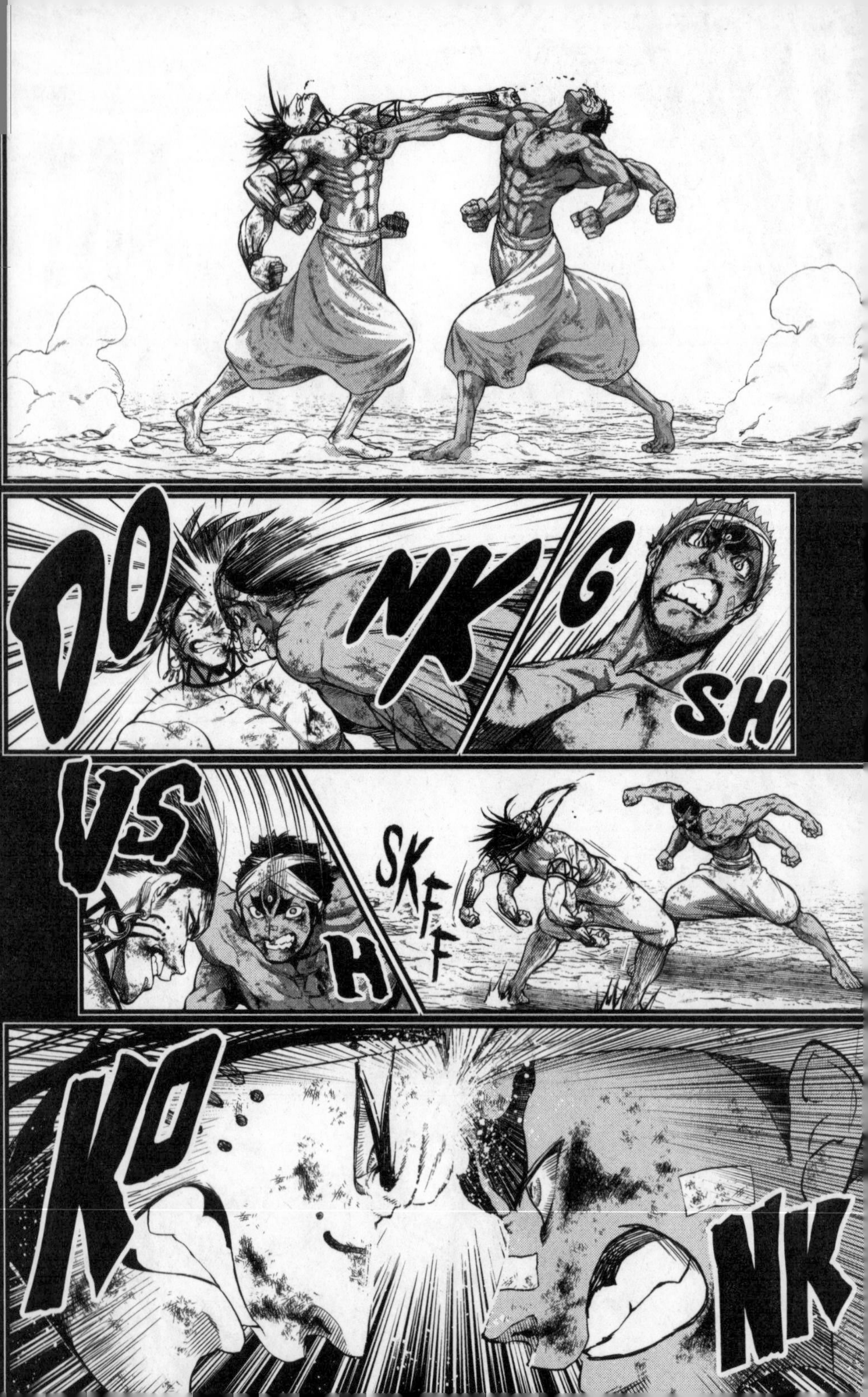
GSH
DONK
SKFF
VSH
KONK

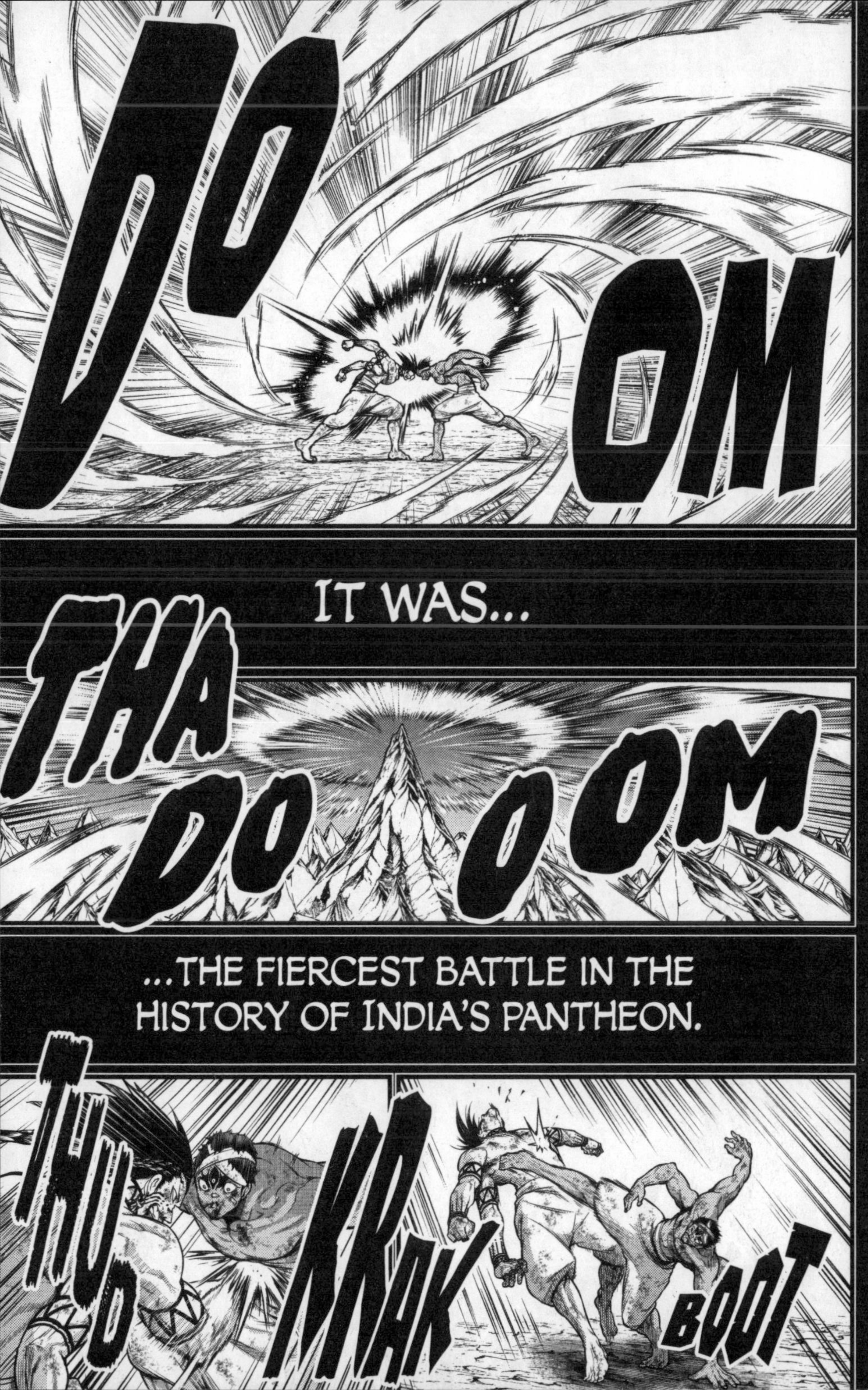
DOOM
IT WAS...
THA DOOOOM
...THE FIERCEST BATTLE IN THE HISTORY OF INDIA'S PANTHEON.
BOOT
WHAK
THUD

THE SOUND OF THESE TWO GODS
FIGHTING ECHOED ACROSS ALL OF INDIA.

THEIR SWEAT POURED DOWN AS HEAVY RAIN.

FOR SHIVA...

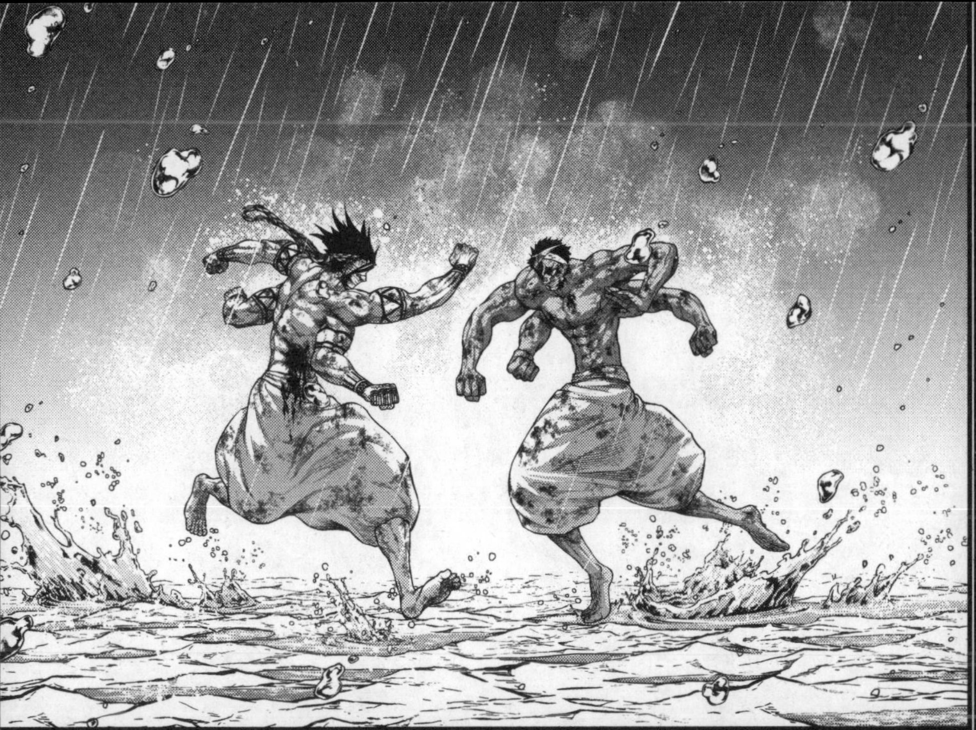

...IT IT WAS THE MOST EXHILARATING...

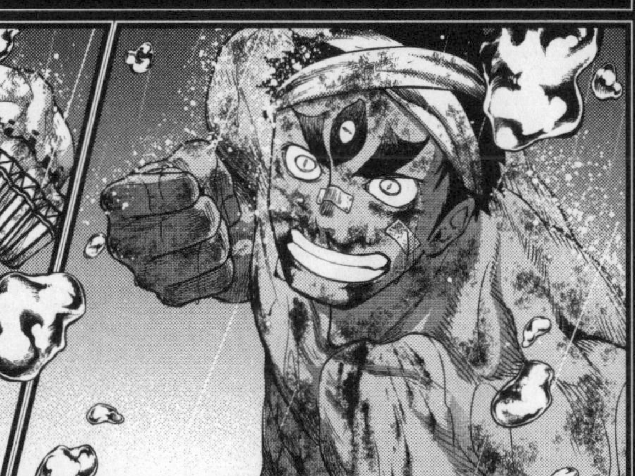

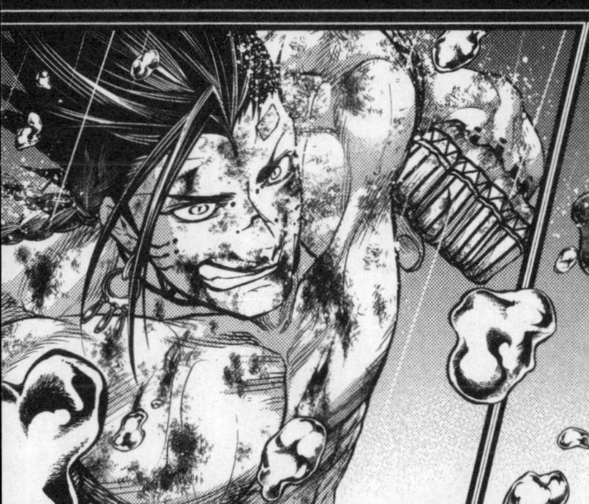

...AND MOST SORROWFUL MOMENT.

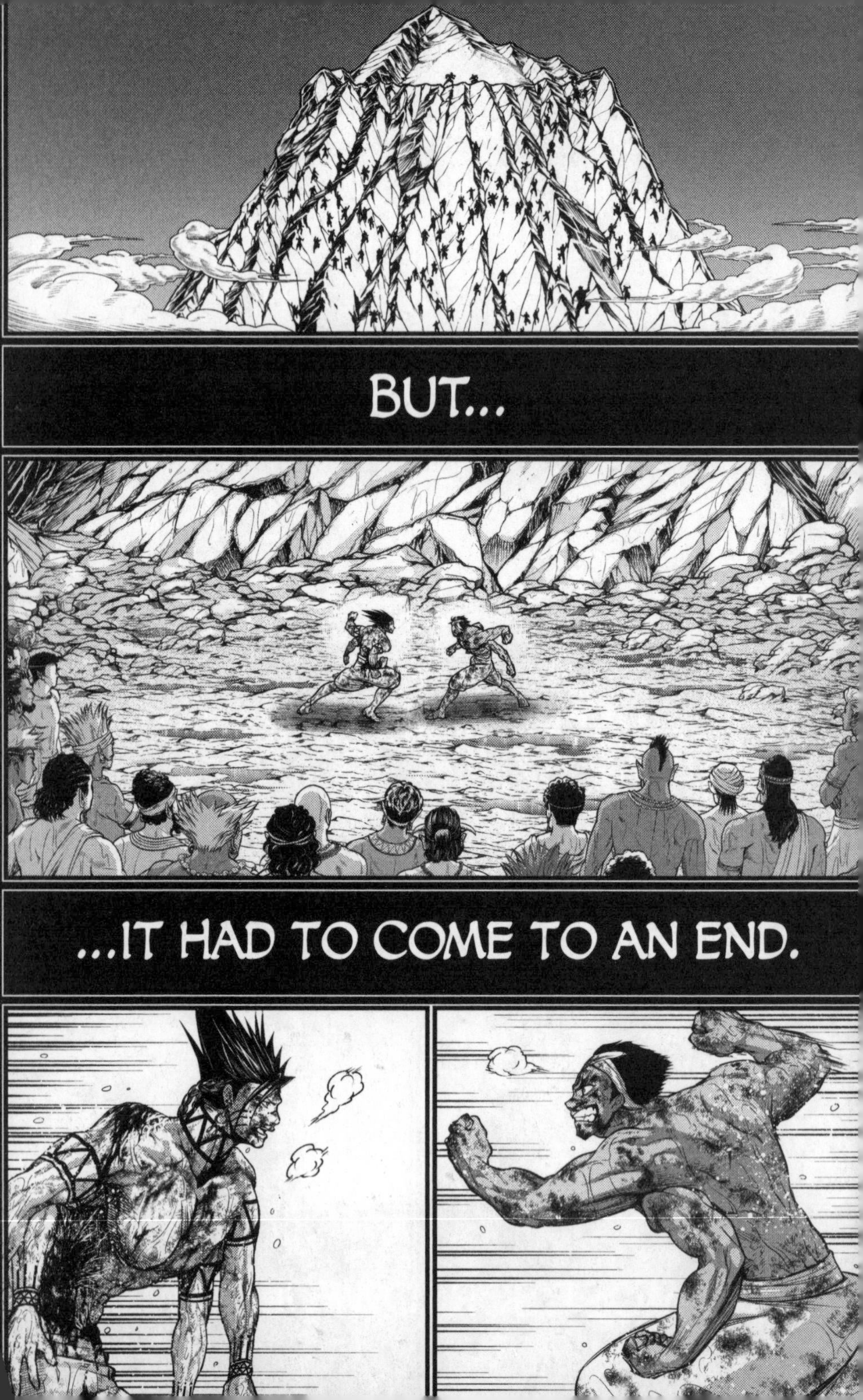
BUT...
...IT HAD TO COME TO AN END.

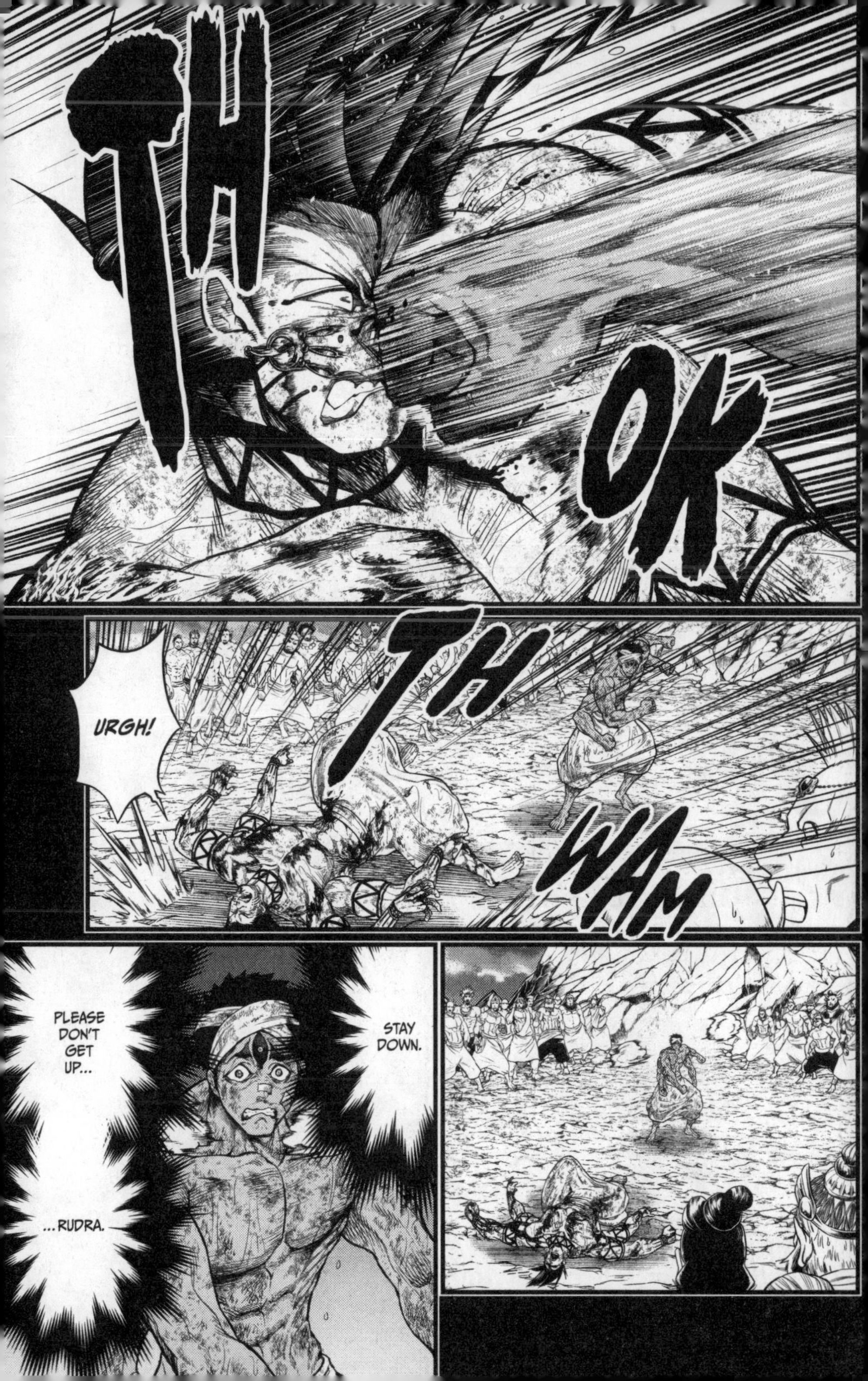
TH
OK
TH
URGH!
WAM
STAY DOWN.
PLEASE DON'T GET UP...
...RUDRA.

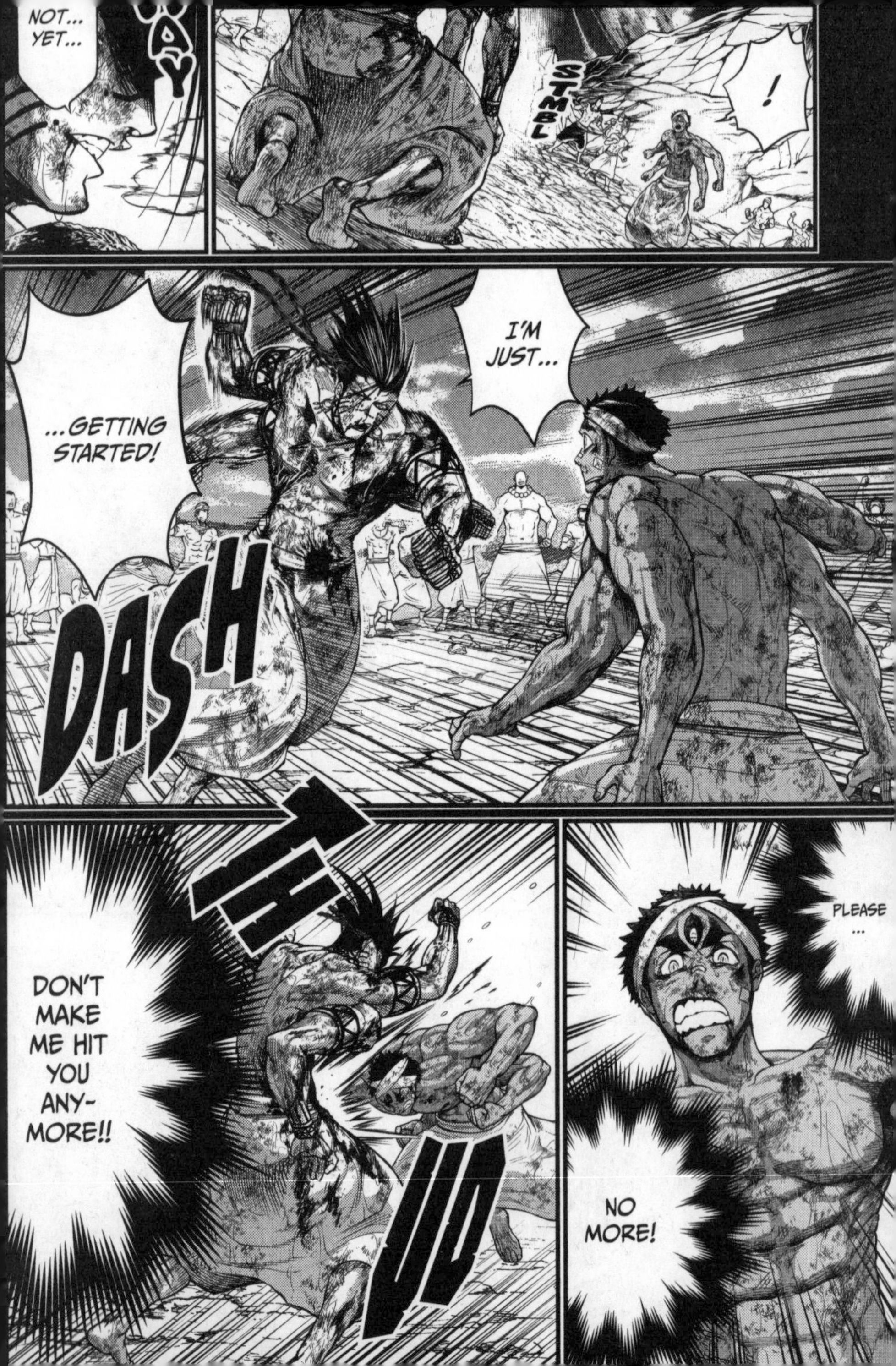
!
STMBL
NOT... YET...
I'M JUST...
...GETTING STARTED!
DASH
PLEASE ...
NO MORE!
TH
UD
DON'T MAKE ME HIT YOU ANY-MORE!!

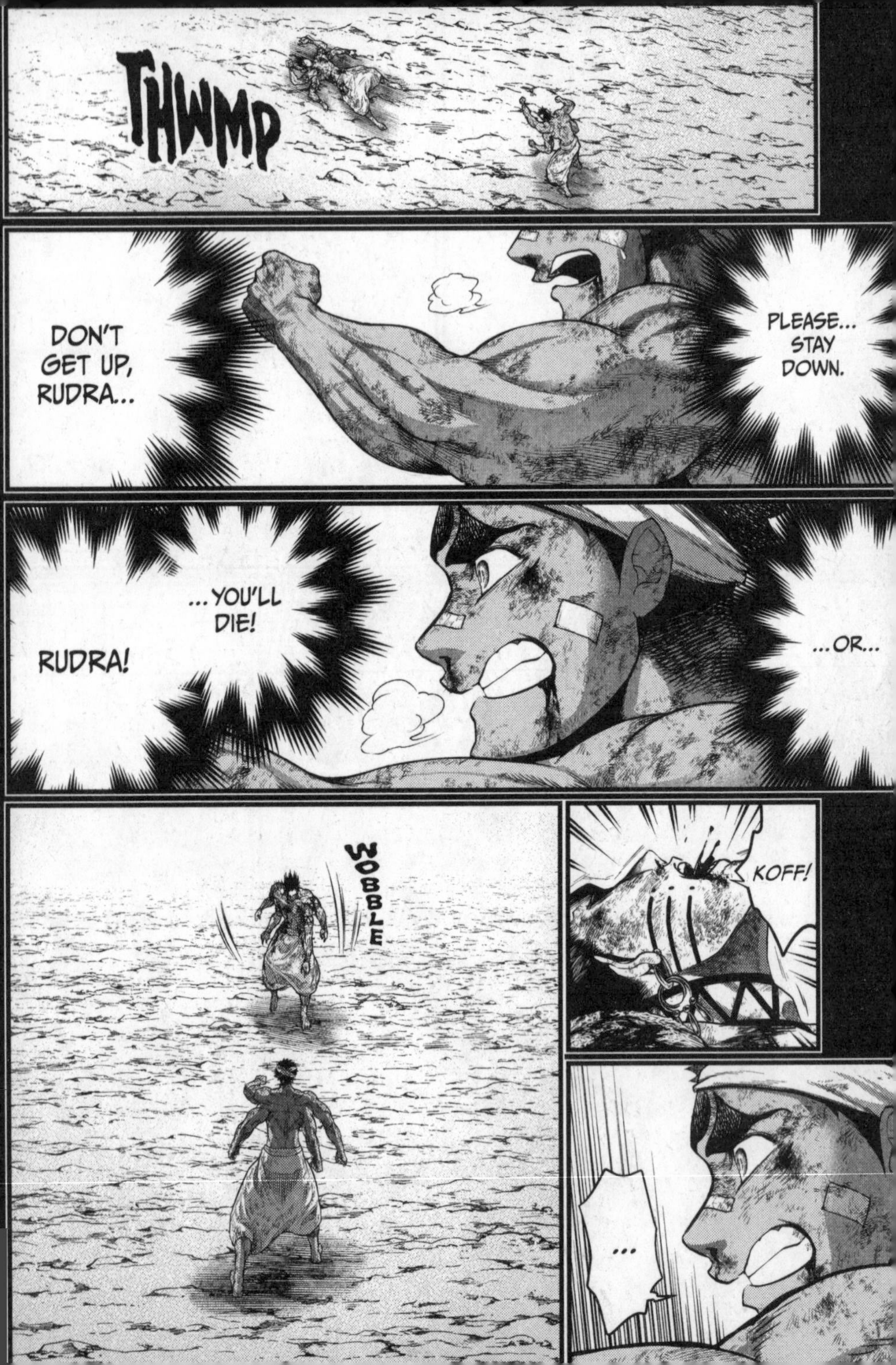
THWMP
PLEASE... STAY DOWN.
DON'T GET UP, RUDRA...
...OR...
...YOU'LL DIE!
RUDRA!
KOFF!
...
WOBBLE

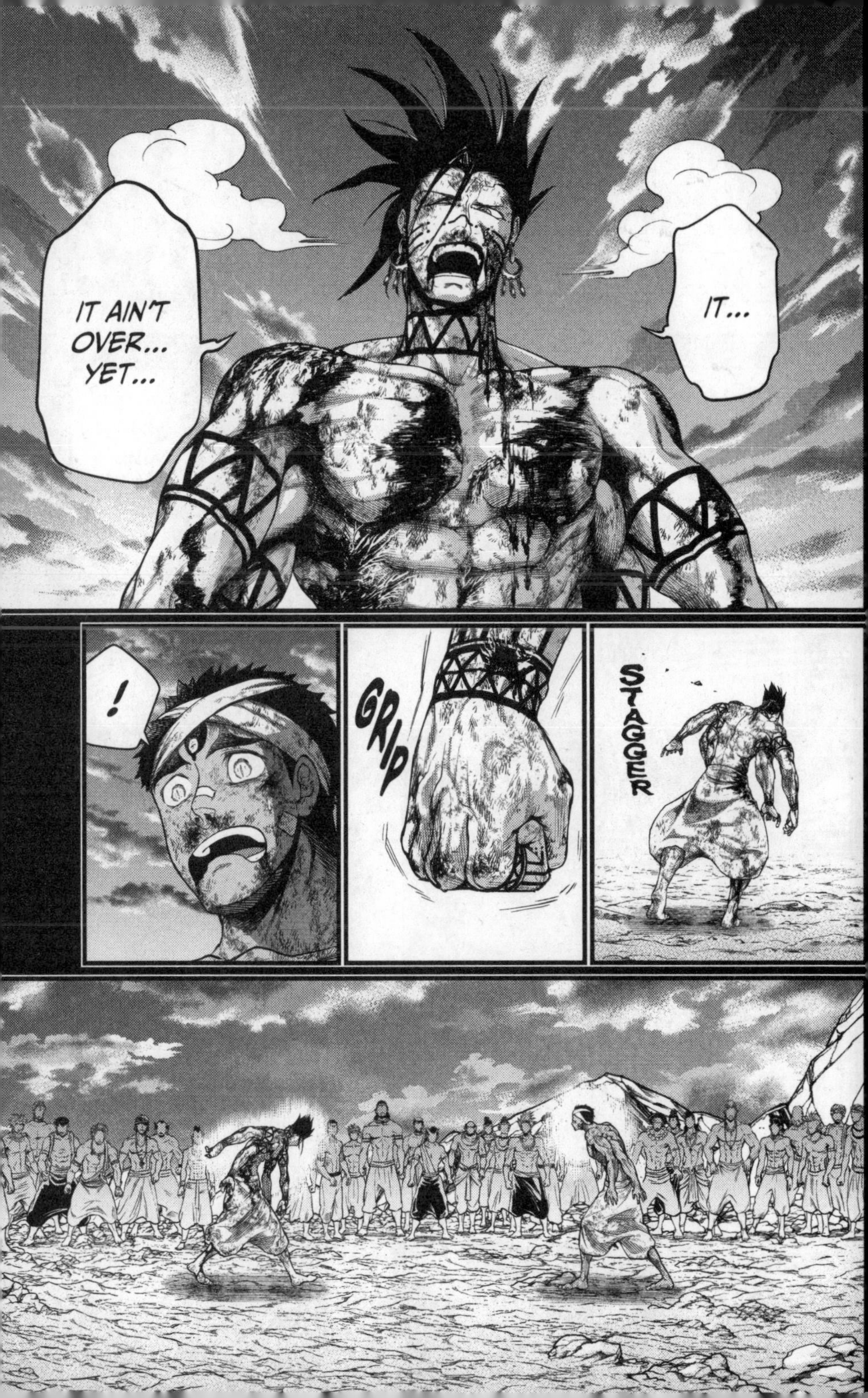
IT...
IT AIN'T OVER... YET...
STAGGER
GRIP
!

I HAVE A DREAM.

...TO STAND AT THE TOP...

...OF INDIA'S PANTHEON.

SHIVA, I WANT...

YOUR NAME'S SHIVA?

I'M RUDRA.

YOU'RE A LOT OF FUN!

...THE GOD OF STORMS.

RUDRA...

...

OKAY THEN.

WELL...

THUMP

YOU'RE CRAZY STRONG!

RUDRA...

YOU W—

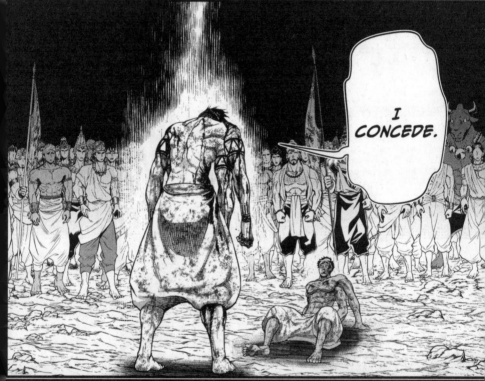

I CONCEDE.

YOU...

...WIN.

SPSH

...

WHAT'RE YOU SAYING...?

R-RUDRA...?

PAT

WHY ARE YOU...?!

...YOU HAVE TO GIVE IT YOUR ALL TOO!

WHEN YOUR OPPONENT IS GIVING IT EVERYTHING THEY'VE GOT...

GRSH

LISTEN TO ME, SHIVA...

...IS WORSE THAN DEATH ITSELF!

PULLING PUNCHES WHEN YOU'RE FIGHTING TO THE DEATH...

IT WAS...

...YOUR...

BUT...

...

RUDRA...

...DREAM...

GUSH

...YOU'RE THE ONE...

WITHOUT A DOUBT...

...YOU IDIOT!

DON'T CRY...

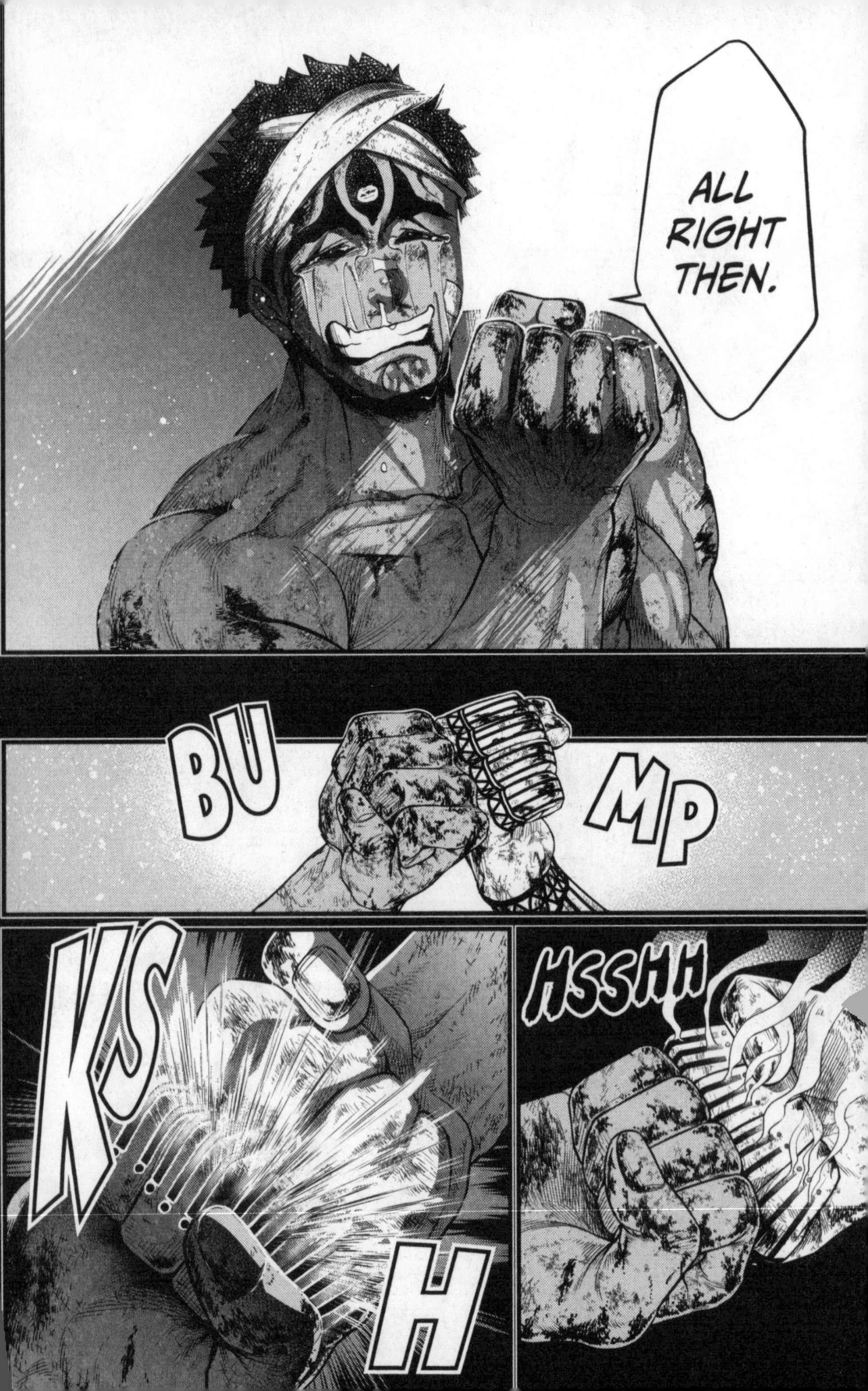
ALL RIGHT THEN.
BUMP
HSSHH
KSH

THAT IS HOW RUDRA LEFT THE GOD REALM OF INDIA...

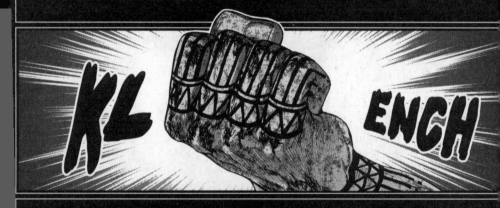

...AND HOW SHIVA REACHED THE SUMMIT OF THE GODS.

BUT HIS VICTORY COST HIM
HIS GREATEST FRIEND.

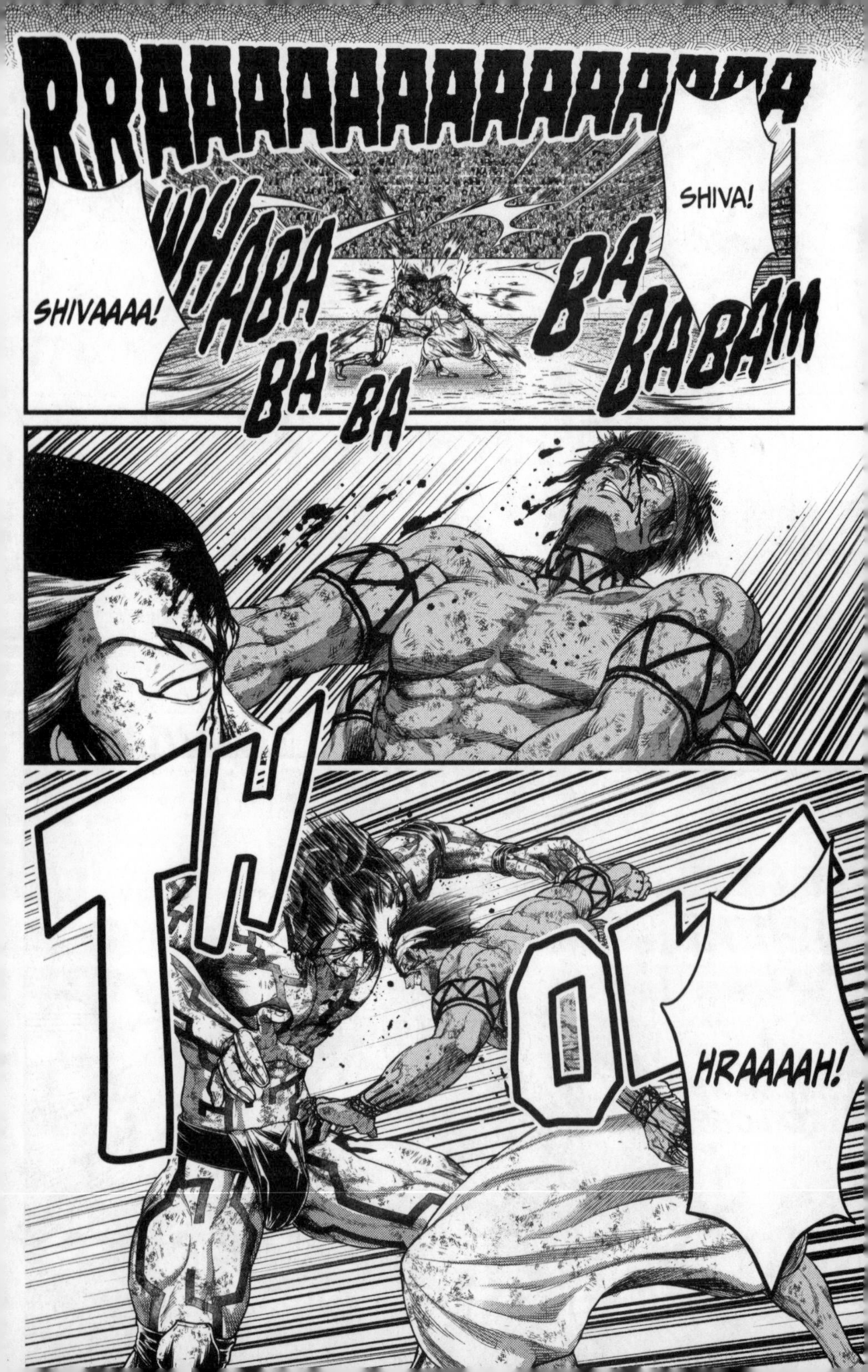
RRAAAAAAAAAAAAAA
SHIVA!
SHIVAAAA!
WHABA BA BA BA BABAM
THOOM
HRAAAAH!

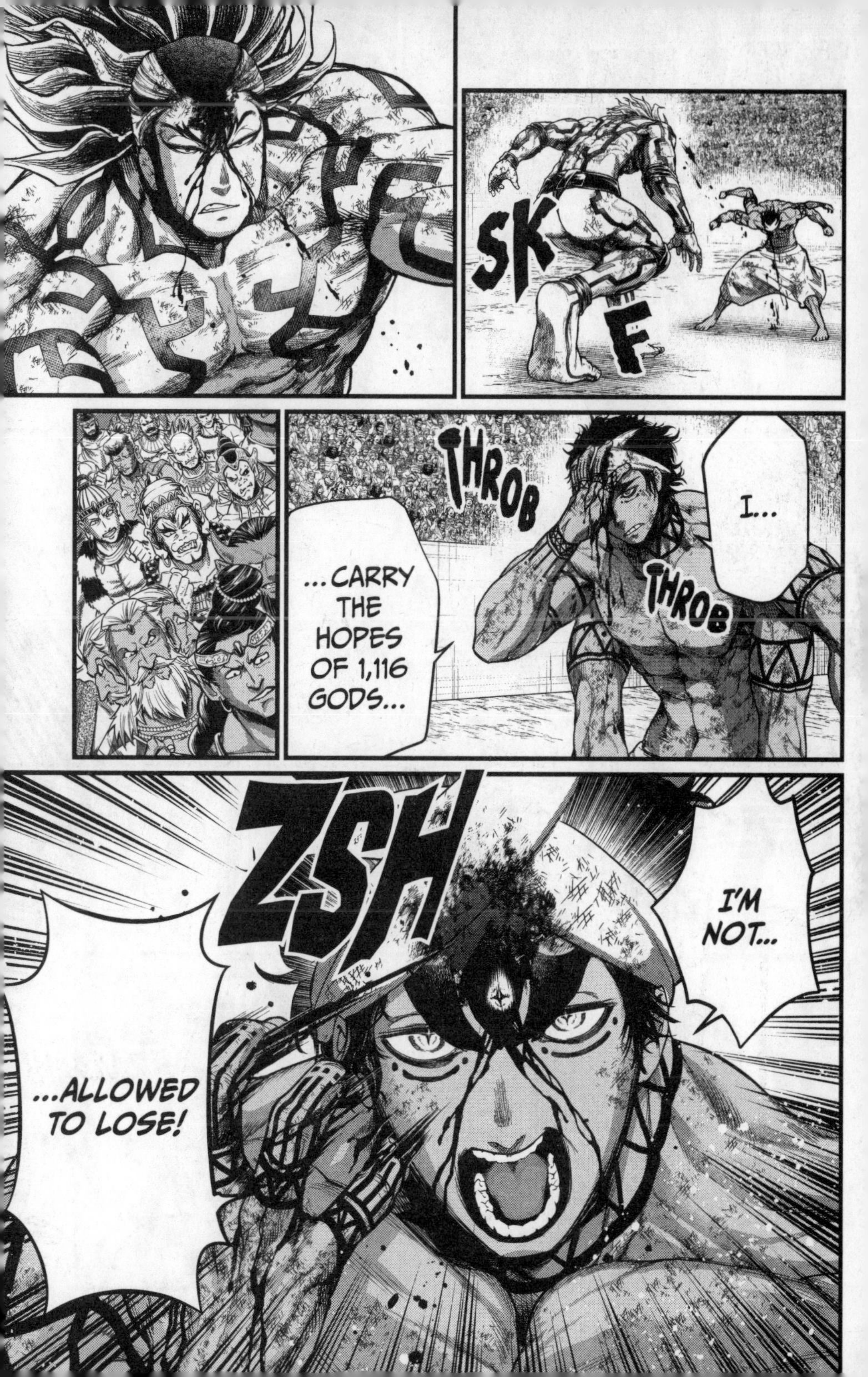
SK
F
I...
THROB
THROB
...CARRY THE HOPES OF 1,116 GODS...
ZSH
I'M NOT...
...ALLOWED TO LOSE!

166

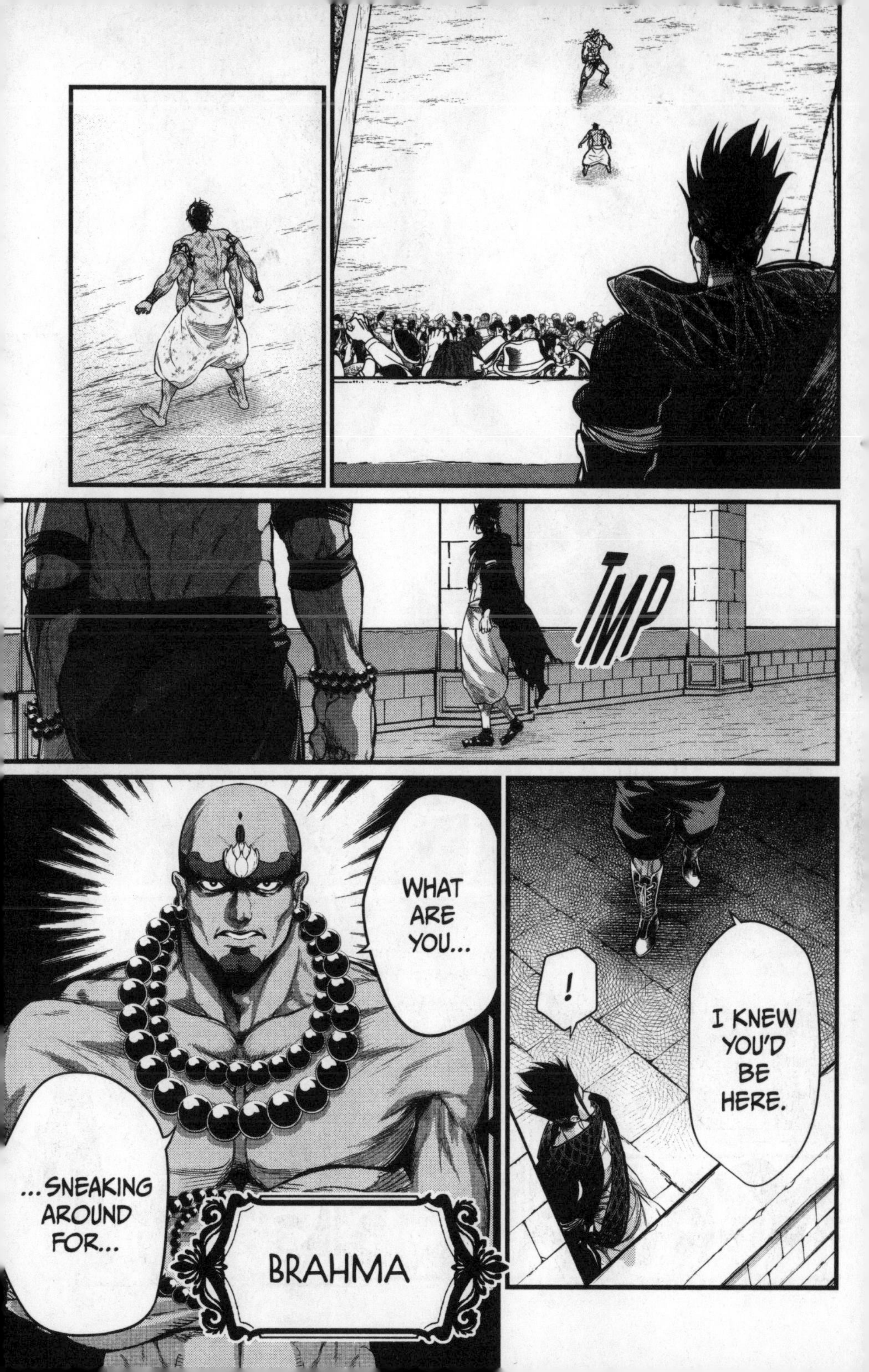
TMP
I KNEW YOU'D BE HERE.
!
WHAT ARE YOU...
...SNEAKING AROUND FOR...
BRAHMA

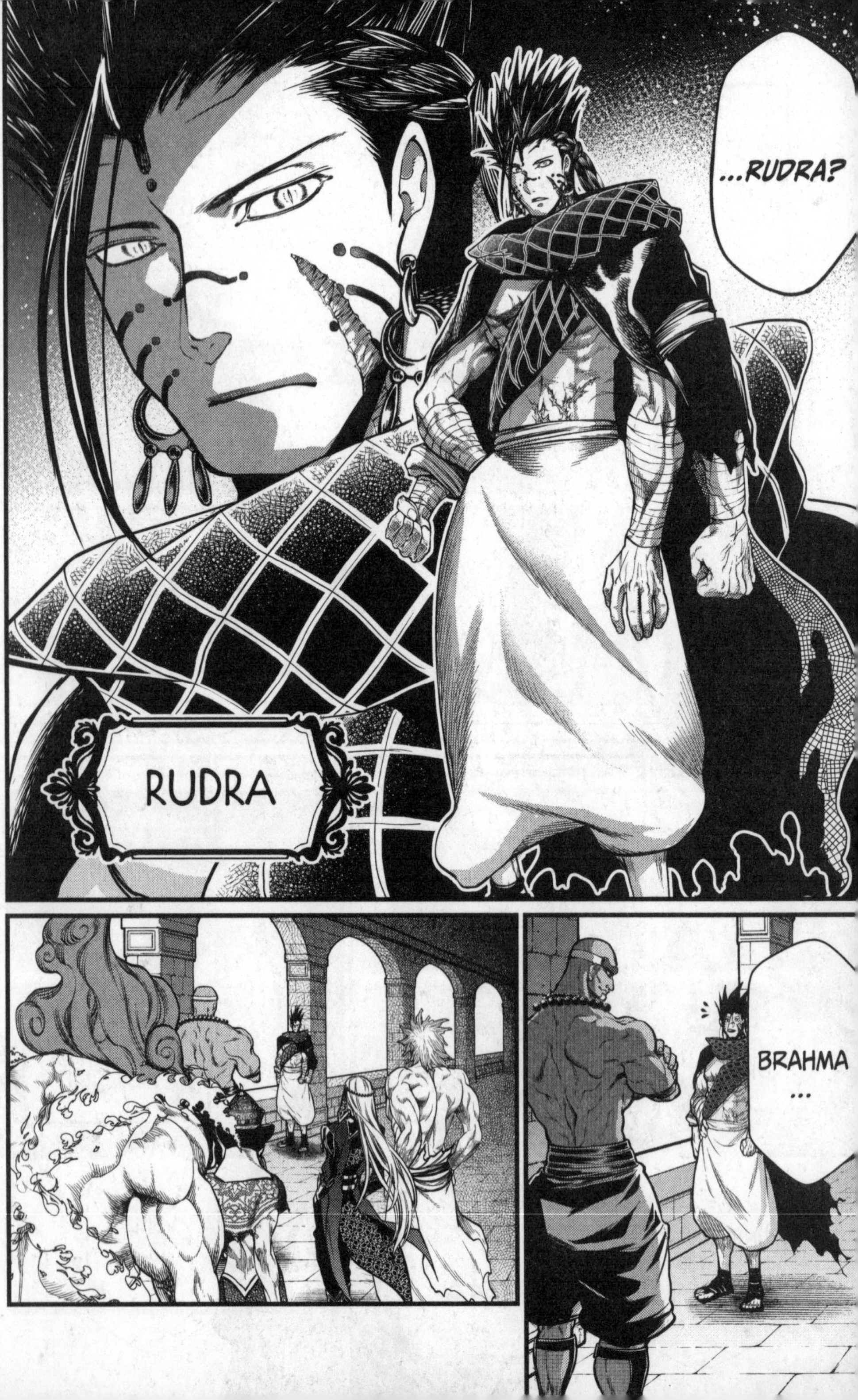
...RUDRA?
RUDRA
BRAHMA ...

INDRA

VISHNU

VARUNA

AGNI

THE GANG'S ALL HERE, HUH?

HEH

WELL, WELL, WELL...

THE HEAD OF INDIA'S PANTHEON, OF ALL PEOPLE...

THROB

TMP

BUT MAN...

SHIVA HASN'T CHANGED ONE BIT!

FIGHTING SO RECKLESSLY!

YOU KNOW HOW HE IS.

...TO USE HIS *FISTS* TO GET TO KNOW HIS OPPONENT.

...ONCE HE'S IN A FIGHT, HE PREFERS...

KNCH

BUT MORE THAN ANYONE...

HE'S THE SWEETEST GUY.

ANYWAY...

THIS IS OUR TOP DOG'S FIGHT.

LET'S SEE IT THROUGH.

YEAH...

RUDRA,
GOD OF STORMS!

RECORD OF RAGNAROK

VOLUME 9
VIZ Signature Edition

Art by **Azychika**

Story by **Shinya Umemura**

Script by **Takumi Fukui**

Translation / Joe Yamazaki
English Adaptation / Stan!
Touch-Up Art & Lettering / Mark McMurray
Design / Julian (JR) Robinson
Editor / Mike Montesa

Shumatsu no Walkure
©2017 by AZYCHIKA AND SHINYA UMEMURA AND TAKUMI FUKUI/COAMIX
Approved No. ZCW-123W
First Published in Japan in Monthly Comic ZENON by COAMIX, Inc.
English translation rights arranged with COAMIX Inc., Tokyo
through Tuttle-Mori Agency, Inc., Tokyo

Printed in Canada

Published by VIZ Media, LLC
P.O. Box 77010
San Francisco, CA 94107

10 9 8 7 6 5 4 3 2 1
First printing, January 2024

PARENTAL ADVISORY
RECORD OF RAGNAROK is rated T+ for
Older Teen and is recommended for ages
16 and up. Contains graphic violence.

YOU'RE READING IT
WRONG!

RECORD OF
RAGNAROK

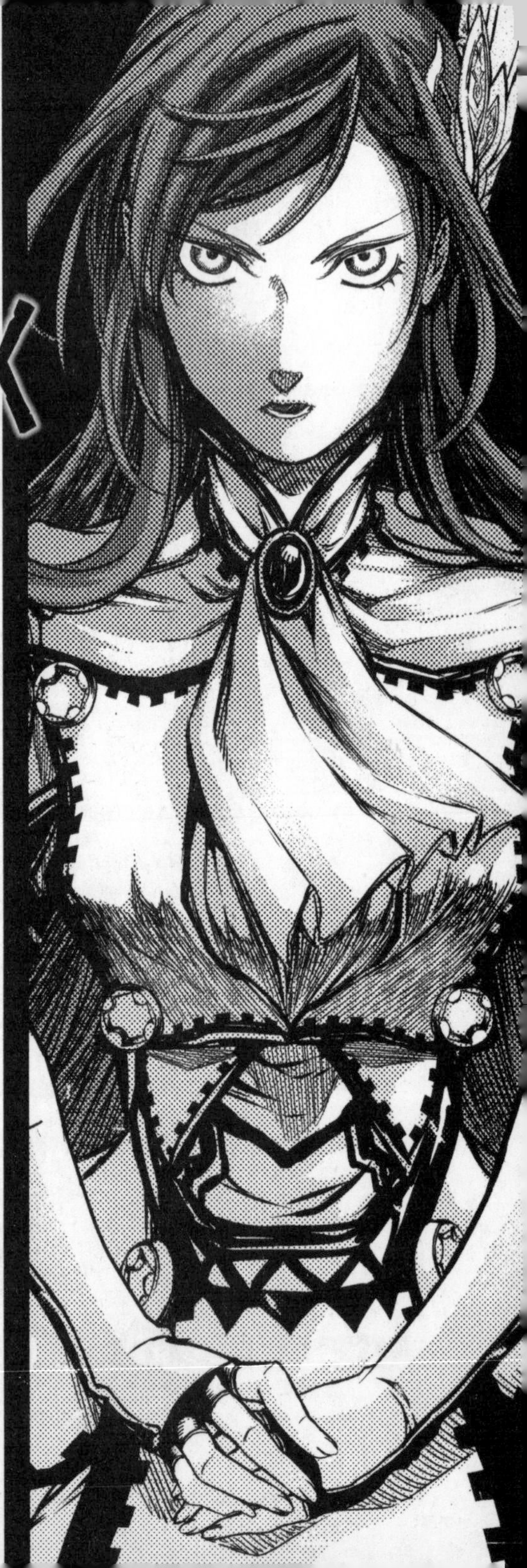

reads right to left starting in the upper-right corner. Japanese is read from right to left, meaning that action, sound effects, and word-balloon order are completely reversed from English order.

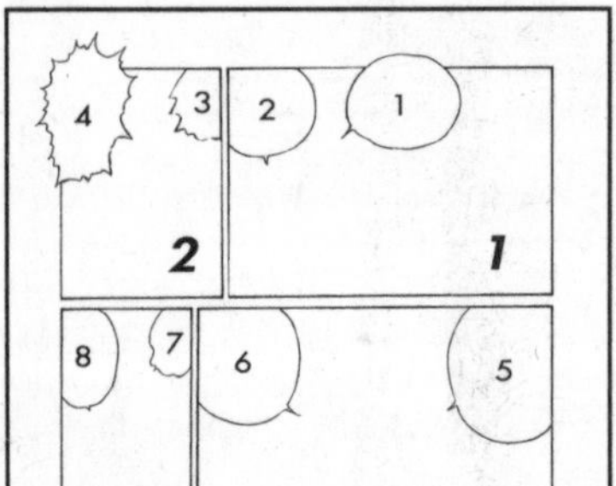

1
2
3
4
1
2
5
6
7
8
3
4
9
5
142

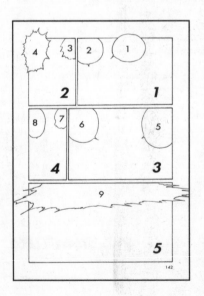